Madness and the Loss of Identity
in Nineteenth Century Fiction

Madness and the Loss of Identity in Nineteenth Century Fiction

JUDY CORNES

McFarland & Company, Inc., Publishers

Jefferson, North Carolina, and London

LIBRARY OF CONGRESS CATALOGUING-IN-PUBLICATION DATA

Cornes, Judy, 1945–
    Madness and the loss of identity in nineteenth century fiction /
Judy Cornes.
        p.   cm.
    Includes bibliographical references and index.

    ISBN-13: 978-0-7864-3224-0
    softcover : 50# alkaline paper ∞

    1. Identity (Psychology) in literature.   2. American fiction —
19th century — History and criticism.   3. English fiction —19th
century — History and criticism.   I. Title.
PS374.I42C67   2008
823'.809353 — dc22   2007027409

British Library cataloguing data are available

Cover image ©2007 Photos.com

Manufactured in the United States of America

McFarland & Company, Inc., Publishers
    Box 611, Jefferson, North Carolina 28640
        www.mcfarlandpub.com

For Frank

Table of Contents

Preface

Children and Identity

When I was about four years old, I spent a great amount of time studying the cover photograph on a magazine that was a particular favorite of my mother's. Though I don't recall the name of the magazine, I am sure that it was one of those women's periodicals so popular in the late 1940s: a time when recipes, fashions, fiction, and stories on current celebrities predominated. It was a time when women who went shopping at the neighborhood grocery store wore hats, tailored dresses, hose, and high heels. It was a period when no proper lady would have been seen in public without gloves and a fancy purse. It was also a day when they usually carried a pack of cigarettes placed neatly in a stylish case, which was often sold with a matching lighter: all a part of the middle class ladies' everyday accessories.

So it was in this type of environment that I can imagine myself once again seated on the living room sofa, balancing my mother's magazine on my lap, totally spellbound by the picture in front of me. And what I saw in that distant past stretched my child's mind beyond the limits of what it could comprehend. On the cover of the magazine was a photograph of a sophisticated, well-dressed lady, properly attired for her day of shopping, driving children to their various activities, and finally enjoying an afternoon cigarette and a cup of coffee with other ladies at the corner drugstore. But there was more. This elegant woman was holding an identical magazine that pictured on *its* cover an identical photograph of the same woman. Likewise, the second magazine revealed this original but duplicated woman holding in turn her own magazine, which of course also featured another but correspondingly smaller twin, one displaying the same magazine. I cannot recall how many of these identical women I could see posing with the selfsame picture of themselves, but the duplicated images went on and on, each photo containing a tinier image of a woman holding a magazine, with an even smaller image of herself holding an even smaller magazine.

At the time, the complex riddle inherent in this picture reminded me of a favorite toy, one consisting of a series of eggs, each one of which could be pried open to reveal an identical egg inside; the object of these maneuvers was to continue unpacking eggs until all of the eggs had been exposed. However, unlike those eggs, which always remained visible, the magazine with its picture on the front gradually dissolved into the distant background, becoming too small for me to see anymore. At last, there were no more images of the woman.

But the images nonetheless remained, imprinted on my child's mind, even as I wondered just who this woman was. Furthermore, unlike the toy eggs that I could actually touch and put back into place, building them up once more so that the largest egg again covered all the smaller eggs, restoring the toy to its original state, the woman on the magazine cover could not be rebuilt in that way. She remained embedded in that cover photograph, forever disappearing down a hole, imprisoned in the photographer's sense of perspective. Because I could not grasp her, because her intangibility kept her just beyond my reach, I was horribly concerned about this woman's identity, and I asked myself which one of these pictures contained the *real* woman. Was she the largest one, the first one that I saw on the cover? Was she the second? the third? the fourth? Was she all of them? None? And, an even more frightening thought occurred to me: suppose she was all of these people, but that she kept losing her own self, getting smaller and smaller, until she finally disappeared altogether? Would that happen to me? Who *was* I? How did I get to be the unique person I was? Would I one day lose myself as this woman had done and simply vanish?

The Courage of the Imagination

These are the kinds of questions that children, the eternal narcissists, ask themselves. And they are the kinds of questions that we adults also address, though less overtly, more self-consciously, for we, too, maintain traces of such self-absorption throughout our lives. The cultural anthropologist Ernest Becker has written that we humans live in constant anxiety, for we are forever aware of our limitations, of the ultimate truth that we all must die. We are painfully aware that our uniqueness is transitory, that our identity is fleeting. In his discussion of mankind's philosophical dilemma, Becker summarizes Kierkegaard's conclusions about our awareness of life and death:

> Anxiety is the result of the perception of the truth of one's condition. What does it mean to be a *self-conscious animal*? The idea is ludicrous, if not monstrous. It means to know that one is food for worms. This is the terror: to have emerged from nothing, to have a name, consciousness of self, deep inner feelings, an excruciating inner yearning for life and self-expression — and with all this yet to die.[1]

And so it is the task of the creative artist to look into a mirror, to be reminded of this "consciousness of self," and then to turn the mirror outward to capture the angst of the rest of mankind: to remind all of us that, no matter how we try to define ourselves as unique individuals, we are ultimately still "food for worms." To accomplish this undertaking requires a special kind of bravery that most of us ordinary mortals lack; great writers have the courage to probe into the human mind and heart. Their courage is born of what Joseph Conrad and Ernest Hemingway have referred to as the courage of the imagination. The best artists, then, dig deep into their own psyches, lay bare their innermost fears, expose those very psychological elements which most of us prefer to keep hidden. Like Hawthorne's Parson Hooper in "The Minister's Black Veil," they bring to light "secret sin" — both theirs and ours; furthermore, like Hooper, they sometimes pay a price for daring to expose man's mortality: this price is all too often loneliness and isolation. By the same token, like Hemingway, they occasionally lose themselves in their created worlds, becoming their own fictional creations — the lady of the magazine cover, the picture within the picture within the picture — until, like Hemingway, they disappear altogether and choose to die rather than remain forever invisible.

This book explores some of these talented, courageous fiction writers of the nineteenth century: those authors who have pursued the twins of identity and madness in order to bring to the surface the hidden fears that plague all humans. I have selected representative British and American writers: some well known (Henry James, Robert Louis Stevenson) some less so (Lillie Blake, Charles Chesnutt). Chapter One examines the supernatural stories of Ambrose Bierce; Chapter Two looks closely at one of Henry James's stories, which delineates a character who has lost himself in time and space. Wilkie Collins is the focus of Chapter Three. Collins probes the dilemma of identity against the background of nineteenth century British society's social restrictions. Chapter Four examines Robert Louis Stevenson, who is obsessed with the problem of identity as a physical and moral disease. Chapters Five, Six, and Seven explore the predicament of nineteenth century minorities — specifically blacks and women — as these individuals try to define themselves against the background of white male persecution. Charles Chesnutt, Lillie Devereux Blake, and Mary Elizabeth Braddon take us into the dark world of uncertainty: a world born out of the knowledge that certain categories of individuals are not allowed the freedom to establish their own identities.

Finally, all of these writers, no matter what their race, gender, or social background, confront the insecurities of a Western world in transition: where to be human is to be aware of the social, cultural, and economic changes wrought by wars and industrialization.

Introduction

> But for me, in my impenetrable mantle, the safety was com-
> plete. Think of it — I did not even exist!
>
> Robert Louis Stevenson,
> *The Strange Case of Dr. Jekyll and Mr. Hyde* [1886]

The Spirit of the Times

An obsession with individual identity pervaded Western world thinking in the nineteenth and early twentieth centuries. Many people were
worried that they might lose themselves in the frightening darkness lying
just beyond the earthbound. The romantic sensibility, which probed the
mystery of identity and which would eventually be linked to early twentieth century psychology, permeated nineteenth century thought and con-
tributed to some of the most prevalent themes of the century's literature.
If the romantics saw the irrational, the perverse, and the absurd as essential aspects of everyday existence, then their works were a reflection of
their insistence on the validity of chaos. The literature of the time reflects
this fascination with the shaky foundations on which rested these authors'
desires for certainty in an unpredictable universe. Even such an optimistic
writer as Walt Whitman demonstrated this paradoxical view prevalent
among many nineteenth century thinkers. Whereas Whitman was
influenced by the Enlightenment tenets to which he had been exposed in
his boyhood, and while he was also a believer in the scientific discoveries
of the nineteenth century, he still had a romantic's eye, a transcendentalist's view of the ephemera of the earthly.

Moreover, the Civil War was a touchstone for many American intel-
lectuals of the mid-nineteenth century. The war further challenged the way

in which they viewed reality, and it made them question the confidence in their earlier beliefs about the world and their place in it. Whitman himself, a medical attendant during the Civil War, had nursed the wounded in makeshift hospitals, and his *Drum-Taps* poems are a sensual, memorable tribute from an aging man to those dying soldiers whom he did not want future generations to forget.

So too, the iconoclastic American writer Ambrose Bierce was forever imprinted with his experience of the horrors of that war. A generation younger than Whitman, Bierce did more than just comfort the mutilated and the dying; Bierce, the soldier, was among the wounded. Nor can other important nineteenth century figures be ignored when one considers the impact that that conflict had on the survivors of the bloodiest war of the century: a war "fought with modern weapons and premodern tactics."[1] These outmoded tactics included infantry charges that had been popular years earlier, when the most utilized weapon was the musket, which had a range of only about eighty yards. But during the Civil War, rifles were the weapons of choice. These were far more effective killing machines, their range being four hundred yards. Thus, such close combat with such efficient weapons resulted in a "mismatch [that] was responsible for some of the most spectacular carnage of the war."[2]

Oliver Wendell Holmes, Jr., son and namesake of the famous physician, poet, novelist, and essayist, was a privileged young man, a Harvard graduate, and, like his contemporary Ambrose Bierce, participated in some of the most horrendous battles of the war, seeing this "most spectacular carnage" again and again. Wounded three times, he always returned to the fighting, and he emerged from the war a changed man, one less sure of himself and of the world around him. He had seen a world blown apart by leaders who were so convinced of the rightness of their cause that they carelessly accepted bloodshed as the natural means to prove just how right they were. In later years, recalling the misguided zeal of these officers, who were perfectly willing to sacrifice thousands on the altar of a "noble cause," Holmes, the jurist, would respond by refusing to rewrite laws that interfered with democracy. He felt that democracy would prevent a repeat of factional disputes that would inevitably lead to violence.[3] Moreover, Holmes ultimately came to see civil liberties not in terms of how they would benefit an individual, but in response to how they would benefit society as a whole. Holmes would come to have a fervent appreciation of the law as written and an equally fervent suspicion of the firebrand's "causes."[4] He knew what such an obsession with causes would lead to; he had seen the apocalypse.

Indeed, the Civil War taught Holmes that individual heroism involves seeing oneself according to a creed of one's own — not according to the dim lights of some half-baked tenets that are as likely as not to get a person killed. Writing in 1884 in "The Profession of the Law," Holmes observed that a thoughtful individual is one who knows that courage involves a willingness to divine the unknowable, to admit that only when he reaches for the unseen will he be living a truly heroic life: "No man has earned the right to intellectual ambition until he has learned to lay his course by a star which he has never seen — to dig by the divining rod for springs which he may never reach.... Only when you have worked alone — when you have felt around you a black gulf of solitude more isolating than that which surrounds the dying man, and in hope and in despair have trusted to your own unshaken will — then only will you have achieved."[5] The diplomat Lewis Einstein, one of Holmes's correspondents, reported that Holmes once told him "that after the Civil War the world never seemed quite right again."[6] Indeed, the war made many citizens question long-cherished beliefs about man's identity, about his place in the universe.

Likewise, the question of identity was just as frequently entwined with the protean tendency accompanying the entrepreneurial excesses of the late nineteenth century Gilded Age. If a person could not claim fame and fortune as his/her birthright, then that person often felt obliged to achieve success through a reshaping of the circumstances of his/her birth. Much nineteenth century literature is filled with the histories of such individuals who overcome the disabilities of being born the wrong social class, the wrong sex, or the wrong race. Like the beginning student of arithmetic who works through a problem, eraser always ready, and indeed finds that multiplication rather than division has been required, these hapless fictional characters assumed that the forging of a new identity simply represented the correction of an error. Unlike the situation of the budding mathematician, however, the error found is not theirs, but rather is the fault of the world at large.

A further reason for this nineteenth century concern with identity may be found in the social mores of the time, which precluded an acceptance of the illegitimate into respectable company. Such dictates focused specifically on unwed mothers. Thus the child born from such a socially unacceptable union might lose her identity because her parents had been unwed at the time of her birth. These illegitimate children, produced as a result of their parents' lapse in moral rectitude, were often forced to redefine themselves in order to become visible to the world at large. This was a world where to be respected one had to be recognized; and to be recognized, one had to render oneself respectable through a fabrication of the circumstances of one's birth. Failing in this endeavor, these children often suffered consequences that were financial as well as social; in essence, they became nonpersons, legally denied their inheritance: their birthright an elusive phantom.

Toward a Definition of Self

Another curious aspect of nineteenth and early twentieth century fiction lies within a dilemma that would subsequently be posed by twentieth century existentialists. If these later philosophers held that individuals define themselves according to the actions that they perform of their own free will, then we can see in some of Henry James's characters a definition of modern existentialist thought. Spencer Brydon in "The Jolly Corner" is an ideal illustration of modern man: mindful of his past, fearful of his future, and paralyzed by a self-loathing born of his inability to identify himself through action.

Nor do these writers always anticipate the future. Many writers of the period embody a fascination with the supernatural. For instance, authors of Gothic fiction often managed to insert at least a hint of metamorphosis into their characters. Joseph Sheridan LeFanu in his 1865 novel, *Uncle Silas*, depicts the rise and fall of the sinister Madame de la Rougierre, who not only mutilates the English language in a grim but humorous fashion, but also is herself physically mutilated at the novel's conclusion, when she is bludgeoned to death as a result of her killer's mistaking her for someone else. In the meantime, however, we are led to believe that Madame de la Rougierre had been known by another name before her incarnation as the wicked governess of the heroine narrator of the novel. While we never learn exactly who she had been or why she had been engaged to live and work in the household of the adolescent narrator, her cloudy past hangs oppressively over the novel, even as she disappears midway through, only to resurface near the conclusion, just in time to be murdered. *Uncle Silas* is a riveting novel, marred only by LeFanu's occasional neglect of plot strands. Despite such oversights, Madame de la Rougierre remains an ideal illustration of the nineteenth century writers' fascination with their characters' identities and the corresponding descent into madness that accompanies these characters' confused states of mind and being. After all, these are individuals whose very names are as questionable and ambiguous as are their pasts.

In short, this obsession with identity had various manifestations. For some nineteenth century writers, it involved *ghosts* or *doubles*—spectres or twins of the living. Often, in such instances, it was a challenge to determine which was the earthly and which was the spirit. For other writers, this fascination involved characters who adopted whole new identities: some became other people altogether. Some became people of a different race; others even changed gender—not literally of course: this *was* the nineteenth century. Rather, through very careful plotting and clever disguises, they posed as individuals of the opposite sex. Some writers depicted characters who were in two places simultaneously; others saw the ghosts of themselves as they had been years before. Thus, the writers I examine are as varied in style and ability as are their methods of dealing with the labyrinth of identity.

Ambrose Bierce and the Riddle of Being

With Ambrose Bierce, we encounter a tormented yet supremely gifted man, one whose youth was forged by a world fractured for all time by the Civil War. Indeed, the absurdity of the war itself was prefigured by John Brown — the unbending, Calvinist, demented abolitionist — and his ill-advised raid on Harpers Ferry, Virginia in 1859. With an army that consisted of only twenty-two men, John Brown was convinced that he could start a major black uprising and bring down once and for all the Southern institution of slavery. Yet Brown fatally miscalculated the enemy forces: "Ninety United State Marines and the militia of seven neighboring communities from Frederick, Maryland, and five more from Baltimore, were brought to Harpers Ferry to crush an armed rebellion that turned out to number twenty-two men."[7] When the uneven confrontation had ended, twenty-four people were dead — ten of them Brown's men; two of these, his own sons. "By any standard the venture was a fiasco of epic proportions."[8]

And Ambrose Bierce himself would be among those who were forever altered by the absurdities of this time: by his knowledge of single-minded, cruel, narcissistic martyrs such as John Brown. In his ever-increasing skeptical worldview that accompanied his personal wartime experience of such senseless, wrong-headed behavior, Bierce resembled

Oliver Wendell Holmes, Jr. and so many other young men of his generation. Already a world-weary 18-year-old in April of 1861, Bierce enlisted to fight for the Union as a member of Company C, Ninth Indiana Volunteers.[9] By the war's end, he had seen hundreds die horrifying, grisly deaths in battle, and he would subsequently move beyond this apocalyptic war to become a hardened cynic, expecting nothing, giving nothing. Fascinated with the absurdity of the macabre events preceding the equally macabre methods of dying, which the Fates bestowed equally upon the ill-fated soldiers of both sides, Bierce came to view the world as a paradoxical combination of reality welded to illusion. And the reality would merge with the illusion in a number of his stories, some set against this Civil War background and some set entirely out of the boundaries of ordinary time. In all of the stories that mingle the real with the surreal, identity becomes a quagmire into which characters soon disappear, lost forever to the world and to themselves.

Indeed, as we read such stories, we get a sense that we are looking at one of those magic slates that were at one time so popular with children. The surface of the slate held a transparent cover that children could write upon, thus making an impression on the surface beneath, where the writing was visible. But when they lifted the cover, the writing would magically disappear, erased forever, giving these children an opportunity to write upon it innumerable times, always aware that whatever they had written might invariably, inevitably be effaced. So it is with the confused characters created by Ambrose Bierce in some of his most remarkable horror stories. These individuals are so puzzled by the riddle of their own identities that not only are they forever redefining themselves and starting over with a "clean slate," but they are also verging on madness as they wipe themselves out again and again.

Overshadowed by the Elder Brother

Henry James, two years younger than Ambrose Bierce, did not serve in the Civil War, for reasons that he never really explained. James's biographer Leon Edel concludes that some obscure wound, which plagued James from about 1862 onward, kept him out of war. Edel speculates that this impairment was probably a back injury.[10] James himself is so vague in writing of this injury that he clouds with suspicion his nonparticipation in the war. There is assuredly room for doubt with respect to his true motives in avoiding service. In fact, the shy, reticent, and passive Henry James, unlike the aggressive and belligerent Bierce, was ill suited to any sort of physical confrontation. In fact, Bierce himself was always less than cordial in his comments about Henry James, whom he saw as cowardly, delicate, effeminate, and impossible to read without a good English translation. In his usual unpleasant, taunting manner, Bierce referred to him as "Miss Nancy James," assuming that his readers would recognize *Nancy* as a slang term for *homosexual.*[11] In truth, Bierce's ill-natured carping about James's writing ability is misplaced and ironic, for much of Bierce's fiction suffers from overkill — the antithesis of the polish and subtlety that we associate with even the most inferior writings of Henry James. Yet both authors were very much a part of their times, and both skillfully depicted motifs prominently featuring doubles, ghosts, and madness.

Additionally, whatever Henry James's sexual taste, James harbored feelings associated with sibling rivalry. As the second child of Henry James, Sr., a year younger than his brother William, James felt a lifelong jealousy toward his brilliant older brother. Moreover, from the days of their youth, William often chastised Henry, challenging Henry's knowledge and criticizing his early writing efforts. Indeed, as a child, Henry James suffered nightmares that were probably subconscious manifestations of his desire to establish his own identity, one apart from the intimidating, hovering shadow of William. Leon Edel describes one of these recurring nightmares that so terrified young Henry:

> He is defending himself, in terror, against the attempt of someone to break into his room. He is pressing his shoulder against a door and someone is bearing down on the lock and bolt on the other side. Suddenly the tables are turned. Nightmare is routed. Terror is defied. It is Henry who forces the door open in a burst of aggression — and of triumph. Now he is no longer afraid. Now he is triumphant.[12]

Henry James's triumph consists of his vanquishing that "someone ... bearing down on the lock and bolt on the other side." He pursues the intruder and chases him from the room and out of his nightmare. He has conquered those fears before they had the chance to annihilate him. He has succeeded in fighting back. Furthermore, it is possible to see his brother William as that figure just lurking outside the door, ready to pounce upon the unprepared Henry, to destroy the younger brother's feelings of self-worth. In the dream, however, young Henry knows his strengths, knows who he is and where he is going. And he wins. Years later, in his early twentieth century story "The Jolly Corner," James would use his childhood nightmare as a point of departure in his depiction of Spencer Brydon, a man trying to recapture himself, even as he is bedeviled by the spectre of his alter ego.

In an ironic historical twist, it was William James who seemed always in search of a focus, shifting from painting to chemistry to natural history to medicine to psychology to philosophy in order to find a way to believe and a vocation with which he was most comfortable. The elder brother even accompanied the naturalist and great self-promoter Louis Agassiz on an expedition to Brazil in 1865.[13] In a further historical connection, William James's contemporary, Ambrose Bierce, shared many of William James's beliefs about the world, notably the Jamesian conclusion that "there is no point of view from which the world can appear as an absolute, single fact."[14]

Though Henry James shared his brother's restlessness, the famous novelist never doubted that he would be a writer. In 1864, at the age of 22, he sent his first book review to the *North American Review*, for which he received a total of twelve dollars.[15] In his story "The Middle Years," James puts his own feelings about art into the dying words of a gifted writer named Dencombe: "'We work in the dark — we do what we can — we give what we have. Our doubt is our passion, and our passion is our task. The rest is the madness of art.'"[16] There may indeed have been a type of "madness" in James's pursuit of perfection, in his drive to formulate out of his own youthful insecurities a lasting record of his own time. And in creating the bedeviled character of Spencer Brydon in "The Jolly Corner," James not only freezes a moment in time but also frees this character *from* time. In depicting Spencer's search for what-might-have-been, he transports us forward, from the early twentieth to the early twenty-first century, as we see in Spencer Brydon all of our own unrealized hopes.

Caught in the Web: What Is a Woman to Do?

Mary Elizabeth Braddon was a British contemporary of Ambrose Bierce, a woman only five years older than Bierce, but just as obsessed with identity as he. Yet for Braddon, the problem of identity manifested itself in a completely different way. Nevertheless, like Bierce, Braddon suffered many dislocations in her private life. If Bierce remained forever haunted by the Civil War, by those blue- and gray-clad demons that were everlastingly crawling towards him through the misty forests, bellies sunk in mud, bloody faces split in two by occasional grapeshot, Braddon had her own devils to contend with.

These monsters, however, were of the more domestic sort. Ms. Braddon spent many years as the live-in mistress of a man named John Maxwell, by whom she had five children before she was eventually given the opportunity to marry him and subsequently to become a respectable woman. The roadblock on the path to their wedding — Maxwell's wife — finally died in a mental home, thus making it possible for Maxwell to legitimize his long-term relationship with his lover. But by then, Ms. Braddon had already lived through fourteen difficult years. During this time, she tried to extricate Maxwell from his financial excesses, a goal she accomplished through writing novels. Meanwhile, she worked under thorny conditions — often during one of her pregnancies — and cared for five other Maxwell children from his legitimate marriage.[17] Ostracized for breaching the socially accepted boundaries of the day, Braddon doubtless felt that it would be a pleasant change were she able to assume a new identity altogether. Such a metamorphosis is exactly the path taken by Lady Audley in Braddon's 1887 novel, *Lady Audley's Secret.*

In addition, as is the case with Bierce's tortured characters, Lady Audley's identity crisis leads to madness. Furthermore, although Lady Audley's identity shift appears more deliberate, more premeditated than those of Bierce's doomed protagonists, Lady Audley does indeed make a decision based on circumstances over which she feels she has no control. These circumstances are born out of her status as a nineteenth century woman with few options besides those offered her by men. While many of Bierce's newspaper articles reveal him to have been sympathetic to women's post–Civil War push for both political and domestic equality,[18] Bierce's short stories are often less concerned with external social issues than with the internal twilight world, the relationship between mind and matter. If Lady Audley orchestrates her own secret world by knowingly opening her personal doors to duplicity, Bierce's characters watch helplessly as these doors swing open of their own volition, forcing these characters to confront a puzzling, terrifying secret world that Bierce never allows them to comprehend fully.

Another nineteenth century author concerned with the slippery issues of woman's identity and its close kinship with women's rights is Lillie Devereux Blake. Her 1874 novel, *Fettered for Life,* explores topics that are especially timely even today at the beginning of the twenty-first century: notably wife beating and wife murder, men's emotional abuse of and sexual exploitation of women, and discrimination in the workplace.

Like Mary Elizabeth Braddon, Lillie Blake was forced by circumstances to support herself by writing. Although legally married to Philadelphia lawyer Frank Umstead and initially not obligated to support herself and their two children, events turned against Blake when her husband of four years shot himself in the head. Umstead left his widow with two young daughters under the age of two and a half. And so Blake turned to fiction, which provided her with the outlet to vent her frustrations against an unjust system bent upon destroying a woman's autonomy.[19]

Nor was it only female authors who were concerned with nineteenth century women's issues. Wilkie Collins frequently deals with the questions of woman's inferior status in nineteenth century England and her subsequent pursuit of a new identity. In many of his novels, Collins sympathizes with the anti-establishment rebelliousness of such courageous women. Collins himself was something of a social rebel in Victorian England, as he lived for many years with a woman to whom he was not married, and he fathered three illegitimate children by a second woman. Nor did he try to keep these two liaisons a secret. In fact, he was quite willing to admit the paternity of his children.

While Collins focuses primarily on gender as the stumbling block to a woman's fulfillment, it was not exclusively gender that stood in the way of a woman's chances for self-satisfaction. Sometimes there were other unfortunate circumstances related to her status at birth that drove her to assume a new identity. We return to American literature with Charles W. Chesnutt's daring novel *Mandy Oxendine*, which he completed around 1896 but which was not published until 1997. In this work, we find a young woman who vows to disentangle herself from her black roots in the Reconstruction South and move some miles away from her birthplace. In the process, she recreates herself as a "white" woman, cavalierly snubbing the Negroes whom she scorns because she knows that this is no world for them — no matter what their sex.

The Restless World of Robert Louis Stevenson

One of the most popular stories published in the past two hundred years is Robert Louis Stevenson's *The Strange Case of Dr. Jekyll and Mr. Hyde*. Dozens of plays and movie versions have been adapted from Stevenson's 1886 tale; most of these have taken many liberties with the original. In fact, many people today know of Jekyll and Hyde only through the innumerable popularizations of the story. Indeed, the work has become so much a part of popular culture that it is not unusual to find individuals who can identify the names Jekyll and Hyde as synonymous with good and evil, though they typically cannot identify which character is the good and which one the evil. Nor are they at all familiar with the original story that Stevenson wrote toward the end of the nineteenth century. Many cannot even identify the name of the author of "Dr. Jekyll and Mr. Hyde," the most popular, abridged title of the tale.

Furthermore, today we often have the Jekyll and Hyde characters depicted in ways that would have made Stevenson pause to consider what his story had wrought. For instance, modern filmmakers have enveloped Messrs. Jekyll and Hyde within diverse racial and ethnic groups. This famous duo has even undergone a gender switch, whereby in one 1971 filmed version, Mr. Hyde has been transformed into an individual named Sister Hyde, a bizarre character that Stevenson could never have conceived of.[20]

But one of Stevenson's less well known stories is also deserving of attention: this probing of the ambiguities of identity is not solely limited to the notorious Dr. Jekyll and Mr. Hyde. To illustrate, in "The Body Snatcher," a work containing much blissfully absurd dark humor, a corpse actually undergoes an identity switch — or at least a body switch. When this alleged transformation occurs, we are left to wonder about the perspicacity of the two odd fellows who have snatched the body in the first place.

When one considers the personality of Robert Louis Stevenson, it is not surprising to learn that he was captivated by the vagaries of the human mind and by the disabilities of both the brain as well as the body that frequently accompany such abnormalities, such personality quirks. Like Wilkie Collins, Stevenson endured the pain of chronic ailments throughout much of his life, his ill health originating from lung diseases, the primary symptom of which was energy-draining, life-threatening hemorrhages. These frequent and often terrifying episodes enervated him and caused him to seek more advantageous climates than that provided by his native Scotland. So too, like Collins, Stevenson sought stability in family relationships. Unlike Collins, however, Stevenson finally opted for marriage, though he appears to have had few illusions about love and romance.

Furthermore, like Collins, Stevenson was always restless, always seeking something beyond the everyday. In this search, he appears to have been as paradoxical, as contradictory as his most famous creation, Dr.

Jekyll and Mr. Hyde. For Stevenson's was a reclusive temperament that nonetheless frequently sought companionship. Even as an adult, he maintained a child-like enthusiasm for life and a desire to be liked by others. He read for the law in order to please his father, an engineer, yet he knew that he could never be content with the kind of prosaic existence that the legal system offered him. As the son of a man with a scientific bent, he was early exposed to the rigors of scientific inquiry. Consequently, he knew that he was temperamentally suited for neither law nor engineering. In addition, Stevenson would suffer emotionally from a serious break with his father, the result of their religious differences. Yet he continued to accept his father's financial assistance, even as he struggled to gain entrance into, as well as recognition within, the competitive world of essay and fiction writing.

Scope of the Book

I have narrowed the focus of my study in two ways: First, I have limited my analysis to British and American fiction from the nineteenth and — in the case of Henry James — the early twentieth centuries. Such a time frame encompasses a number of important trends in intellectual thought: in America, the Second Great Awakening; in Britain and America, the ascendance of intuition and mysticism accompanying the Romantic movement; in America, the Civil War; in Britain and America, the battle for civil rights for women; in America, the questions of slavery and later, of Reconstruction; in America, the rise of the robber barons; and finally, in Britain and America, the beginnings of modern psychology. All of these trends are reflected in various works of this period, often manifested by characters either in search of or running from themselves.

Second, I examine problems of identity by adopting the following criteria: I look at the extent to which these novels and stories reflect confusion or downright evil. Sometimes this pursuit of identity is either the cause or the effect of insanity. Nor do I limit myself to *living* individuals. Occasionally, I find that identity switches occur between the living and the dead: even, at times, between the dead and the dead.

Yet I am not concerned with works that treat duality of personalities in a totally symbolic fashion, nor am I interested in the motif of *doubling* as such. *Doubles* are found throughout literary history; these are not necessarily associated with problems of identity. Nor am I interested in twins, unless these are identical twins who also happen to suffer from a bizarre type of identity confusion.

Sometimes such symbolic representations become stereotypes with no more than one dimension to their characters. Often, their presentations are simply one aspect of hoary plots that propel the narrative forward, but accomplish little else. In the skilled hands of authors such as Henry James and Joseph Conrad, these symbolic individuals usually transcend types to become much more than cardboard cutouts, but such people are not as fascinating to watch nor as challenging to analyze as the insidious, twisted, and clever characters who dwell within a hazy, often ghost-ridden underworld. Nor are they as intriguing as those characters who are victimized by their surroundings and so are forced to live in a world over which they have no control. Like a person in a nightmare, suspended in air, simultaneously unable to come down from the heights but fearful of falling, these characters have no identity because society refuses to give them one, refuses to allow them to land gently on firm ground. It is with these characters and their stories that I am most concerned; these are the subjects of this book.

The Modern Mind and
the Silent Impermanence of Cyberspace

Today, at the beginning of the twenty-first century, we live in an age that has also become obsessed with identity. Like Sandra Bullock in the movie *The Net* (1995) we fear that we may have all traces of ourselves wiped away with one computer keystroke: our names, faces, Social Security numbers, backgrounds — all disappearing into cyberspace — only to be replaced by the vital statistics of some Other, perhaps someone with a sordid past and a criminal record.

Such deterministic thinking may also be seen in the writings of the brilliant nineteenth century mathematician, scientist, philosopher, probability expert, and eminently peculiar thinker, Charles Sanders Peirce. Peirce argued that *habit* is what conditions all things in the universe. Without habitual actions, our behavior would be purely arbitrary, random, purposeless. In other words, our habits are what give us our identities. So too, this very sameness reveals itself to those around us as "the set of repeated behaviors observable in us."[21] Peirce also observed that no organism can act in a totally predictable way, but rather "has the potential to produce a variety of responses to a given stimulus.... But those responses cannot be random, since if they were, law would not be possible."[22]

According to Peirce's principles of pragmatism, then, our identities are formed by our habits, which are, ipso facto, recognizable by others. Yet, the very fact of our having an identity leaves us unable to transform it, because such transformation would result in chaos. According to Peirce's philosophy, the universe is gradually moving "toward a condition of absolute law, or complete determinism, in which chance will disappear and all habits will be perfectly fixed."[23] If this sounds something like eighteenth century Chain of Being rationalism and the movement toward a perfect society created by a mechanistic, perfect God, it also anticipates the naturalistic thinkers of the late nineteenth and early twentieth centuries.

Today, our computer-driven lives force us into an odd combination of mechanistic, naturalistic, yet romantic, thinking about who we are. On the one hand, we are saturated with movies and television shows dealing with possession, reincarnation, spectres that come and go, with ghosts, angels, and other sundry creatures that dwell in unearthly realms. All of these manifestations of the romantic fascination with the mystical remind us of elements of the nineteenth century Gothic novel.

In addition, like many nineteenth century writers whose romantic sensibilities led them to a passionate embrace of melancholy, we often dwell, like supreme narcissists, on our own misery, searching for an elusive sort of joy around which to center our existences. We seek identity in the amount of pleasure that we find in our lives. And ironically, the more we pursue this euphoric state, the faster it recedes from us. Yet at the same time, we fear depression, consuming hundreds of thousands of dollars worth of anti-depressants each year in an effort to hide from ourselves and from others what we see as a moral weakness. And so the phrases *emotional maturity* and *emotional intelligence* become synonymous with successful adult behavior, while the concept of *therapy* is one from which we shy away when it is applied to the *mental* rather than to the *physical*. Far better to be physically handicapped than emotionally handicapped, we tell ourselves, for the latter succeed neither in their jobs nor in their private lives.

Fearful of the chaos, then, that we attempt to dispel by swallowing mood-altering pills, we seek to become those predictable creatures of habit described by Charles Sanders Peirce. In this connection, about one century later and well into the twentieth century, we found ourselves striving to be what futurist Alvin Toffler called "modular man." Toffler introduced this concept in his book *Future Shock*, which was first published in 1970. Today his commentaries on the fragmentation of human relationships appear even more prescient than Toffler could have anticipated when he first wrote them. There is a certain amount of comfort and freedom in such modular relationships, suggested Toffler in 1970:

> In a modular relationship, the demands are strictly bounded. So long as the shoe salesman performs his rather limited service for us, thereby fulfilling our rather limited expectations, we do not insist that he believe in our God, or that he be tidy at home, or share our political values, or enjoy the same kind of food or music that we do. We leave him free in all other matters — as he leaves us free to be atheist or Jew, heterosexual or homosexual, John Bircher or Communist. This is not true of the total relationship and cannot be. To a certain point, fragmentation and freedom go together.[24]

As Toffler set out quite clearly, our lives have become so segmented that we find ourselves plugging in to others according to those interchangeable modules so familiar and therefore so comforting to us because so predictable and so inherent in modern technology. We do indeed identify ourselves and others out of rote habit; we have a certain module that we plug into casual acquaintances, such as a familiar supermarket checker or the person who delivers our mail on a regular basis. Yet we have a different module for our co-workers. Even here, there is a hierarchy: some fellow employees we see every day and work closely with; others we know by sight but not by name, since they might work in a different department and have offices on different floors. Finally, we even have a module for family members, some of whom we are closer to than others. In short, we are "fixed" in much the same way as Peirce defined our beings in the nineteenth century.

But we live in a world much different from Peirce's, for we also know that we can symbolically be eliminated from the universe by a careless data entry operator, by a cunning computer hacker, by the introduction of a computer virus. Thus, we are in many ways as insecure about ourselves and about our stability in the cosmos as were those nineteenth and early twentieth century individuals who floated in the fog of chance and randomness. By looking at these characters in the contexts of their time and place, we can perhaps put our own idiosyncrasies into perspective and consequently better understand the world that we have inherited from these tortured people.

• *One* •

The Nightmare World
of Ambrose Bierce

Fiction has nothing to say to probability; the capable writer
gives it not a moment's attention, except to make what is related
seem probable in the reading — *seem* true.
Ambrose Bierce, *Examiner*, May 22, 1892

The Return of the Dead

San Francisco is the setting of "A Watcher by the Dead," one of
Ambrose Bierce's most provocative horror stories. It is a city in which
Bierce lived and worked for many years and consequently knew quite well.
It was, and is, a city of dislocated, heightened, and then — suddenly — of
devastatingly flattened landscape: a city where one might easily become
disoriented, dizzy from looking over the edge, uncertain of who one is and
where one is. The time is the latter half of the nineteenth century, when
post–Civil War San Francisco was a wild, violent, polluted, anxious place;
where a person was as likely to be murdered on the street as to dine in an
elegant restaurant with a beautiful view of the city. It was also a time when
the prevailing romantic sensibility in art allowed the intrusion of the irrational, indeed asserted the validity of the illogical, in human life.

Early in the story, Bierce introduces us to three friends, two of them
doctors and one a medical student. They are discussing the superstitious
awe that the living often feel toward the dead. One of these three, Dr.
Helberson, is an arrogant, self-absorbed man who challenges the other
two by asserting that no man can spend the night with a dead body in a
vacant house and not go completely mad. A second man, the student

named Harper, accepts the challenge, arguing that he has a wealthy friend who is completely fearless and who will gladly wager with Dr. Helberson. The third conspirator, Dr. Mancher, agrees to play the corpse. All three of these men of science are convinced that they will have a roaring good time at the expense, both literally and figuratively, of Harper's friend, a Mr. Jarette. One other noteworthy point is important here: Helberson tells both Mancher and Harper that Jarette looks enough like Mancher to be his twin. This tidbit becomes significant in light of the fact that the prevailing motif involves doubling, identity confusion, and madness. Moreover, the prevailing tone underscores the uneasiness that accompanies our dread of our own baser instincts. Ultimately, the work challenges our preconceptions about who we are and about what it takes to make us question our place in the scheme of things.

Bierce establishes this questioning tone at the outset; he tells Part I of the story from the point of view of Jarette himself, a man who, when we first see him, has already made the bet and is preparing to settle in with what he assumes is a dead body. The conversation described above does not occur till the flashback in Part II. Furthermore, the story's narrative structure is organized so that its climax is a stunning surprise: a reversal of what readers have been expecting. Yet Bierce is never surprised by the madness of daily life nor by the paradoxically commonplace twists that often lead to madness. When we first learn that Mancher and his "victim" Jarette look enough alike that they might be twins, we file this information away, paying little attention to the possible consequences of such a resemblance.

But the nightmarish world of Ambrose Bierce does not allow our attention to lapse for long. Part I, which focuses on Jarette trying to remain composed even as he is perversely fascinated by the body with whom he is sharing a deserted room, is filled with much Gothic, unsettling detail. We learn, for instance, that the room in which Jarette has been locked by the three pranksters "was not in the front of the house, facing a street. It really faced nothing but a high breast of rock, the rear of the building being set into a hill."[1] So Jarette is walled off from outside contact by the structure of the building itself and by the hilly San Francisco backdrop. Moreover, it is clear that Jarette is uneasy, despite all of his outward composure. In fact, when we last see him at the end of this first episode, he is inspecting the lit candle, which is the only light in this room. Apparently agreeing with the cliché that discretion is the better part of valor, he looks closely at the candle and, noting that if it remains lit, it will last about one more hour, he blows out the flame. But he performs this action only after he has carefully checked on and pocketed a good supply of matches. Jarette is a prudent man, but he will soon discover that prudence is not enough to keep him from confronting his worst fantasies.

These horrible visions truly begin by Part III which, like Part I, is told from the point of view of the increasingly distressed Jarette. Now in total darkness and thinking that he has heard noises, he stumbles through the room till he locates the unlit candle on the floor, lights it, and focuses once again on the still-undisturbed, covered body on the table. But now the candle appears considerably shorter, even as time seems contracted, for Jarette notes to his surprise that it is only half past nine, fifteen minutes since his ordeal began. Priding himself on being a rational man, Jarette chastises himself: "...the greater the number of variations which he played upon the simple theme of the harmlessness of the dead, the more insupportable grew the discord of his emotions."[2]

We cut to Part IV. It is early the next morning, and Helberson and Harper are about to witness the outcome of their jolly little joke. What they see in these early morning hours as they walk toward the scene of their fun of the previous night is a frazzled man who they assume is Jarette. His hair has suddenly turned completely white, and he is running from the empty building where he has been held captive all evening. When they go inside the apartment, they discover the corpse of Dr. Mancher. So it seems that Dr. Mancher has indeed played the part of the dead man to its perfect completion, while his "twin" Jarette has escaped, doubtless killing Mancher in a fit of terror and pique at the bad taste displayed by the three frolicsome friends. Since Helberson and Harper are prudent men, they immediately decide that now would be a propitious time to tour Europe. Accordingly, they scurry away, seemingly secure in the knowledge that their part in this wild scheme will never be discovered. But Ambrose Bierce's view of the world is too bitter to allow them to escape for long. If he leads us to believe that our lives are made up of a series of bad jokes, then the jokes will ultimately prevail, turning inward in order to attack us more efficiently.

It is precisely this reversal that occurs to the two living pranksters who have fled the country; they find that they cannot run away forever. Seven years pass between Parts IV and V. Ordinarily, we think of the number *seven* as having some mystical but lucky significance. Likewise, *seven* suggests *completion* or the ending of a task — something finished, over, done with, whether for good or ill — as in the seven days of creation, the seven wonders of the world, the seven cardinal virtues, and the seven deadly sins. But Bierce is not an author who grants his characters the luxury of good luck; neither is he one to give them a feeling of completion, a sense that their troubles are over. During the intervening seven years, Helberson and Harper have felt themselves secure, even as they have been pursuing their true vocation as gamblers rather than physicians.

One day, they are sitting on a bench in New York, enjoying the sort of casual conversation that occurs among those who are sublimely content with their lot in life. The fact that our two intrepid heroes have been suddenly shifted from San Francisco to New York is doubtless owing to Bierce's trenchant sense of humor, for Helberson and Harper have previously been intent on getting as far away as possible from the scene of their joyous fun at another poor fellow's expense. Consequently, upon their return from their extended sojourn in Europe, they have settled in New York, figuring that a continent will now forever separate them from the results of their earlier stouthearted behavior. But Bierce always delights in irony that is both comic and cosmic. And indeed, though Helberson and Harper have heretofore been able to run without fear of being discovered, they are about to learn that they have vaulted over their last hurdle and landed on a sharp nail of remembrance and retribution.

This deathless memento enters the tranquil scene as a sort of ghost, a reminder of their cloudy past, of their moral amnesia. And with this ghost we have reached the end of the twisted path that Bierce has constructed, for the ghost takes a thoroughly ambiguous route to announce his presence and define his identity. Despite the vast distance that Helberson and Harper have traveled from the site of their original misstep in California, the apparition has found them.

This question of identity becomes especially vexing to Harper and Helberson because Bierce has earlier made it appear that Dr. Mancher, who had assumed the identity of the corpse, was himself killed by Jarette. But perhaps not. Cavalierly introducing himself to the astonished duo who have been enjoying their day, our ghost politely tips his hat, thereby revealing his frost-white hair. In so doing, he also reveals the following astonishing information: "'I beg pardon, gentlemen, but when you have killed a man by coming to life, it is best to change clothes with him, and at the first opportunity make a break for liberty.'"[3] On closer inspection of this spectre, our erstwhile physicians recognize — or think that they recognize — none other than Dr. Mancher. Or do they?

"Who the devil are you?" said Harper, bluntly.

The stranger came nearer and, bending toward them, said in a whisper: "I call myself Jarette sometimes, but I don't mind telling you for old friendship, that I am Dr. William Mancher."

The revelation brought Harper to his feet. "Mancher!" he cried; and Helberson added: "It is true, by God!"[4]

Here, of course, Harper and Helberson are convinced that they recognize Mancher, just as they had been certain that they had seen Jarette running from that abandoned building seven years earlier. However, the strange, white-haired apparition now standing before them does not seem at all certain about who he is, for in response to Helberson's exclamation, "'It is true, by God!'"[5] the odd man makes an equivocal statement.

"Yes," said the stranger, smiling vaguely, "it is true enough, no doubt."

He hesitated and seemed to be trying to recall something, then began humming a popular air. He had apparently forgotten their presence.[6]

Key words in this description are *recall* and *forgotten*, as though Bierce were trying to paint a portrait of a man forgetful, remote, distanced from reality. Yet, at this point, both Helberson and Harper are as prepared to accept the presence of the man claiming to be Dr. Mancher as they had previously been ready to believe that it was Jarette who had survived the evening's festivities. What Bierce does not allow them to comprehend is the possibility that this demonic phantom is something altogether different from what their senses perceive. We already know that Mancher and Jarette look enough alike to be twins. We also know that Bierce, ever the darkly playful illusionist, has provided us with enough tantalizing information that we might create a number of imaginative scenarios, all of which could explain the surprise twist now confronting Harper and Helberson.

For instance, we might at first assume that the stranger now facing the other two must indeed be Dr. Mancher, for he recognizes both Helberson as well as Harper. Therefore, we must conclude that it could not be Jarette, who quite possibly never met Helberson. However, Bierce does not let us off that easily; in the conversation between Helberson and Harper in Part IV, Helberson alludes to at least a brief acquaintance with Jarette, when he loftily informs Harper, "'If your friend had not irritated me by the contemptuous manner in which he treated my doubt of his endurance — a purely physical quality — and by the cool incivility of his suggestion that the corpse be that of a physician, I should not have gone on with it. If anything should happen we are ruined, as I fear we deserve to be.'"[7] So Jarette had indeed met Helberson; had, in fact, treated the physician haughtily and would doubtless remember what the evil doctor looked like, even seven years later. Who, then, is this strange man with the distracted, even disinterested, air? If it is Mancher, as the spectre first suggests, then he did in fact trade places with Jarette and has apparently been posing, every now and then, as Jarette. If, however, upon seeing a terrified man run from the vacant building, Harper initially made the correct identification, then this person is Jarette, and Jarette has won the bet; he *did* survive the night with a dead man.

Yet the issue becomes even more complicated when we remember the bolted door, to which we are introduced in Part I. When Jarette first enters the room and moves toward the "corpse," the door closes, followed by "a grating, as of a key turned with difficulty, and the snap of a lock bolt as it shot into its socket."[8] So Jarette has been tightly fastened inside the room by some unseen person or persons outside the door. Then, in Part III, Jarette does a curious thing. As he becomes more and more distraught, trying his best to maintain a calm, rational attitude in spite of his increasingly unsettled mental state, he crosses "over to the door" and tests it "by turning and pulling the knob with all his strength. It did not yield and this seemed to afford him a certain satisfaction; indeed, he secured it more firmly by a bolt which he had not before observed."[9] Why Jarette would be comforted with the knowledge that not only is he secured into this room from the outside but also that he has ensured his further imprisonment by fastening another bolt from the inside remains one of the many perverse puzzles in this story. However, such apparently senseless behavior will become an important aspect of the story's final scene, as we try to determine whether the crazed man accosting his two old friends is indeed Mancher, as he initially claims to be.

One important clue to the identity of this odd fellow who reunites with Helberson and Harper in New York lies beyond that carefully fastened and bolted door. The man who at first identifies himself as Mancher adopts an accusing tone as he recounts the history of that fateful night. He claims that he had decided to play a further prank on Jarette by coming to life; he thus leads his fellow conspirators to conclude that Jarette had indeed died of fright. But his final revelation in this connection is what is most enlightening about Mancher's true identity, as he complains, "And afterward — well, it was a tough job changing places with him, and then — damn you! you didn't let me out!"[10] If we assume that Mancher, spread upon the table, had neither been able to hear the bolt turning from the outside nor had any recollection of turning that bolt from the inside, then his surprise and anger at being unable to exit quickly appear genuine. In short, we might suppose from this evidence that Mancher is indeed the accuser in this instance.

Alternatively, Bierce provides us with a further clue that this man might instead be Jarette, when the intruder offers this parting shot to his increasingly dumbfounded listeners: "'I hope Sharper here paid over Jarette's money like an honest stakeholder.'"[11] Maybe the stranger is hoping that Harper has not gambled away all of the money that should rightfully be the stranger's own reward. However, a mere seven years earlier, Jarette had been quite young, "not more than thirty — dark in complexion, smooth-shaven, with brown hair. His face was thin and high-nosed, with a broad forehead and a 'firmness' of the chin and jaw which is said by those having it to denote resolution."[12] Jarette's appearance in this opening scene, then, would appear to contradict the possibility that it is indeed Jarette now standing before Helberson and Harper, for we are told that the man approaching the two gamblers is "courteously lifting his hat from locks as white as frost."[13] Yet to further complicate matters, the man whom Helberson and Harper had seen running from the house had been "smooth-shaven" with a bloodless face, "his hair frost-white."[14] This is the man whom Helberson and Harper had thought that they recognized as Jarette. That Jarette had been "smooth-shaven" only hours earlier is a fact that we have been told in Part I.

On the other hand, another possibility presents itself here. Perhaps Mancher/Jarette truly does not know *who* he is. This likelihood might account for the fact that Mancher/Jarette has previously made the astonishing revelation that sometimes he calls himself Jarette, though in truth he is Dr. William Mancher. Maybe on that spooky evening, Jarette had removed the cover from the corpse, whereupon Mancher, having tired of the immobility accompanying his role as the dead, rose from the table. Jarette might then have seen himself, his "twin," arising from the dead and died from the shock.

Or perhaps Jarette did not die from shock, but instead became so enraged at seeing his double ascending to a sitting position that he killed Mancher and ran madly from the house, lest his deed be discovered. Whoever this odd fellow is, he tells Harper and Helberson that he is now employed as "High Supreme Medical Officer of the Bloomingdale Asylum; it is my duty to cure the superintendent."[15] That Jarette/Mancher has become a lunatic is apparent from this statement, the last sentence of the story. This inhabitant of the Bloomingdale Asylum has doubtless escaped and has found great joy in tormenting those who had formerly tormented him.

But do these two ex-physicians really care about Jarette/Mancher? Do they indeed allow themselves to be tormented by the stranger? Concerning these two doctors cum gamblers, Cathy Davidson offers the following analysis:

> Bierce's protagonists are usually known by their failures, failures that show the limits and the limitations of a particular character's particular perspective. In this respect the test passed sometimes proves nothing. Survival becomes an accident of obtuseness in a few stories such as "A Watcher by the Dead," a tale that shows two characters, Doctors Helberson and Harper, who do not even recognize that they have been tested at all.[16]

Is Bierce, then, simply playing a clever joke on the reader? Is he asking us to believe that these events took place exactly as the narrator has described them? Are we to understand that, since the two obtuse jokesters, Helberson and Harper, take Jarette/Mancher at his word, that we are to do likewise without question? Or are the "twins" of the story symbolic of something else? When we recall that many nineteenth century horror stories use ghosts in a non-literal way, exposing them only as representations of the unconscious drives and desires of the characters who have the misfortune to be visited by these spooks, we then have another way of looking at "The Watcher by the Dead." It is certainly possible that the character of Jarette is having nothing more than a bad dream, and that this nightmare involves his entering a room where his Other Self lies upon the table. Thus, through his obsessive fears of encountering his own mortality, he is inexorably drawn to the prone figure, until at last he sees this figure, his mirror image, rise and move toward him. Our primal fascination with our own deaths is consequently displayed here; we can open the curtain upon our own funeral to see what the world would be like without us. But this way lies madness, and Bierce refuses to provide us with the comfort of knowing which of our nightmares are indeed real and which simply illusory manifestations of our subconscious urges.

Another pattern worth considering when one examines "A Watcher by the Dead" involves the doppelgänger concept, or the *double-goer*, as in the German and Dutch translation of the term. Reference to this idea may be traced as far back as 1821, when the German composer and writer E. T. A. Hoffman wrote a short story called "Die Doppelgänger." So this concept was prevalent in the nineteenth century and was probably a theory known to Bierce. A doppelgänger is the apparition of a living person, a double, sometimes referred to as a hellhound who pursues the living; sometimes called, on the other hand, a guardian spirit. Yet this guardian is not always one placed on earth to bless its earthly double. In fact, the hellish undertone of the doppelgänger allusion climaxes in Part V, where Jarette/Mancher playfully addresses his former tormenters by parodying their names, by giving them titles that he considers more suitable to their personalities: "'Didn't I say you were Drs. Hell-born and Sharper?'" inquired the man, laughing. *Did* he say this? If so, when? Under what circumstances? Did he know from the beginning who these men were and what game they were playing? So too, is the stranger merely enjoying his own little joke, his own play on words, or are Helberson and Harper themselves symbols of the demons that pursue all of us in our darker moments, ready to attack our misguided sense of well-being?

Likewise, if we examine the Jarette/Mancher duo in connection with the hazy world of the doppelgänger, we see that an analysis of such *doubling* leads to another solution of the riddle of identity in this story. Suppose that Jarette and Mancher are really two sides of the same person, one side the physical body; the other, the guardian spirit. On that fateful night, one side, the physical, destroyed the other, the spiritual, but in so doing, rid himself of one half of his identity, leaving him with only an incomplete sense of who he was and what he was doing in that building late at night. If the flesh and the spirit are forever at odds, as the Puritans have always argued, then here the *flesh* has clearly won the struggle, leaving what remains a man with no ethical compunction whatsoever. Moreover, from that time forward, Jarette/Mancher has suffered from a split in his personality, sometimes calling himself Jarette, but other times convinced that he is Dr. William Mancher. Small wonder that he now resides in Bloomingdale Asylum, floating in the twilight of a translucent but dimly lit sky, bereft of any moral weights to bring him back to the sanity of earth.

By the same token, Drs. Hell-born and Sharper (a.k.a. Helberson and Harper) might themselves be a doppelgänger and his earthly counterpart, with Sharper the physical, the one with the sharp, clearly defined edges, the one who actually suggests that Jarette be the guinea pig for their horrid laboratory experiment in playing with the dead. His doppelgänger is Helberson, the son born of hell, the spirit who accompanies him as he moves through the same dark landscape as Jarette/Mancher.

In the Introduction to *The Complete Short Stories of Ambrose Bierce*, Ernest Jerome Hopkins writes of the critical consensus that Bierce is, ultimately, a pessimist: "The verdict of 'pessimism' of course depends upon the point of view. Bierce himself would have denied it, stating that to scourge stupidity and hypocrisy was not pessimism but the reverse. In an age when all values are being questioned, Bierce's definition of 'white' as 'black' is very near the essence of modern thought.'"[17] In response to Hopkins's conclusion, one must agree that Bierce does indeed define good and evil as two sides of the spinning coin which, when looked at in the midst of its rotation, seem to be one and the same, like those familiar two-faced masks of comedy and tragedy. Furthermore, Bierce's sardonic view of our weaknesses, our isolation, our fragmented lives, and our dissociation from reality, appears quite modern. There is humor in Ambrose Bierce, but his humor arises from his realization of the cosmic irony that permeates all action, from his knowledge that a grim joke is being played on the world's inhabitants, but that the joke has no punch line because it has no ending.

Furthermore, Bierce's conviction that the world is a disorienting place, a conviction born of his own uncertainty with respect to the facts of our tenuous existence in a fragile world, may have been exacerbated by Bierce's unlucky encounter with a bullet in 1864. During a Civil War skirmish, Bierce, an able Union soldier, received a head wound, compliments of a rebel sharpshooter.[18] The bullet remained in his head, and, although in a few months Bierce recovered sufficiently to rejoin the fighting, the aftereffects would linger. He suffered from recurrent headaches, dizziness, and a feeling that he was living in a twilight world where it was impossible to distinguish between the living and the dead. "It is not uncommon for survivors of a major trauma — and a bullet wound to the head would certainly qualify — to feel themselves living a sort of posthumous existence, not entirely convinced of their own survival."[19]

In sum, then, it is possible to look at the major characters in "A Watcher by the Dead" as people who are not only "not entirely convinced of their own survival" but also not entirely convinced of *who* are they, assuming that they are, indeed, still among the living.

The Journey of Jehnry

Bierce pursues this concept of the doppelgänger in another of his most chilling stories, "One of Twins." Unlike "A Watcher by the Dead," which is told in the third person, this one achieves verisimilitude from the outset through its use of the first person, epistolary point of view. Its epigraph tells us that what we are about to read is "A Letter Found Among the Papers of the Late Mortimer Barr." But this is no ordinary letter, nor is it one that we would welcome. Significantly, it is a communication received by a man who is now deceased; moreover, there is no commentary appended by Mr. Barr as to the authenticity of the story told by the author of this letter. Bierce leads us to assume that Barr considered it important enough to preserve among his other papers, but Bierce denies us the certainty of knowing what opinion the late Mr. Barr held concerning both the author and the tale that this writer was driven to tell. Bierce's manipulation of point of view, then, is impersonal but shrewd, calculated to distance us from the first person "I" of the narrator, while simultaneously drawing us into the story. Because we know so little about the storyteller, we want to learn more about what he has to say.

The first thing he tells us is that he is a twin; in fact, he and his brother had so resembled each other that it was impossible to tell them apart. Henry reports that, as a child, he could never be sure just *what* his name was: "I speak of my brother John, but I am not at all sure that his name was not Henry and mine John."[20] Like the blending of the two identities of Jarette/Mancher in "A Watcher by the Dead," the identical twins in "One of Twins" are such a composite that their parents and friends had called them both by the combined name of *Jehnry*. With this imaginative designation, Bierce reveals his sardonic fascination with the possible complications that result from such similarities in appearance.

By the same token, Bierce also introduces the possibility of a doppelgänger when his storyteller, either Henry or John, confesses that even he is not quite certain which name had been originally assigned to him, thereby implying that there might very well be a *double goer* lurking somewhere in his background. To illustrate, addressing the late Mortimer Barr, the narrator describes his hazy identity: "You knew my brother John — that is, you knew him when you knew that I was not present; but neither you nor, I believe, any human being could distinguish between him and me if we chose to seem alike. Our parents could not; ours is the only instance of which I have any knowledge of so close resemblance as that. I speak of my brother John, but I am not at all sure that his name was not Henry and mine John."[21] In addition, Henry presents another tantalizing fact when he confesses: "We were regularly christened, but afterward, in the very act of tattooing us with small distinguishing marks, the operator lost his reckoning; and although I bear upon my forearm a small 'H' and he bore a 'J,' it is by no means certain that the letters ought not to have been transposed."[22] Thus, the two brothers were "branded" as infants, but which brand belonged to which brother is unclear. Furthermore, the very process of tattooing involves a puncture of the skin and, as the events in the brothers' lives will demonstrate, their identities not only blend but also bleed into one another. As in "A Watcher by the Dead," *Death* stalks the phantoms that flicker throughout this tale.

So, as with the Jarette/Mancher split in "A Watcher by the Dead," we are once again in a twilight mist of confusion. We are not only puzzled by the identities of Henry and John, but we are also uncertain about the person of Mortimer Barr, specifically his relation to the twins. Nor do we ever learn much more about the mysterious Mr. Barr, save that he was a good friend to Henry and John; that, on the deaths of their parents, he helped both young men get jobs in San Francisco; and that he later nurses Henry back to health following an emotional trauma. Nonetheless, at this point, Henry relates one significant but ultimately ominous fact: that he and John did not live together in San Francisco (again we ascend these dizzying city heights) nor did they often see each other, each pursuing his own individual lifestyle, each associating with his own acquaintances.

These separate lives will soon lead to complications as chilling in their own way as the torturous paths taken by either Mancher or Jarette following the death of one of them, whoever it might be. To begin, since few of Henry's friends know John and vice versa, Henry describes an incident in which such confusion of identities leads him to receive an invitation to dine at the home of a man who mistakes him for John. Claiming to have no idea who this host might be, Henry nevertheless replies to the man's invitation with the following odd bit of information: "'You are very good, sir, and it will give me great pleasure to accept the invitation. Please present my compliments to Mrs. Margovan and ask her to expect me.'"[23] Here, if we are alert, we might say to ourselves, "Aha! So our narrator Henry alleges that he does not know this man. If that is the case, how does he know the man's last name?" Bierce, of course, has the answer to the puzzle, and the answer is as stupefying in its uncanniness as the Jarette/Mancher solution to the riddle of the corpse had been in "A Watcher by the Dead."

At first, Henry appears puzzled himself, as he muses to the reader: "But how had I known that this man's name was Margovan? It certainly is not a name that one would apply to a man at random, with a probability that it would be right. In point of fact, the name was as strange to me as the man."[24] Furthermore, when Henry goes to his brother's business the following morning and tells him of the strange dinner invitation that he had received the night before, brother John rejoins with an equally odd story concerning Margovan, who it seems is rapidly becoming a mutual friend. According to John's account, Margovan is a good friend who works in the same office. They had met that morning at work, exchanged greetings, and John then informs Henry that a peculiar impulse had overcome him, as he had asked Margovan: "'Oh, I beg your pardon, Mr. Margovan, but I neglected to ask your address.' I got the address, but what under the sun I was to do with it, I did not know until now. It's good of you to take the consequence of your impudence, but I'll eat that dinner myself, if you please."[25] Mental telepathy? Not quite, for the phenomenon just described by the narrator goes one step further than mental telepathy. These are twins who are not just transferring thoughts to one another; these are twins who actually *know* things that only the other one should know. However, in due course, only one of the twins actually becomes engaged to Mr. Margovan's daughter. It is John who has been going to the Margovans' dinners on a regular basis and who naturally has become enamored of Miss Margovan, informing his brother Henry of both his infatuation and the impending marriage.

But the cynical Ambrose Bierce, following his own autobiographical inclination, rarely allows his characters much opportunity to enjoy love and romance. Nor will Miss Margovan find happiness with John Stevens, for Henry, the ever-perceptive twin, happens to see "one day on Kearney street a handsome but somewhat dissipated-looking man whom something prompted me to follow and watch, which I did without any scruple whatever."[26] As often happens in Ambrose Bierce's world, people move as though they are wandering on circular paths that return them to their original beginnings; by the same token, they act without volition. So it is in this instance with Henry Stevens, as he is compelled to follow this seedy individual to a logical, but unplanned, conclusion.

What Henry sees as he trails this man is what appears to be an assignation between the furtive stranger and an attractive woman. In addition, Henry informs us that there is something familiar about the woman, though he also adds that he has never seen her before. And yet, "I now felt the necessity of extreme caution, for although the girl was a stranger it seemed to me that she would recognize me at a glance. They made several turns from one street to another and finally, after both had taken a hasty look all about — which I narrowly avoided by stepping into a door-way — they entered a house of which I do not dare state the location. Its location was better than its character."[27]

This young woman is, of course, Julia Margovan, whom Henry meets for the first time the following week and immediately recognizes as the lady he had seen in a decidedly compromising situation. Like many other Ambrose Bierce creations, Henry is a character who enjoys the darkly ironic absurdities of existence; consequently, when he meets his brother's betrothed, he playfully alludes not only to his own status as a man with a "double" but also to the probability that Miss Margovan herself has a dou-ble. Knowing that she has been caught in a situation that no decent woman could excuse on any grounds whatsoever, she can offer only a lame ques-tion:

> "Was she very like me?" she asked, with an indifference which I thought a little overdone.
> "So like," said I, "that I greatly admired her, and being unwilling to lose sight of her I confess that I followed her until — Miss Margovan, are you sure that you understand?"
> She was now pale, but entirely calm. She again raised her eyes to mine, with a look that did not falter.
> "What do you wish me to do?" she asked. "You need not fear to name your terms. I accept them."[28]

Despite the unfortunate Miss Margovan's acquiescence to Henry's supe-riority in the matter of good timing and fortunate location, Henry is will-ing to be gracious about the whole thing and to ease her off the hook with a minimum of pain. Thus, he tells her gallantly, "'You have nothing to fear from me but suc h opposition to this marriage as I can try to justify on — on other grounds.'"[29] So Henry does not divulge to his twin the facts of Miss Margovan's perfidious nature and active libido. Yet, as with "A Watcher by the Dead," this is a story of identity and madness. And we know that it will end tragically, for as usual, Bierce offers his characters no way out.

The tragic conclusion is precipitated by Henry's knowledge of John's ill-conceived engagement; in point of fact, on the very next evening, it is Henry who first hears the horrifying cry of his brother, which "seemed to come from the street outside my window."[30] Moreover, as is reportedly the case with many identical twins, Henry has a presentiment of the shriek before he actually hears it. In addition, he hears it more than once, the noise seemingly emanating from the misty, foggy outside air but nevertheless coming from no precise, discernible location. Then, as though he were in that twilight world halfway between sleeping and waking, Henry starts walking down an obscure street, one previously unknown to him. Indeed, his destination is a place that heretofore he has never visited, a place the location of which he is not consciously aware. But, arriving at Mr. Margovan's home, he relates that he is met with "a subdued confusion of voices."[31]

The cause of this confusion is the death of the betrothed couple. Julia Margovan lies in one room, dead many hours as the result of poison. In another room is Henry's twin John, not yet dead but about to join Julia, for his demise is imminent, bleeding as he is from a recently inflicted chest wound, the result of a strategically aimed pistol shot. We can guess at the parts of the story that have been omitted. The unhappy Miss Margovan, distraught over Henry's discovery of her secret life, has decided to end that life. The equally unfortunate John, having made his own discovery of the body and unable to bear the sight of it any longer, has retreated into another room and removed himself from this world in a more violent manner than the way taken by his beloved.[32] But Henry has not yet finished his story. Evidently, the wife of the mysterious Mortimer Barr had spent the subsequent six weeks nursing Henry back to health following his traumatic encounter with the dead. So too, the shock had been so great that Henry claims to have been delirious during that time.

Yet in the succeeding years, Henry appears to have recovered sufficiently to resume his ramblings about the city. On one of these recent nights, Henry tells us, something leads him to the spot where he had witnessed the provocative encounter between the doomed Julia Margovan and her gentleman friend. And, lo and behold, whom does Henry spot but the very same man of dubious rectitude that he had spied entering that seedy establishment, accompanied by Miss Margovan. To Henry, this man appears to be somewhat the worse for wear, since the narrator describes him as "terribly altered — gray, worn and haggard. Dissipation and vice were in evidence in every look; illness was no less apparent. His clothing was in disorder, his hair fell across his forehead in a derangement which was at once uncanny and picturesque. He looked fitter for restraint than liberty — the restraint of a hospital."[33] Bierce's word choice here is astute. In describing this apparition's hairdo, Bierce gives us a word that looks as if it should mean the opposite of *tidy*, yet in affixing the prefix *de* to a word that sounds much like *arranged*, Bierce reminds us of both the unkempt appearance as well as the madness of the man, he who is the focus of Henry's immediate attention.

Likewise, Henry is the focus of this gentleman's gaze. Nor is this ghastly looking creature at all pleased to see Henry — or is it Henry? Terrified that he has seen a ghost, the man now facing "Jehnry" utters the following imprecation: "'Damn you, John Stevens!'"[34] Here he makes a half-hearted attempt to attack the narrator, the "one of twins," but instead falls headfirst into the gravel. Not especially concerned with the agitated stranger's fate, the narrator informs us that he walks away. Yet, as usual, there is a postscript to Bierce's tale; furthermore, as usual, the postscript is cryptic. The last paragraph ties some, but not all, of the loose ends: "Somebody found him there, Stone-dead. Nothing more is known of him, not even his name. To know of a man that he is dead should be enough."[35]

These final observations are particularly significant, mentioning as they do the issues of anonymity ("not even his name") and of the ultimate, irrevocable fact of death ("that he is dead should be enough.") As he does in "A Watcher by the Dead," Bierce brings us around in a circle, so that we end where we began: unsure of whether the narrator is Henry or John (as the recently deceased man had called him). Therefore, as in the previous story, we remain unaware of just who it is that is dead. And once again, we are reminded that Bierce's world is one that often resembles our own, where our sense of self is extremely fragile, where we must constantly reassemble ourselves in order to feel worthwhile and secure.

In fact, Bierce had a gift for drawing us into the events, to make us feel these incidents as surely as if we had been present. For instance, a number of Bierce commentators have pointed out that one of Bierce's most common literary techniques may be found in his development of the "mimetic tale." In his critical study of Bierce, Roy Morris Jr. cites another Bierce scholar, M.E. Grenander, who describes such a tale as one "in which a particular sequence of events is skillfully organized to reproduce in the reader a similar emotion that mimics that of protagonist."[36] This was a trick, observes Morris, that Hemingway would learn from Bierce, one of many ways in which Hemingway was indebted to Bierce in motif and style. As a matter of fact, both "A Watcher by the Dead" and "One of Twins" are "mimetic tales," for in both we feel emotions that mimic those, not just of the protagonist, but of the person from whose point of view we are hearing the story as it unfolds. In the case of the former story, we are with each character in turn as the points of view shift. In the case of the latter, we are forever with "Henry" as he relates his bizarre journey into the world of the peculiar.

Moreover, in "One of Twins" this mimetic quality is augmented in much the same way as in "A Watcher by the Dead": through the suggestion of a doppelgänger motif. Are Henry and John, then, representative of a man and his double? If so, which one is the earthly and which one the spirit? It is possible to imagine that the narrator, who thinks that his name might indeed be Henry, is the earthly, and that his *double goer* or his shadow self is John. If so, then Henry deliberately destroys that part of the self that wants to marry. By destroying John, Henry brings into the open his doubts about the worth of Julia Margovan and also secures his terrors about a commitment to another. The cry of alarm that Henry hears just before he discovers the harrowing scene of double suicide could very well be his own cry of angst as he confronts his own darkest dread. But what reason, then, is there for the death of the strange man, the luckless escort of the late Miss Margovan? In the commonplace, everyday world in which realistic, explicable events occur, we could naturally question how the stranger would even have recognized "John" Stevens under any circumstances, for presumably he never saw his stealthy follower, who might have been John's identical twin. Perhaps, following the double tragedy, he had seen a newspaper photo of the two victims; then, years later, he thought that he recognized one of these victims, this "ghost" on the street. But perhaps not. It is also possible that Miss Margovan's erstwhile squire is "Jehnry's" conscience, the small nagging voice warning him that women are trouble, and that this one is no exception. With the death of this portion of his moral sense, then, Jehnry achieves a kind of peace, as though an unseen spirit had performed an exorcism by killing his would-be attacker.

Yet, in the nether world of Ambrose Bierce, such catharsis as an exorcism may bring does not signify a completion, for in Bierce's world we can never be certain of anything. "To know of a man that he is dead should be enough" is the narrator's final resolve. Perhaps such knowledge should be enough for us as well.

Lost at Sea

Bierce does not limit his hallucinatory world to the enigma of physical resemblance; rather he sometimes explores the riddle of spectral evidence. So too, this concept of *doubling* can occasionally apply to *name* recognition as much as it does to *physical* recognition. Such identical names can lead to a crisis of doubt, to a faltering step into the unknown. Bierce pursues this riddle in "A Psychological Shipwreck." Here, we are left to question our own memories, which can at best be unreliable and at worst, terrifying. As he does in "One of Twins," Bierce presents a first person narrator who tells his story one step at a time, in a straightforward linear style, just as he recalls it.

From the first paragraph, Bierce's darkly ironic sense of humor comes again to the forefront, as his narrator sets the scene for his coming adventure. He had formerly been a partner in the mercantile house of Bronson and Jarrett, of New York. He is the only surviving member of this firm, his partner Bronson having passed away following the firm's failure the previous year. It is typical of Bierce to establish a causal relationship between these two facts, for the narrator informs us that Zenas Bronson died because he had been "unable to endure the fall from affluence to poverty."[37] The image of Mr. Bronson tumbling headlong from a fancy, high-rise office building to the squalid, cluttered tenements below is doubtless a picture that Bierce wants us to imagine.

But before Bronson's unfortunate fall from grace, Mr. Jarrett had undergone an unusual event, one that he is about to relate. It involves a sea voyage from Liverpool, where Jarrett had gone on business for the firm, and it ends in a most peculiar, unsettling way. Not that its conclusion is anything that Jarrett had anticipated when he embarked, for he is convinced at the outset that a long boat journey will have a calming effect. Deciding that a leisurely ocean trip is just what he needs to settle his nerves, Jarrett books passage for New York, not on a passenger steamer, but "on the sailing vessel *Morrow*, upon which I had shipped a large and valuable invoice of the goods I had bought."[38] Clearly, Jarrett had believed that a ship devoid of bothersome fellow travelers would allow him time to himself. And indeed, there are only two other passengers: "a young woman and her servant, who was a middle-aged negress."[39]

But these other two are enough to complicate Jarrett's life forever. Bierce's stories are often peopled with characters who exemplify the old maxim embodying our most fervent, escapist desires: "You can run, but you can't hide." An early hint of such complications surfaces when the young Englishwoman explains why she has a black servant; and further, why this servant is accompanying her from England. This domestic worker was originally from South Carolina, having lived with a husband and wife who had subsequently settled in England, but who had had the misfortune to die on the same day in the home of the Englishwoman's father.

Yet this unlucky couple had also seen to it that their black servant should continue to live with the Englishwoman's family. All of this detail appears somewhat interesting to the narrator, yet the fact that really intrigues him is the name of the husband, the man from South Carolina. His name was William Jarrett, which, as the storyteller reminds us, is "the same as my own. I knew that a branch of my family had settled in South Carolina, but of them and their history I was ignorant."[40]

Here we have a different kind of *doubling* than we have previously examined in Bierce. Whereas both "A Watcher by the Dead" and "One of Twins" involve a physical duplication and its accompanying thrust into a dizzying whirlpool of fear and confusion, "A Psychological Shipwreck" suggests a duality emanating from identical names. That Bierce found an irony and a wry amusement in such a coincidence is evident from an observation that he made when, as a young soldier fighting in the Civil War, he was involved in a skirmish in which a member of his regiment, the Ninth Indiana Volunteer Infantry, was killed by a cannon shot. Bierce is typically caustic in his description of his comrade's unusual manner of death, as well as intrigued by the ironic coupling of names. The soldier was a man named Abbott, who "was lying flat upon his stomach and was killed by being struck in the side by a nearly spent cannon-shot that came rolling in among us. The shot remained in him until removed. It was a solid round-shot, evidently cast in some private foundry, whose proprietor had put his 'imprint' upon it: it bore, in slightly sunken letters, the name 'Abbott.'"[41]

Such a grotesque correspondence is one that Bierce finds amusing; moreover, while the same sort of correspondence is alluded to in "A Psychological Shipwreck," the connection between the two fictional Jarretts is more oblique than it had been in the case of the real-life Abbotts. Nonetheless, the spectral presence of the recently deceased William Jarrett of South Carolina hovers over the upcoming events, even as the living William Jarrett is about to describe them.

This earthly William Jarrett, partner in the equally earthly mercantile house of Bronson & Jarrett, is bound for New York from Liverpool on the sailing ship *Morrow*, a name that will come to have symbolic significance. The young Englishwoman to whom he freely confesses an attraction is named Janette Harford; here the similarities between Jarrett and Janette are also worth remembering. Also significant is the fact that Jarrett is unable to define precisely the feeling that he gets when he is with Janette. Whatever this emotion is, it is a transcendent one, for whenever he bores into Janette's eyes, he has an Emersonian moment, as though he were making the shapes and colors of the world disappear: "Ship, ocean, sky — all had vanished. I was conscious of nothing but the figures in this extraordinary and fantastic scene."[42] Then — darkness — and, upon regaining his ability to make out shapes in the twilight, Jarrett perceives an eerie stillness followed by the mind-numbing feeling that the ship is sinking, even as the fascinating Janette is "torn from my grasp."[43]

But no ordinary shipwreck, this, for when Jarrett awakens, he has inexplicably been transported to a different ship, this one the steamer *City of Prague*. Bierce's denouement is filled with the dislocations and doublings that we have come to expect as one of his most prominent motifs. Jarrett's companion on the *City of Prague* just happens to be an acquaintance named Gordon Doyle, who also just happens to be the fiancé of Janette Harford. Doyle informs his dumbfounded listener that, three weeks previous to their current, peculiar conversation, he and Jarrett had boarded the *City of Prague*, while Janette had gone with her black servant to sail on the *Morrow*. But the *Morrow* never comes (an undoubtedly deliberate, grotesque pun on Bierce's part), and our hapless Jarrett is left alone to tell his bizarre tale.

The similarities between names, objects and events in this story are numerous. Not only is there the duplication of the name *William Jarrett*, but there is also the Jarrett/Janette resemblance. In addition, similarities exist in the histories of Janette and her servant: both had endured the deaths of the people who had been entrusted with their care. Moreover, the husband and wife in each instance had died on the same day. Nor do the likenesses end there. Shortly before Janette Harford disappears into the murky mists of time and space, Jarrett sees her reading a book: evidently arcane but nonetheless known to the narrator, for he refers to it as "that rare and curious work."[44] A popular book called *Denneker's Meditations*, it is as awkwardly written as it is peculiar. Yet Bierce quotes from this work, perhaps to suggest a further kinship between Jarrett and Janette, a kinship of souls, if not of blood. In point of fact, *Denneker's Meditations* sounds much like the sort of transcendental stuff reportedly read by Poe's Ligeia and her spooky lover: "To sundry it is given to be drawn away, and to be apart from the body for a season; for, as concerning rills which would flow across each other the weaker is borne along by the stronger, so there be certain of kin whose paths intersecting, their souls do bear company, the while their bodies go fore-appointed ways, unknowing."[45]

But Janette has evidently enjoyed these circumlocutions enough to absentmindedly buy a duplicate copy, for the recently awakened Jarrett notes that Doyle has his own on board this ship: the vessel that they are ultimately, but inexplicably, traveling on together. Doyle tosses him the book; he is evidently unimpressed with Janette's reading tastes, for he tells Jarrett, "It's a rum lot, Janette gave it to me; she happened to have two copies. Want to see it?"[46] What Jarrett sees, of course, is the book fall open to the page on which is found the selfsame, convoluted passage that had so bewitched the now lost Janette. For as Jarrett concludes his story, "the *Morrow* was never heard from."[47] (192) So the *Morrow* had indeed been lost at sea, along with Janette Harford. But Jarrett had been on the *City of Prague* all along, or so his friend Doyle had apprised him following Jarrett's returning consciousness from a long period of delirium. How Jarrett came to fancy himself on the *Morrow* is a mystery that Bierce leaves for us to ponder, but he gives us many clues regarding the dual nature of these proceedings, so that we are not really surprised that Jarrett has simultaneously been on board both vessels, perhaps through some sort of astral projection. Further, we are again reminded of the fragility not only of our own psychological states — thus the title "A Psychological Shipwreck" — but also of our own mortality, for we are admonished that, in all likelihood, our morrows, like the ill-fated ship, will never arrive.

In a 1991 dissertation, Stephen Nacco speculates that "A Psychological Shipwreck" should be read "in the context of Bierce's paradigm for ancestral doubling."[48] Nacco alludes to the distant relationship suggested between Janette and Jarrett, though the family ties are not as clearly delineated as he seems to think. For instance, Bierce does not have his narrator directly report that Janette herself had relatives in South Carolina. Additionally, Nacco studies in detail the name of the ill-fated ship, the *Morrow*, with respect to its symbolic orthography and its suggestion of a doppelgänger. He possibly stretches interpretation a bit when he argues that the word *Morrow* is almost (but not quite) a palindrome. What keeps it from actually being a palindrome, of course, is the difference between the first and last letters. Nonetheless, Nacco interprets the reason for this difference when he introduces the concept of Jarrett and Janette as mirror images, "except for the distinction of the 'm' at the beginning and its inverted version, the 'w' at the end. Ultimately, Jarrett will discover that Janette Harford is his female mirror image, an almost perfect replication of himself with the exception of gender. Thus, the 'w' stands for the woman and the 'm' represents the man."[49]

Of Civil War Soldiers and Ghostly Encounters

Many of Ambrose Bierce's stories are set against a Civil War and post–Civil War background. It was a war that Bierce would recall, auto-biographically, again and again, often through a gauzy screen colored with the red of uniforms recently pierced with bullets and swords, the brown of soldier-engulfing mud, the green of irrevocably infected sores, and the white of blinding, apocalyptic light. Three of these stories, "A Resumed Identity," "A Man with Two Lives," and "The Mocking-Bird," trace the efforts of a number of these soldiers to come to terms not only with their battlefield experiences but also with their wartime loss of a vital aspect of their very existences.

The Disadvantages of Being Dead

As with many of Bierce's stories of the supernatural, "A Resumed Identity" leaves us with some questions with respect to actual happenings. For one, we are never told just when the story's events are unfolding. "A Resumed Identity" begins, fairy-tale-like, with the information that what we are about to discover happened at some vague past time: "One summer night a man stood on a low hill overlooking a wide expanse of forest and field."[50] Such bucolic imagery is misleading, though, for this unnamed man soon discerns the movement of horse soldiers followed by dozens of infantry regiments, "marching in column, with dimly gleaming rifles aslant above their shoulders. They moved slowly and in silence."[51] Truly perplexed by the fact that he cannot hear this surge of fighters as they trudge north-ward, he at last concludes that these silent phantoms must be moving in a direction that results in his being in an acoustic shadow: "If you stand in an acoustic shadow there is one direction from which you will hear nothing."[52] Having satisfied himself as to a plausible explanation for this eerie sight, the man briefly turns away. When he turns back to look again, the columns of soldiers have disappeared. He can only wonder at the swift movement of such a slow army.

Like so many Bierce characters who are trapped outside of ordinary time and space, the man remains disconcerted by the sight that he knows he has just seen: "Minute after minute passed unnoted; he had lost his sense of time. He sought with a terrible earnestness a solution of the mystery, but sought in vain."[53] By the second part of the story, we begin to follow the threads that will finally lead to a solution of this mystery. This part introduces us to a real, concrete character, a physician named Dr. Stilling Malson, who is returning home from a night spent visiting a patient. As the doctor and his horse pass by the site of the Stones River battlefield, they encounter another traveler, this one on foot. From the side of the road, he approaches the horseman and greets him with a military salute, moving his right hand to the brim of his hat. Yet Dr. Malson notes that there are many peculiarities about this stranger, among them the fact that "the hat was not a military hat, the man was not in uniform and had not a martial bearing."[54]

Moreover, the doctor is even more dumbfounded by the nature of the conversation initiated by this odd man, who has materialized out of nowhere. What especially puzzles Dr. Malson is the stranger's line of questioning, which specifically addresses such military topics as the location of armies and the whereabouts of battles. Furthermore, Dr. Malson is implicitly accused of being the "enemy." When the man identifies himself as a "lieutenant, of the staff of General Hazen"[55] (a noted Civil War general to whom Bierce himself was assigned in 1863 as a topographical engineer[56]), Dr. Malson stays resolutely impassive. Nonetheless, something does stir within his professional memory, some recollection of the science of the mind, so he inquires if this ex-soldier is wounded. Upon hearing the stranger's reply — that he had received a head wound and had been unconscious for some time — "the doctor did not immediately reply: he was recalling much that is recorded in the books of his profession — something about lost identity and the effect of familiar scenes in restoring it."[57]

But this soldier of the Federal Army has lost more than just his identity. He has misplaced years, unaware that they have even gone. To the doctor's question concerning his age, the man replies without hesitation, "'Twenty-three.'" At this, the doctor rejoins, "'You don't look it; I should hardly have guessed you to be just that.'"[58] Impatiently brushing aside Dr. Malson's judgment, the man informs the doctor of the marching troops that he had just seen on the road. Malson, of course, knows that such an action would have been impossible, so his reply suggests bemusement at the man's hallucinations: "'Why, really,' said the physician, with an amusing consciousness of his own resemblance to the loquacious barber of the Arabian Nights, 'this is very interesting. I met no troops.'"[59] Stunned by such a peremptory brush-off, the man turns from Dr. Malson and wanders "very much at random, across the dewy fields, his half-penitent tormentor quietly watching him from his point of vantage in the saddle as he disappeared beyond an array of trees."[60]

The reason for Dr. Malson's half-penitent condition is the result of the physician's certainty that this man is a patient from the local hospital, an inmate who has apparently worked loose from the cords that have, for many decades, held him fast in that institution. From the unkempt civilian attire to the lined and aging face, this strange man has demonstrated all the symptoms of one who has lost himself somewhere in the past. Nonetheless, this tormented soldier is in the process of recovering some of what he has been missing, for he is about to make a horrible discovery that will eventually destroy him.

This revelation occurs in the third and final part of the story, where the sole focus shifts again to the Man With No Name. Still staggering from his encounter with the physician, who has seemed to him strangely distant and noncommittal, the man sits upon a rock and feels his worn and furrowed face, puzzled as to the cause of its odd leathery feeling. He recalls his recent wounding in a Civil War battle, but cannot reconcile his extremely altered appearance with the incontrovertible fact that "a mere bullet-stroke and a brief unconsciousness should not make one a physical wreck."[61] Shortly after he has allowed himself to ponder this conclusion, his attention fixes on a nearby monument, which could be a metaphoric representation of the man himself, as he notes that it "was brown with age, weather-worn at the angles, spotted with moss and lichen."[62] So too, as with Shelley's centuries-battered masterpiece of stupendous decay in "Ozymandias," this more recent edifice is one on which "Time had laid his destroying hand."[63]

Yet what is even more awesome to our unnamed hero is the inscription on the memorial, for it is both tribute and remembrance to Hazen's Brigade and to his soldiers who had died on that spot, Stones River, December 31, 1862. His memory vivid and alive with the image of his fellow Stones River comrades, he "fell back from the wall, faint and sick. Almost within an arm's length was a little depression in the earth; it had been filled by a recent rain — a pool of clear water."[64] In a perverse, parodic reversal of the revelation awaiting the beautiful god Narcissus when he falls in love with his youthful, stunning reflection in a pool, this aging fellow crawls toward his own likeness and is driven to madness and death by what he sees mirrored there: "He uttered a terrible cry. His arms gave way; he fell, face downward, into the pool and yielded up the life that had spanned another life."[65]

On the level of surface realism, we can surmise that the anonymous protagonist has been suffering from trauma-induced amnesia since the battle of Stones River in 1862. We may further assume that this battle occurred three or four decades earlier. Roy Morris, Jr. suggests that in this story the man has lost "a good forty years."[66] Moreover, in the intervening years, the veteran has mislaid his previous identity as a young soldier. Yet Bierce rarely leaves us nestled upon such a comfortable, easy, surface reading. Symbolically, we are led to believe that this man's earlier self has never truly vanished but has continually remained next to him, like a shadow self or a doppelgänger. His more recent self, having wandered away from a nearby hospital, has returned to the scene of the Stones River conflict. The battle site, long since forgotten by this recent self, jars something in the spectral shadow, which has for years accompanied and pursued him but has always been just beyond the reach of his consciousness. Therefore, it is this newly emerging shadow that holds the odd conversation with Dr. Malson; it is this shadow that believes he has been a patient for just a few months at the local hospital.

But when shadow and substance merge, as they do at the end when he sees his horrifying reflection in the pool, the Man With No Name dies. His identity at last complete, the old veteran cannot face the knowledge that for all of these years he has been only a partial human and that a vital part of him has forever belonged to the monument commemorating the fallen soldiers of Stones River. Becoming whole once again, he cannot reconcile his two selves. Truth hits him hard, like lightning, and blinds him by its luminous white bolt. His knowledge of his "true" identity offers no comfort. Like Narcissus, he is benumbed by what he sees in that pool. Unlike Narcissus, however, he does not see the outer world solely as a reflection of his own ego; rather, he sees it as having robbed him of ego: he remains forever nameless. Becoming whole again while simultaneously losing whatever self-esteem he has clung to through the years, he gives up his renewed life. Regaining his past, he forfeits his future.

He Forgot to Duck

When we turn to "A Man with Two Lives," we again see Bierce's sardonic humor and his sense of the absurd at work, as he probes the puzzle of an old veteran with the childishly singsong, alliterative name of David Duck. The story's narrator tells us that this ancient but revered man is commonly referred to by his numerous admirers as "Dead Duck." The man with the clichéd, but accurate, moniker tells his own story. It seems that in 1866 he had been a soldier assigned to carry military dispatches through hostile Indian territory. For two days and nights, he had hidden from the Indians' gunfire, but on the morning of the third day, "I remember, rather indistinctly, that in my desperation and delirium I sprang out into the open and began firing my repeating rifle without seeing anybody to fire at. And I remember no more of that fight."[67]

What the unfortunate Mr. Duck does remember is emerging naked from a river and traveling northward till he reaches his destination, Fort C.F. Smith. However, our storyteller informs us that, somewhere along the way, he has lost his dispatches. Something else has apparently been lost as well, for when the intrepid Duck, clad now in nothing but his feathers, approaches an old friend at the fort, Sergeant William Briscoe, the sergeant wants to know who the devil he is.

> "'Dave Duck,' I answered; 'who should I be?'
> He stared like an owl.
> "'You do look it,' he said, and I observed that he drew a little away from me. 'What's up?' he added.
> "I told him what had happened to me the day before. He heard me through, still staring; then he said:
> "'My dear fellow, if you are Dave Duck I ought to inform you that I buried you two months ago.'"[68]

So here we are again: in that nether world that Bierce so often creates. If Dave Duck is dead and buried, the victim of Indian ambush, as duly reported by Sergeant Briscoe, then who is the man speaking to Briscoe? If the sergeant had indeed found Duck's bullet-riddled body, scalped and "somewhat mutilated otherwise, too"[69] on the selfsame spot where Duck had reported his Indian encounter, then is this particular Dave Duck an imposter, as Sergeant Briscoe accuses him of being? When Briscoe turns on Duck, demanding to know who Duck *really* is, Duck replies plaintively, "'I'd give something to know.'"[70]

But Dave Duck is doomed never to know with certainty. Indeed, he is never allowed the luxury of finding his very own burial spot. He is, however, reunited with his clothing, courtesy of the increasingly skeptical Sergeant Briscoe, as well as with a few letters that were found in this clothing, which was removed from him before he was buried. Since it is apparent to the officers at the fort that the unlucky Duck is deranged, if not downright dangerous, he is forthwith imprisoned in the guardhouse, from which he subsequently escapes a week later in order to embark on a fruitless search for his own body.

So, just who *is* David Duck? Why is he so "universally respected,"[71] as the narrator tells us at the outset of the story? As with other stories in which Bierce explores the riddle of identity, there appear to be two David Ducks; once again we have a man and his *double*. And which David Duck is telling the story? Perhaps he was reborn that evening when he scrambled naked from the river, a baby just emerging from the womb, but with all his memory still intact, and his clothing, dispatches, and personal letters awaiting him at the fort. Whoever he is, David Duck has become a Rip Van Winkle, 1880s style. And, like Rip Van Winkle, once he has settled upon an identity with which he is comfortable, he is happy to tell and retell his story. In fact, as with the case of Rip, he relates his tale so often that it has crystallized into the story we now have: the journey of "A Man with Two Lives."

What Happens When a Man Has Killed His Other Half

"The Mocking-Bird," also set during the Civil War, involves two brothers. As in "One of Twins," Bierce probes the psychological effects of being a twin, and the concomitant problems that erupt as a result of the blending of twin identities. So too, as with Bierce's story of the ill-fated twin civilians, this narrative takes us through a dark landscape of mist, confusion, and subsequent horror: all of this seen through the terrified eyes of Private Grayrock, a Union sentinel who has lost his bearings in a dark forest and is now fearful of enemy attack. His is the uneasy edginess that comes from the commonplace, universal feelings of being disoriented, no matter what the time, place, or circumstances. It is the type of heart-pounding terror that can leave a person breathless, with mouth dry and skin damp.

As a result of these feelings of helplessness, Private Grayrock fires blindly at the first sound he hears. Unable to see his target, he is nonetheless able to hear answering shots from his fellow soldiers, arranged in picket lines on either side of him. In addition, Private Grayrock — good soldier, expert marksman, and dutiful sentinel — is convinced that he has hit something. Consequently, he becomes increasingly frustrated by his fruitless attempts to find evidence that he has brought down his quarry.

Exhausted and disappointed, Private Grayrock at last rests against a pine tree and neglects his sentry duty when he falls asleep. It is in his subsequent dream that we see Grayrock's wistful desire to return to an earlier, less confusing time: a time when his country was not at war, when he was not lost and abandoned in the forests of blood, when he knew who he was and where he was. For Private Grayrock dreams that he is once more a child, walking with his twin brother, "in paths of light through valleys of peace, seeing new things under a new sun. And through all the golden days floated one unceasing sound — the rich, thrilling melody of a mocking-bird in a cage by the cottage door."[72]

But Grayrock's dream of peace had soon turned into a world of darkness when his widowed mother died, leaving him and his beloved twin at the mercy of two warring relatives, who cruelly separate them, each one taking one of the brothers. Grayrock's brother "William (the dreamer) went to live in a populous city in the Land of Conjecture, and John, crossing the river into the Enchanted Land, was taken to a distant region whose people in their lives and ways were said to be strange and wicked."[73] And John receives the beautiful mocking-bird, whose beautiful, plaintive song will forever remind him of his hurt and loneliness, of his loss of William, the dreamer: of the loss of his other self. Although the brothers at first try to communicate by letters, their separation further widens with William's move to an even more distant city. Then contact ceases altogether. Still dreaming, Private Grayrock hears the voice of the mocking-bird, whose melancholy refrain underscores Grayrock's deep sadness.

Upon awakening, Grayrock sees a mocking-bird fly from out of a laurel thicket, perch above his head, and sing to him its joyous song. For a brief moment, he feels as though dream and reality are one, that he has become the child he once was before war and killing and dread of the unseen became his twin, became his identity. But in the macabre world of Ambrose Bierce, childhood is a phantom, an ephemera, a cruel mockery that haunts the adult because it refuses to disillusion him. Bierce's mature man knows that he can never recapture his past, nor would he want to, because the past is a reflection of what we all become in the present: sick of our very existence but afraid to reveal our fears.

Such is the state of Private Grayrock, whose moments of effervescent awe in the presence of the familiar mocking-bird last only briefly. Their brevity is underscored by Grayrock's determination to daydream no more as "he pulled himself together, picked up his weapon and audibly damning himself for an idiot strode on."[74] But his strides do not take him very far, for Private Grayrock is about to find the man he killed. The aim of sharpshooter Grayrock had indeed been on the mark, for the recipient of his bullet is his twin William, a Confederate soldier. William had been the "one to whom he gave his heart and soul in love."[75]

Only now do we realize why Grayrock had searched so fervently for evidence of the man he killed. He was looking for his lost self, for that part of his childhood remembered with fondness, before the death of their mother had forever separated him from William, from his heart and soul. Upon his discovery that his wartime obligations have caused him to annihilate his other self, Private Grayrock commits suicide, completing the circle that had begun with the death of his mother and that had ended with the death of judgment accompanying the absurdities of war. "At roll-call that evening in the Federal camp the name William Grayrock brought no response, nor ever again thereafter."[76] Both halves of the Grayrock brothers are now dead: one plus one equals nothing.

Closely analyzing this work in his dissertation, Stephen Nacco sees the Grayrock twins as emblematic of the tragedy of the Civil War, of the way in which it divided families. Further, he suggests that John represents the artistic half of an individual and William the logical part. But "the war separates the two halves of the single human mind, utterly disrupting the individual psyche."[77] Additionally, Nacco makes some comparisons between "The Mocking-Bird" and "One of Twins." He pursues the concept of the ancestral bond suggested in many of Bierce's stories, notably those dealing with *twins* and *doubling*. Moreover, continues Nacco,

> On a more thematic level, Bierce's twins form a symbiotic relationship that makes both members incapable of achieving any true individuality. Appropriate to "The Ancestral Bond," heredity unifies modern humankind into a single entity capable only of perpetuating communal misery. With respect to identical twins, neither possesses free will, as the fate of each is dependent on the flaws and quirks of human biology.[78]

Stuart Woodruff offers a further interpretation of "The Mocking-Bird." Woodruff mentions a discussion that Bierce had with his friend Walter Neale: a conversation in which Bierce maintained that individuals are made up of many personalities and that each of these personalities is a different aspect of these individuals' emotional, psychological, and intellectual development. Woodruff concludes that the underlying meaning of "The Mocking-Bird" lies in the statement that he made to Neale concerning the conviction that man cannot achieve immortality because these multiple identities could not survive. With respect to his own situation, Bierce remarked to Neale: "'When I ask myself what has become of Ambrose Bierce the youth, who fought at Chickamauga, I am bound to answer that he is dead.'"[79] In truth, Bierce's observation here could apply just as well to "One of Twins," "A Watcher by the Dead," "A Resumed

Identity" or "A Psychological Shipwreck" as it does to "The Mocking-Bird." In each of these stories, someone dies; yet it is equally true that in each of these, Bierce plants confusion. We can never really be sure if our perceptions of the story's events are correct or if our deductions about the outcomes are definitive.

Some Conclusions

Ambrose Bierce and the Critics' Overview

In his 1962 dissertation, Lawrence Berkove examines Ambrose Bierce's indebtedness to the philosophy of the Stoics, but he offers the following caution with respect to Bierce and the mind of the Stoics:

> The sayings of the Stoics appeal mainly to the intellect; Bierce's stories, however, appeal both to the emotions and the intellect, and the emotional appeal is the more powerful. When the reader's emotional turbulence subsides, he will have left from the story its stoical core, inviolate in its validity, unaffected by the story's pathos or the reader's passion, unshakable, and enduring. But, in addition, he will also have left to him Bierce's legacy, a re-aroused sympathy for his fellow man based on a sharpened awareness of man's demonstrated limitations.[80]

What is especially provocative about Berkove's study of Bierce in general and about this passage in particular is his exploration of the motifs of *doubling*, *identity*, and *madness* in Bierce's stories. Specifically intriguing throughout the dissertation is Berkove's judgment on Bierce as a largely misunderstood writer, one who was often misjudged as a mere imitator: a descendent of Edgar Allan Poe, imbued with cynicism and a misanthropic taste for and delight in the macabre. Rather, Berkove sees Bierce as a man with a strong core of humanitarian instincts, but one who is ever aware of one tragic fact of life, the fact "that man never won, that death was his usual portion and pyrrhic victory his utmost possibility."[81]

Certainly, Bierce's concern with the confusion resulting from an individual's search for identity reflects not only these humanitarian ideals but also the uncertainties inherent in an imperfect world. The idea that man is a frail being with decided limitations is not by any stretch an original one.

In fact, Ernest Hemingway, who was in some respects deeply indebted to Bierce, would posit a similar philosophy in many of his stories, novels, and essays. The later writer also believed that "man never won, that death was his usual portion." Yet Hemingway never wrestled with the concept of identity as Bierce did: never wrote stories of the supernatural as such, in which a person's identity keeps shifting till we are unaware of just who is who. However, Hemingway, with his sparse, simple style, often explored the source of courage in his imperfect world by magnifying his own personal light of bluster and bravado to a dazzling but blinding extent. Bierce, with his often overwrought, ornate style, spoke of courage by understating the consternation that frequently accompanies an individual who has lost his way and has therefore lost his hope. Both searched for identity in a world where nothing seemed to matter, but Hemingway was more the nihilist. Bierce believed in the power of language to persuade and to convey a moral lesson, albeit often a gruesome one. Hemingway distrusted language and so found definition and meaning in physical ritual. Both writers committed suicide, but Hemingway was deadly earnest and not at all secretive about his deed. Bierce crept away without a trace and probably with a wry, ironic chuckle at the tremendous joke he was playing on everyone concerned, although he left enough hints to family and friends for them to assume that he was quitting this world of his own volition.

Despite the fact that Bierce's vision frequently lacks Hemingway's dark despair, many students of Bierce's work agree that Bierce was a paradoxical combination of the realist and the romantic, a believer in the power of reason but one who was also convinced that reason could take one only so far. Bierce had read Darwin and believed that there were limits to man's ability to overcome the circumstances that the fates tossed in his direction. Thus, Bierce had many elements of naturalism tied to his romantic's view of the validity of the irrational.

Many critics agree that Bierce was a writer who would have been more at home in the twentieth century than in his own time, for Hemingway was not the only modern writer whom he influenced. According to Stephen Nacco:

> His [Bierce's] particular brand of supernatural and nihilistic fiction, as well as his acerbic journalistic style, ultimately endures as a literary influence whose disciples include H. L. Mencken. In addition, his more humorous stories, and his original application of the grotesque to the traditional western tall tale genre, foreshadow the works of such writers as the North American black humorists of the 1960's along with that of the contemporary South American magic realists, such as Jorge Luis Borges.[82]

So too, Bierce's modernity stems from his recurring demonstration that *reason* is not enough to save us from ourselves. He pits his supposedly rational protagonists against an absurd world filled with incongruity and incomprehensibility. And these reasonable men are invariably defeated, often by their own hubris, as they believe that they can beat the most bizarre, frightening circumstances, that they can beat the world at its own game. But this is a fixed game played by a universe with cards hidden in its sleeve.

And yet, Bierce's characters are forever surprised by their defeat — if they live. Such is the doom of Mancher/Jarette at the conclusion of "A Watcher by the Dead": a man, whichever one he is, now residing in the local asylum. Cathy Davidson asserts that Bierce's "stories can be read as allegories of the dangers of faulty perception, dangers to which all men are liable."[83] Likewise, Davidson makes some valid observations about the way in which Bierce perceives the nature of reality. We may apply her conclusions to our previous look into the way in which Bierce deliberately obfuscates questions of identity in a number of his protagonists. According to Davidson:

> In many of these stories (particularly the "ghost" stories), Bierce does not intrude with an "objective" or "rational" explanation for the extraordinary perceptions or clearly non-rational responses of his protagonists. He does not maintain rigid distinctions between "real" and "fictitious" or "perceived" and "imagined" occurrences.[84]

Therefore, according to Davidson, in the world of Ambrose Bierce, "no one can say what is, objectively, real."[85]

Bierce was also influenced by the theories of Charles Darwin and by the scientific determinism accompanying these theories. Many Bierce scholars have pointed out Bierce's naturalistic bent, a leaning that so often goes along with scientific determinism. Stuart Woodruff examines the paradox involved in Bierce's worldview that "man, innately selfish, engaged in an endless series of wars which destroyed the capable and strong while preserving the feeble and incompetent."[86] Likewise, Bierce, with his mixture of realism and naturalism tempered with romanticism, saw medical science as possessing an odd irony, even as malevolent nature was involved in weeding the unfit out of her garden:

> Scientific progress and discovery had managed to prolong man's life, but in so doing, had intensified the struggle for existence through overpopulation and increased competition. The basic paradox was that the very means by which man would save himself and improve his lot multiplied his problems instead of solving them.[87]

Given Bierce's dour view of man's absurd, untenable position in the impersonal universe, it is small wonder that all the stories dealing with dislocation of being in both time and place, as well as those focusing on identity confusion, end tragically.

Edmund Wilson has posited that Bierce's only real character is Death.[88] In fact, Wilson sees this obsession with death as a tiresome weakness in Bierce's writing: "The executioner Death comes to us from outside our human world and, capriciously, gratuitously, cruelly, slices away our lives. It is an unpleasant limitation of Bierce's treatment of violent death that it should seem to him never a tragedy, but merely a bitter jest."[89] Yet that is precisely the point. To Bierce, the Fates have played a terrible, cosmic joke on mankind.

One writer who was able to relate quite well to Bierce's despairing worldview was the superb but haunted literary critic Newton Arvin. Like Bierce, Arvin was from a small community in Indiana; furthermore, like Bierce, Arvin was a misfit, a man at odds with his Middle Western upbringing and with his father's sternly rigid discipline. In addition, like Bierce, Arvin was a troubled man who nevertheless loved words and the lasting impression these words could create. Both men became alcoholics; both were fascinated with the idea of self-destruction. Arvin made at least two unsuccessful attempts at suicide. Bierce, dying alone, somewhere in the isolation of the West, succeeded where Arvin failed. Yet significantly, the resemblance that Arvin himself saw was not between himself and Bierce but between his own despised father and Bierce. In fact, Bierce had grown up in rural northern Indiana at about the same time as Arvin's father.

Toward the end of his tormented life, Arvin began to do research into his ancestry. As he turned over the soil that contained his midwestern roots, he discerned the similarities between his father and Bierce. In a letter he wrote to Edmund Wilson, Arvin explained how he himself interpreted Bierce, for Arvin succinctly summarized the sterility not only of Bierce's background but also of his own heritage as well as that of his father. It was a background that Arvin was forever convinced existed as a deterrent to the intelligence and creativity of the sensitive artist. As Arvin told Edmund Wilson: "These qualities of bitterness, cynicism, and emotional aridity strike me as very characteristic of the men who grew up in the Middle West in those dreary decades from say the forties on to the seventies and eighties; it was a cultural trait, a form of self-protection, an almost desperate form of indemnification."[90]

More than forty years separated Bierce from Newton Arvin, the homosexual scholar who, even as he was filled with guilt and self-loathing, was also able to penetrate so brilliantly both the anguish and the genius of Hawthorne, Melville, Whitman, and Longfellow. Although it appears that the aggressive, masculine, heterosexual Bierce would have little in common with Newton Arvin, there lingered in the ghost of Ambrose Bierce a reminder to the shy, reclusive Arvin that we can never leave the past behind, that what we were is what we will become and what we will remain. In short, Bierce would continue to transcend time and place, to speak to later generations — to those who would also come ever so reluctantly to face their own inner demons and perhaps be equally terrified at what they saw.

• *Two* •

Henry James
and the Examined Life

The power to guess the unseen from the seen, to trace the
implication of things, to judge the whole piece by the pattern,
the condition of feeling life, in general, so completely that you
are well on your way to knowing any particular corner of it —
this cluster of gifts may almost be said to constitute experience
... Therefore, if I should certainly say to a novice, "write from
experience, and experience only," I should feel that this was a
rather tantalizing monition if I were not careful immediately
to add, "Try to be one of the people on whom nothing is lost!"
Henry James "The Art of Fiction" [1884]

The Man Who Might Have Been

At fifty-six, Spencer Brydon, protagonist of Henry James's story "The
Jolly Corner" (1908), is a man well past middle age. He has reached
that stage of life where a person often pauses to look back, to take stock
of what has been accomplished, to examine what has happened in the
years between adolescence and the approach of old age. Yet, as James
first presents him, Spencer does not appear to be a man who worries
inordinately about the passing years. He is, in fact, a taciturn man, not
given to long, idle conversations, nor is he a man to enter into emotional
commitments. Therefore, he hesitates to answer acquaintances when
they ask him upon his return to America from his life abroad what
he thinks of all the changes that have occurred in New York since he
moved away thirty-three years before. He keeps his thoughts to himself,
except when he speaks briefly to Alice Staverton, an understanding, patient

companion and friend of his youth, with whom he has many shared memories.[1]

In addition to those moments with Alice, Spencer also communicates in short conversations with Mrs. Muldoon, the woman who daily opens the windows and sweeps the dust out of his boyhood home. In fact, Spencer has returned to New York expressly to see about his property there; at the time of his return, he is leasing two houses in New York.

But Spencer Brydon is a restless, unhappy man — not from any definite, visible causes, but because he has come to that point where he has begun to question those blank spots in his existence. Like a person who connects the dots in order to complete the picture, Spencer needs to see something tangible in order to be whole. There are vacancies in his past that he needs to fill in with some meaning, even as he questions his own perceptions of the present. Though he is a self-absorbed man, not really given to introspection, he notes with interest that, from the outset of his return to America, nothing is as he had anticipated it would be:

> He actually saw that he had allowed for nothing; he missed what he would have been sure of finding, he found what he would never have imagined. Proportions and values were upside-down; the ugly things ... of his far-away youth, when he had too promptly waked up to a sense of the ugly — these uncanny phenomena placed him rather, as it happened, under the charm; whereas the "swagger" things, the modern, the monstrous, the famous things, those he had more particularly, like thousands of ingenuous inquirers every year, come over to see, were exactly his sources of dismay.[2]

Most of James's New York stories contain nostalgia for a lost time, for the simplicity of the New York of James's boyhood in the 1840s. "The Jolly Corner" may be read as just such a story, with Brydon representative of the author himself, a man who regrets his lost, prepubescent innocence. Thus when Brydon returns to New York, he is disgusted by what he finds. The New York that he encounters is no longer the New York he remembers: it has been tainted by industry, by a burgeoning population, and by the machinery of progress.

But the changes that have occurred during his thirty-three-year absence are not the only source of Spencer's dismay, for something distressing is about to happen to him: something that will disturb his self-perception and leave him a fragmented man, even less sure of himself. This occurrence is associated with his former dwelling. Spencer is having one of his two New York houses broken up into apartments; but the other one — the one located on "the jolly corner," the one where he was born and the one associated with his youth — holds more fascination for him. It is here "where various members of his family had lived and had died, in which the holidays of his overschooled boyhood had been passed and the few social flowers of his chilled adolescence gathered."[3] James's description here is crucial to our understanding of Spencer's character, for with "his overschooled boyhood" and "his chilled adolescence" we can see a cerebral man, one who tries not to give in to sentiment, to nostalgia, or to emotional confessions. Yet for all that, this house on "the jolly corner" will force him to face himself and to question his very identity, to confront the man he has become and to taunt the man he might have been. It is not coincidental that this is the house that Spencer refuses to allow to be destroyed, to be cut up into modern apartments. There is something waiting for him in that house and Spencer knows what it is.

Spencer Brydon and the Opposite Sex

Mrs. Muldoon also suspects that a spooky presence is lurking in the old house. She informs Spencer that she will not go creeping about the place at night; however, she is unaware that Spencer has deliberately neglected to apprise her of his own nighttime prowling. For Spencer Brydon is searching for one particular apparition. And like John Marcher in James's "The Beast in the Jungle," Spencer has a lifelong feminine associate; Spencer's is the loyal but steadfastly asexual Alice Staverton, who empathizes with Spencer's crisis and who has the temerity to share with him her grasp of those inner demons that he hesitates to acknowledge.

What Spencer sees in that house is his own phantom. It is Spencer Brydon as he would have lived his life had he remained in New York: had he not, as he tells Alice, "given it up."[4] Likewise, Spencer compares himself to a crushed flower as he thinks of the world he left behind in order to live abroad. He confesses to Alice that he might have made a lot of money in New York, yet it isn't the wealth that would have been the attraction had he stayed. What is at issue for him is that

> "it's only a question of what fantastic, yet perfectly possible, development of my own nature I mayn't have missed. It comes over me that I had then a strange *alter ego* deep down somewhere within me, as the full-blown flower is in the small tight bud, and that I just took the course, I just transferred him to the climate, that blighted him for once and for ever."[5]

Moreover, this "blight" that has shaded Spencer's moral center has taken the form of various avenues of dissipation; such moral lapses have been Spencer's raison d'être for over thirty years. Still, he adamantly assures Alice, the ever-steady confidante, "'I know at least what I am.'"[6] Yet knowing *what* he is may not be the same as knowing *who* he is; therefore, in his attempt to explain and to justify his past, Spencer describes to Alice only the externals:

> "I've not been edifying — I believe I'm thought in a hundred quarters to have been barely decent. I've followed strange paths and worshipped strange gods; it must have come to you again and again — in fact you've admitted to me as much — that I was leading at any time these thirty years, a selfish frivolous scandalous life. And you see what it has made of me."[7]

Even so, this explanation does not completely satisfy Spencer, who hesitates to shock the maidenly Alice with the sordid specifics of his "selfish, frivolous scandalous life." As a consequence of this reticence, every night he surreptitiously creeps around the large, old house — a dwelling embodying seventy years and three generations of memories. During the day, he is the sophisticated, cosmopolitan Spencer Brydon, who renews old friendships and is well received, albeit only superficially well liked. But more and more he comes to realize that his daylight self is not the *real* Spencer, that his real life is found solely within the empty chambers of the house.

There is much in the fiction of Henry James that could be classified as romantic, and many passages in this tale reflect components of the Gothic horror story and share a number of stylistic characteristics with Robert Louis Stevenson, a writer whom James admired. There are also elements of Emersonian transcendentalism. To illustrate, in the following description of the dichotomy between Spencer's day persona and his night persona, one can imagine Emerson himself sitting amidst the grass, flowers, trees, and streams, meditating on the beauties of becoming a "transparent eyeball":

> He projected himself all day, in thought, straight over the bristling line of hard unconscious heads and into the other, the real, the waiting life; the life that, as soon as he had heard behind him the click of his great house-door, began for him, on the jolly corner, as beguilingly as the slow opening bars of some rich music follows the tap of the conductor's wand.[8]

By the same token, if there is an ideal world — more real, more perfect — than the one Spencer inhabits with his casual friends, it is a safe, private, pristine world. But it is simultaneously delicate, fragile, breakable, and valuable. James uses the apt metaphor of *crystal* to describe the enclosed, womb-like place that Spencer is driven to visit night after night. Daniel Mark Fogel comments on Spencer's desire to return to his origin by analyzing the way in which James describes this longing in the final section of the story. Fogel examines the imagery of Spencer being picked up from "an interminable grey passage" and then being situated "at that dark other end of his tunnel." Fogel interprets this "grey passage" and the "dark other end of his tunnel" as a "symbolic birth canal."[9] But before he can be reborn, Spencer must continually return to his home on the Jolly Corner. Here is his reality, which he feels ever more powerfully each time he enters the house and places his walking stick on the marble floors:

> On this impression he did ever the same thing; he put his stick noiselessly away in a corner — feeling the place once more in the likeness of some great glass bowl, all precious concave crystal, set delicately humming by the play of a moist finger round its edge. The concave crystal held, as it were, this mystical other world, and the indescribably fine murmur of its rim was the sigh there, the scarce audible pathetic wail to his strained ear, of all the old baffled forsworn possibilities.[10]

Nonetheless, as the last phrase of this passage suggests, it is the self that Spencer renounced years earlier, that possibility of another life, which Spencer is seeking. And it is this other self that is also creeping through the house at night. Spencer even envisions himself as a hunter stalking his prey over mountains and through deserts, ready to strike and defeat the enemy lurking behind doors. Indeed, a complete identity confusion and reversal ensues as Spencer pictures himself as the apparition, feared by this phantom who has remained in the house throughout the years of Spencer's exile: "People enough, first and last, had been in terror of apparitions, but who had ever before so turned the tables and become himself, in the apparitional world, an incalculable terror? ... It made him feel, this acquired faculty, like some monstrous stealthy cat."[11]

The Terror of the Other

Despite his escalating feeling of strength and authority, Spencer feels increasingly dislocated, blind, helpless. In his search for his other self, he is losing the persona that he has adopted for over thirty years. He knows that this spectral presence is pursuing him, but nowhere can he find it: "He was kept in sight while remaining himself — as regards the essence of his position — sightless, and his only recourse then was in abrupt turns, rapid recoveries of ground. He wheeled about, retracing his steps, as if he might so catch in his face at least the stirred air of some other quick revolution."[12]

One manifestation of this disorientation may be seen in his determination to get beyond his compulsion to return each evening to the house. But the more he tries to stay away from the house, the more he is drawn to it, like a man who has resolved not to eat a forbidden food, but then gorges himself with it when he finally gives in to temptation. So it is with Spencer. Having forced himself to remain distant from the house for three nights, he returns more obsessed than ever, now convinced that he is being followed and is thus no longer the hunter, no longer the "monstrous stealthy cat" on the prowl, but rather the prey. Moreover, Spencer is thrilled that the presence is finally holding his ground, that the ghost is aware that something important is happening for him: "So Brydon argued with his hand on the banister and his foot on the lowest stair; in which position he felt as never before the air chilled by his logic."[13]

And thus Spencer's logic dictates that he is both the hunting animal as well as the animal being hunted. He is outside looking in and inside looking out. James's telling phrase for this, Spencer's mental state, is "duplication of consciousness."[14] Additionally, Spencer feels a narcissistic thrill in his anticipation of confronting this worthy foe, as he speaks to himself:

> "He has been dodging, retreating, hiding, but now, worked up to anger, he'll fight"— this intense impression made a single mouthful, as it were, of terror and applause. But what was wondrous was that the applause, for the felt fact, was so eager, since, if it was his other self he was running to earth, this ineffable identity was thus in the last resort not unworthy of him.[15]

Within these two previous passages, we find an important clue, one vital to understanding the essential nature of Spencer Brydon, for he is indeed a man who can chill the air by his logic and by his self-absorption. Like Marcher in "The Beast in the Jungle," he is an aloof, detached person, one who in the past has not been given to introspection. Indeed, Spencer has heretofore been concerned almost exclusively with his own self-seeking pleasure. And this desire for a thrill continues, especially as he feels himself drawing ever closer to his other self. So too, the motif of the *double* intensifies with James's description of Spencer's elated realization that he is now both the *fearful* as well as the *feared*.

In addition, this man, who has spent most of his life drifting, soon realizes that he must act immediately in order to prove to both of his selves that he is not afraid. James uses the phrase *holding on* as a symbol of Spencer's nature. Spencer Brydon had left America because there were things in his youth that left him feeling empty, vacant, like the appearance of those rooms in his childhood home upon his return. So, in one sense, there is nothing left of his past to "hold on to." For instance, when Spencer escorts Alice through the old house, explaining to her that he prefers to leave the place empty while simultaneously not divulging that he visits the house each evening, he emphasizes that nothing remains, nothing even worth stealing:

> He only let her see for the present, while they walked through the great blank rooms, that absolute vacancy reigned and that, from top to bottom, there was nothing but Mrs Muldoon's broomstick, in a corner, to tempt the burglar. Mrs Muldoon was then on the premises, and she loquaciously attended the visitors, preceding them from room to room and pushing back shutters and throwing up sashes — all to show them, as she remarked, how little there was to see.[16]

So herein lies a paradox. If there is in fact "little to see" in the house, if all is vacancy and empty rooms, then there is nothing for Spencer Brydon to "hold on to," nothing at all to draw him back to the place night after night. Yet Spencer desperately wants to *act*, to hold on to *something*, to reinvent himself by facing that awesome Presence.

And so when Spencer realizes that his phantom has turned on him, he reacts like an animal at bay that is cornered and has no choice but to fight. So he steels himself against flight, aware that he must finally act, must finally *do something*. Here James anticipates the twentieth century existentialists, those who insisted that a meaningful existence can only be derived from positive action, that all else in the universe is a meaningless shell, much like Spencer's old dwelling. Indeed, James describes it as "the great gaunt shell."[17] Thus, as Spencer thinks about his ghostly adversary, he feels

> the sense of a need to hold on to something, even after the manner of a man slipping and slipping on some awful incline; the vivid impulse, above all, to move, to act, to charge, somehow and upon something — to show himself, in a word, that he wasn't afraid. The state of "holding-on" was thus the state to which he was momentarily reduced; if there had been anything, in the great vacancy, to seize, he would presently have been aware of having clutched it as he might under a shock at home have clutched the nearest chair-back.[18]

Vacancy, emptiness — a world unfurnished, unused, ugly, dusty, with rooms closed and left unattended — this is the life that the uncommunicative

Spencer feels he has left behind, even as he embarks each evening on his surreptitious journey into the past.

Yet what nags at Spencer is the coldness of it all, the chill accompanying the Spencer Brydon of both past and present. For if a man gives himself form and substance through meaningful action, then Spencer fears that he is truly insubstantial, a series of dots that have not been connected. And so he resolves to face the apparitional foe, to brace himself against running away from it, to define his identity through positive action, to continue to hold on to whatever it is that keeps him from sinking into anonymity. "He had stiffened his will against going; without this he would have made for the stairs, and it seemed to him that, still with his eyes closed, he would have descended them, would have known how, straight and swiftly, to the bottom."[19] Spencer even uncharacteristically romanticizes himself, imagining that he is a knight about to go into battle with a sword drawn and ready.

Beyond the Door

But this romantic courage is short-lived, for at this moment Spencer is appalled at the sight of a closed door, a door that he knows he had left open only minutes before. Try as he might, he cannot convince himself that he had absent-mindedly closed the door. For Spencer is a man who dislikes surprises; he likes to keep his views open. So now Spencer faces another challenge; he must decide whether or not he has the courage to open the door. He realizes that he is at the point that he has both dreaded and feared because behind that door is the self he has been seeking: "Ah this time at last they *were*, the two, the opposed projections of him, in presence; and this time, as much as one would, the question of danger loomed."[20]

That Spencer conceives of both of his selves as *projections* is significant, for Spencer Brydon is remote and separated, even from himself. And these opposing projections imply two things: first, that Spencer is fighting an ongoing battle with himself, despite his public persona — the surface savoir faire and world-weariness that he shows to acquaintances; second, that Spencer sees himself only as a figure in a kind of stereopticon slide show projected on the wall — disembodied, adrift, unreal. Finally, in a decision in keeping with his lifelong determination not to commit himself, Spencer resolves not to act, not to open the door. Even as he resolutely resolves to make this indecision, however, Spencer is filled with self-loathing, all the while he is rationalizing that it is *discretion* that keeps him from acting.

Once again, we see that James has defined Spencer through *negation*; he has shown us Spencer not through what he does, but through what he does not do. Furthermore, James also reveals a salient fact about his protagonist: that in order for Spencer to come to grips with himself, he must first stop running and hiding from those terrors associated with the person he might have been. He must be willing to open those doors, to look inward, not only in search of himself but in search of an honest relationship with others.

And truly, at this moment, Spencer — the loner who has heretofore furtively and stealthily hidden his nocturnal rounds from prying outsiders — actually wants companionship. Having tried to persuade himself that he is using "discretion" in not opening that door, he also wants desperately to call for help. Yet he feels trapped. He looks out upon the empty street, its vacancy mirroring all that has gone wrong in his world, its darkness a metaphor for his abysmal ignorance of what his life might have meant to him had he only opted to exercise freedom of choice. Nor is *darkness* the only metaphoric element. The *closed door* represents Spencer's missed opportunities, his inability to act decisively, and his decision to excuse his past indecisions by referring to this weakness of character as *discretion*.

So Spencer runs from the closed door, runs down several flights till he comes to what he pictures as his escape: the vestibule. Yet here we are presented with another metaphor, this one reminiscent of some primal drive, something that Spencer has pushed down and tried to bury, but which now resurfaces as an image of drowning. Here we have Spencer trying to annihilate some part of himself through a submerging of himself. At the same time, however, *water* is also a symbol of a return to one's origins; even as we drown, we are reborn.

> At the end of two flights he had dropped to another zone, and from the middle of the third, with only one more left, he recognized the influence of the lower windows, of half-drawn blinds, of the occasional gleam of street lamps, of the glazed spaces of the vestibule. This was the bottom of the sea, which showed an illumination of its own and which he even saw paved — when at a given moment he drew up to sink a long look over the banisters — with the marble squares of his childhood.[21]

At this moment, Spencer knows that, when he reaches the bottom of the sea, he will be back in his childhood, a time filled with images of the cold hardness of marble. But it was also undoubtedly a time of silence, not unlike the stillness one associates with the creatures who live and die under water. So too, the memories called forth by these black and white slabs provide an ease and comfort to Spencer. But James does not let his hero off so easily, for there is another reversal here involved in Spencer's reasoning. Since these marble designs are in the vestibule, not only do they suggest to him a new beginning as exemplified by his childhood recollections, but they also point him to a way out: an escape from the terrors of his house. And he is determined to run from that closed door.

Now another reversal occurs. As Spencer resolutely heads for the front door and freedom, he notes with dismay that the vestibule door is open — a door that he remembered closing. It had been relatively easy for him to leave the previous door secure, to resist the temptation to open it. Yet here is one not so easy to ignore; someone or something has opened it, thus allowing easy access into and out of the vestibule. And what Spencer sees, of course, standing in that entryway, is his own presence, the man he might have been. And what that presence conveys to Spencer is shame and embarrassment at having to gaze upon Spencer, so much so that the phantom covers his face:

> Rigid and conscious, spectral yet human, a man of his own substance and stature waited there to measure himself with his power to dismay. This only could it be — this only till he recognized, with his advance, that what made the face dim was the pair of raised hands that covered it and in which, so far from being offered in defiance, it was buried as for dark deprecation.[22]

Having prepared to take an adversarial position, Spencer is caught off guard by another reversal and is subsequently revolted by the spectre's hiding his face. Such a signal leaves Spencer feeling apprehensive as he experiences "the sense of his adversary's inscrutable manoeuvre."[23] Spencer is completely overcome by what he sees projected in the vestibule — the awful realization that his ghostly counterpart cannot face his other self, cannot bear to look at Spencer Brydon, the triumphant sophisticate, he who has just returned from a glorious thirty-three years among the cosmopolitans. At first, Spencer tries to persuade himself that the spectre is unable to face his alter ego because this unearthly vision is loathe to look upon Spencer and to see how successful Spencer Brydon has become:

> That meaning at least, while he gaped, it offered him; for he could but gape at his other self in this other anguish, gape as a proof that *he*, standing there for the achieved, the enjoyed, the triumphant life, couldn't be faced in his triumph.[24]

But again a reversal occurs, as the hands of the spectre drop from the face, allowing Spencer to see the visage that he had so dreaded to confront. As he stares at the other man, he convinces himself that he and this ghost have no resemblance whatsoever. He is angry that he has wasted his time stalking such a prey: one who, after all, is no part of himself and thus undeserving of his attention. James uses an economic metaphor in describing Spencer's state of mind:

> He had been "sold," he inwardly moaned, stalking such game as this: the presence before him was a presence, the horror within him a horror, but the waste of his nights had been only grotesque and the success of his adventure an irony. Such an identity fitted his at *no* point, made its alternative monstrous. A thousand times yes, as it came upon him nearer now — the face was the face of a stranger.[25]

Yet the stranger still has a mysterious power over him, for the apparition now menacingly approaches Spencer, who retreats and faints, overcome by the terrors he had both sought and repulsed:

> Then harder pressed still, sick with the force of his shock, and falling back as under the hot breath and the roused passion of a life larger than his own, a rage of personality before which his own collapsed, he felt the whole vision turn to darkness and his very feet give way. His head went round; he was going; he had gone.[26]

That Spencer acknowledges "the roused passion of a life larger than his own" is vital to our understanding of what is happening psychologically. Yet at first he vehemently rejects any suggestion of a relationship between himself and the spectre, as he gradually comes back to life.

When Spencer awakens, he discovers that he is the object of the ministrations of two motherly ladies: Alice and Mrs. Muldoon. For the first time since his return to New York, he feels absolutely at peace: passive, desperate to reach out for help. But there is still something lurking in the shadows that frightens him. Having confronted what he insists to Alice was a "beast," a creature that was not himself, he repeatedly denies the reality that Alice herself knows exists. For Alice has also seen the presence. Moreover, she knows that it is indeed Spencer, even as she patiently listens to his arguments to the contrary. Spencer is not the first man to refuse to examine himself carefully and honestly:

> "He's none of *me*, even as I *might* have been," Brydon sturdily declared.
> But she kept the clearness that was like the breath of infallibility "Isn't the whole point that you'd have been different?"
> He almost scowled for it. "As different as *that*—?"

Her look again was more beautiful to him than the things of this world. "Haven't you exactly wanted to know *how* different? So this morning," she said, "you appeared to me."[27]

The Woman's Touch

The ever-perceptive Alice urges Spencer to accept one essential truth about his situation: that this phantom with the bowed head and the grim, frightened aspect represents Spencer as he would have been had he remained in New York. She reminds Spencer that this apparition is an unhappy man, albeit a wealthy one, to whom things have happened and for whom she feels affection, just as she is fond of the returning Spencer. And Spencer grudgingly remembers two physical features of his double, both of which he shares with his Other: the poor, fading eyesight and the two missing fingers on one of his hands. Alice has also recognized these characteristics, as she tells Spencer in the final scene of the story. Referring to the spectre's eyeglass, she observes:

> "His great convex pince-nez — I saw it, I recognized the kind — is for his poor ruined sight. And his poor right hand —!"
> "Ah!" Brydon winced — whether for his proved identity or for his lost fingers.[28]

These two characteristics exhibit incontrovertible evidence that he and the spectre are one: the weak eyes representative of the darkness that is notably associated with ignorance; the missing fingers representative of the consequences of greed. Daniel Mark Fogel suggests that the spectre exemplifies "Spencer Brydon's worst self [and] ... the most destructive potentials of American national identity, for it has succumbed to 'the rank money-passion,' has been 'hammered so hard and made so keen' by its conditions, and has been cruelly marked by the violence of the American lust for power — the apparition's missing fingers."[29]

These missing fingers might also have some autobiographical significance. Leon Edel suggests that the tale encompasses James's experiences as an American in Europe and that, in so doing, it assumes an importance as a personal myth "by which James announced to himself that had he stayed at home the hand that held the pen might have been crippled, but he might also have been a titan of finance, a remodeller of old houses, a builder of skyscrapers — even as this enterprising side of himself was about to remodel his writings in the New York Edition."[30]

Ultimately, James holds out the hope that Spencer just might be able to reconcile himself to the holes in his past by means of his acceptance of Alice's unconditional love and understanding. At the story's conclusion, though Spencer declares somewhat melodramatically that the phantom may have temporarily frightened him into an obsessive, paralyzed stasis, he also avows that his erstwhile bête noire lacks the pleasure of Alice's companionship. Agreeing with her long-time friend's estimation, and feeling obligated to provide him with a validation of his own self-esteem, Alice provides Spencer with one last, comforting comment. In the story's final sentence, she reassures him:

> "And he isn't — no, he isn't —*you*!" she murmured as he drew her to his breast.[31]

So finally it appears that Spencer Brydon has come to terms with what he had formerly been and what he has become over the years. Though James does not allow an easy, happily-ever-after ending to his story, he does reveal the ways in which *acceptance* may become a fact of life for anyone willing to face down the past. And what of Spencer's ongoing relationship with Alice? James leaves us with no answers, though we can be fairly certain that the Fates have not mapped out a torrid affair for these two, hovering as they do on the far side of middle age and on the even farther side of romantic, swept-off-their-feet passion. But both appear to be content at last. Perhaps that is enough.

Spencer Brydon and the Issue of Sexual Identity

Alternatively, perhaps contentment is something that will forever elude Spencer. A further slant on this story lies within the fairly extensive critical consensus with respect to Spencer's homosexuality in "The Jolly Corner." Some have suggested that Spencer is a homosexual, desperately trying to grasp his heterosexual "other" as he frequents the Jolly Corner. Spencer's wild, dissipated lifestyle during his self-imposed European exile is often viewed as evidence of the excesses of his perverted sexuality. Eric Savoy suggests that James has written a narrative in keeping with the Gothic tradition in which "the troubling of gender and sexual identification is most evident, most clearly traumatic."[32] Savoy argues that the double in "The Jolly Corner" represents Spencer's long-repressed desire to be "normal," to return as his heterosexual American counterpart. If we follow

Savoy's reasoning, we might assume that Spencer conjures this apparition because he has long desired a different sexual identity.

Yet it must be remembered that Spencer is terrified by the spectre that he has called forth, even to the point of fainting, all the while denying that the spectre resembles him in any form. As Savoy explicates Spencer's dilemma:

> The Gothic horror is, I would say, *doubled* when Brydon, in his recoil from this monstrous other, is incapable of reading it simply as a sign. This failure to read what he has "written"— what he has produced discursively — results in the undoing of his precarious homosexual identity, his inevitable *identification* with that excluded, abjected other.[33]

Moreover, when we insert Alice into this picture, we begin to understand that she has known all along about Spencer's sexual deviancy, but that she has resolutely, and perhaps obtusely, waited all these years for Spencer to return and to renounce his previous dissolute lifestyle. For instance, shortly upon Spencer's return to New York, he and Alice have a curious conversation about the sort of person Spencer might have been had he remained in America. When we once again examine Spencer's choice of a flower as a metaphor for his own stunted, unnatural development and as a sign of his growing self-awareness, we can deduce the oblique sexual references. It will be remembered that he confesses to Alice his understanding of what might have happened to him had he stayed there, "'I might have been ... something nearer to one of those types who have been hammered so hard and made so keen by their conditions.... It comes over me that I had then a strange *alter ego* deep down somewhere within me, as the full-blown flower is in the small tight bud, and that I just took the course, I just transferred him to the climate, that blighted him for once and for ever.'"[34] In the ensuing conversation, then, which is only ostensibly about money, we can now read James implying a normal, sexual function for Spencer; had he not retreated to the decadent wilds of Europe; indeed, had he, as a young man, stayed with Alice, he might have approached her on a different level — on a level that is not quite so Platonic. Both appear to have in mind this idea of a less studied, more emotional and physical relationship — one that might have been — when they speak of Spencer's recent and formerly "blighted" existence as a patron of the evil influences rampant in Europe:

> "And you wonder about the flower," Miss Staverton said. "So do I, if you want to know; and so I've been wondering these several weeks. I believe in

the flower," she continued, "I feel it would have been quite splendid, quite huge and monstrous."

"Monstrous above all!" her visitor echoed; "and I imagine, by the same stroke quite hideous and offensive."

"You don't believe that," she returned; "if you did you wouldn't wonder. You'd know, and that would be enough for you. What you feel — and what I feel *for* you — is that you'd have had power."[35]

Alice's mention of the "power" that Spencer might have possessed at one time may be read in this context as sexual prowess in the heterosexual sense, his "flowering" seen as something splendid, though Spencer significantly protests that he perceives these blossoming buds as "monstrous, hideous, and offensive." Perhaps he is, then, capitulating to his European self, to that person who, he admits to Alice, has "not been edifying — I believe I'm thought in a hundred quarters to have been barely decent."[36]

Yet Spencer continues to probe Alice, to peer closely into her psychological understanding of him. He wants to know what she knows; more specifically, he wonders if she would have liked him as Spencer Brydon, the American who never left home. In spite of himself, he is reassured by her answer: "'How should I not have liked you?'" To this, Spencer replies, somewhat noncommittally: "'I see. You'd have liked me, have preferred me, a billionaire!'"[37]

Spencer's rejoinder here substitutes money, and the power associated with money, for sex. That is, heterosexual behavior equals a normal, staid, secure life, which in turn equals the acquisition of money, which therefore equals power. Moreover, the construction that Spencer gives to his question invites further analysis on the basis of the language he uses. The parallel structure at first suggests ideas of equal importance, yet Spencer negates such equality by pausing after he has initially chosen the verb "liked" in order to substitute a stronger verb, "preferred." With the climactic emphasis on his second choice, then, we can see how Spencer wants a strong affirmation from Alice, one of reassurance that she has indeed chosen him and waited for him, forsaking all others. Nor does the wise Alice desert him at this moment, for her repeated reply is what he thinks he has been waiting for, though Alice does not pick up on his word "preferred":

"How should I not have liked you?" she simply asked again. He stood before her still — her question kept him motionless. He took it in, so much there was of it; and indeed his not otherwise meeting it testified to that. "I know at least what I am," he simply went on; "the other side of the medal's clear enough.... I've followed strange paths and worshipped strange gods; it must have come to you again and again — in fact you've admitted to me as much — that I was leading at any time these thirty years, a selfish frivolous scandalous life. And you see what it has made of me."[38]

What the life has made of Spencer is something that his American self is afraid to face, hence the fact that the spectre hides his face upon seeing Spencer, as though an immensely bright white light were being shone in his face — a lightning truth too powerful for the American Spencer to face. For Spencer Brydon, the world-weary European, has done things that he wants to confront as well as to deny. This duality of desire is thus illustrated in his feeling that he is both pursuer and pursued as he creeps around the vacant house at night. When this chase climaxes with the confrontation in the vestibule, we see even more clearly the horror of the American spectre, he who knows that something has gone terribly wrong with the world of Spencer Brydon:

> Rigid and conscious, spectral yet human, a man of his own substance and stature waited there to measure himself with his power to dismay. This only could it be — this only till he recognized, with his advance, that what made the face dim was the pair of raised hands that covered it and in which, so far from being offered in defiance, it was buried as for dark deprecation.[39]

No matter how much Spencer tries to tell himself that the American apparition is afraid to face the success of his European counterpart, the fact remains that Spencer is ultimately physically overcome by the conventional life represented by his American self, a collapse from which he must be rescued by the presence of two such matronly ladies as Alice Staverton and Mrs. Muldoon. Eric Savoy makes a valid point about the story's conclusion:

> We leave Brydon in the firm control of Alice, who is properly understood not simply as co-author of the ghostly double, but as the agent of heterosexual compulsion; what his life will be with Alice, in his embodiment of this long-repudiated otherness, is a matter for speculation; and this, I suggest, is the Gothic nightmare of "The Jolly Corner." The effect of Brydon's Gothic melancholia, his extreme psychosis, is that he cannot accommodate difference or plurality.[40]

Yet many critics of this story do not share Savoy's reading of the pessimistic conclusion. For instance, Daniel Mark Fogel argues "that there is a real moral victory at the end of the tale."[41] In fact, Fogel does not read any homosexual elements into the story, but rather he focuses on the economic aspects of Spencer's lost life. On the other hand, *money, power,* and *sex* were frequently equated in the nineteenth century, with much

Victorian-era pornography couched in economic terms, specifically in the use of the verb *spent* as synonymous with the male climax. So when one examines Spencer Brydon's unfinished life, it is tempting to see Spencer the European as impotent in more than one sense, his powerlessness extending beyond the monetary.

But does Spencer then come to terms with both of his selves? The answer to this is arguably in the negative, and possibly lies in the dialogue between Spencer and Alice that concludes the story. Alice's responses to Spencer's queries concerning which one of the "Spencers" she likes better are equivocal. At first, she tells Spencer that she had pitied the apparition because "'He had been unhappy, he had been ravaged.'"[42] When Spencer replies defensively that "he" too has been ravaged, she concedes that she has not really liked the spectre better. Then, finding that he cannot get a definite response from her with respect to her feelings, Spencer concludes, somewhat obscurely, that '"He has a million a year ... But he hasn't you.'" To this, Alice responds comfortingly, '"And he isn't — no, he isn't —*you!*'"[43]

The final image of Alice and Spencer offers an intriguing reversal of gender expectations, with Spencer now acting as the consoling mother to Alice, rather than the other way around. Indeed, while Alice murmurs words of reassurance to Spencer, we are told that "he drew her to his breast."[44] This, the last line of the story, comes as a surprise to the reader, for the three pronouns seem to be all wrong: the masculine subject as well as the possessive pronoun should be feminine, while the feminine direct object should be masculine. After all, since it is Alice who is offering consolation to Spencer, she should be the one offering the breast. But here it is the sexually confused Spencer who is acting the feminine role.

When one examines "The Jolly Corner" from an historical perspective, it becomes clear that Spencer's difficulty in defining himself as masculine is an outgrowth of the fin-de-siècle gender crisis, which affected both sexes. This crisis had been precipitated in part by the nineteenth century women's rights movement in France, England, and the United States. As a reaction to a philosophy that many men saw as a threat to their masculine supremacy, a countermovement grew in both the United States and England, one that attempted to reassert the distinct divisions between the roles and spheres of men and women.

"The Jolly Corner," written in 1908, comes at this time of transition, uncertainty and subsequent reaction. Elaine Showalter sees the changing times in this way:

But the process of upheaval, the redefinition of gender that took place at the turn of the century, was not limited to women. Gender crisis affected men as well as women, and the fantasies of a pitched battle for sexual supremacy typical of the period often concealed deeper uncertainties and contradictions on both sides. It is important to keep in mind that masculinity is no more natural, transparent, and unproblematic than "femininity." It, too, is a socially constructed role, defined within particular cultural and historical circumstances, and the *fin de siècle* also marked a crisis of identity for men.[45]

And so "The Jolly Corner" ends on a problematic note, leaving many doubts about Spencer Brydon's ability to find his way back out of the dark, womb-like security he so cherishes. He is still seeking himself, unable to get beyond his sexual confusion, even as he offers himself as a motherly nurturer to Alice at the conclusion of his pathless journey.

• *Three* •

Wilkie Collins
and Social Constraints

I have always held the old-fashioned opinion that the primary object of a work of fiction should be to tell a story ... but it is not possible to tell a story successfully without presenting characters: their existence as recognisable realities being the sole condition on which the story can be effectively told.
Wilkie Collins, "Preface," *The Woman in White* (1861)

No Name at All

The setting of Wilkie Collins's novel *No Name* is Great Britain in 1846: a patriarchal society, imbued with a rigid social hierarchy, dedicated to the proposition that not all men are created equal. Moreover, no woman was *ever* created equal to any man. Into such a world comes Magdalen Vanstone, the young heroine of *No Name* (1862), one of Wilkie Collins's finest novels. It is unfortunate that *No Name* is often overlooked: ignored, for instance, by critics who have favored the spellbinding story of *The Woman in White* (1861) as well as Collins's excellent detective novel, *The Moonstone* (1868).

It is true that *The Woman in White* has some of the most complex, compelling characters in modern literature: for example, the crafty Count Fosco. Likewise, while *The Moonstone* is one of the most carefully constructed novels in English literature, it lacks the superb characterizations and the breathtaking narrative flow of either *The Woman in White* or *No Name*. For instance, Miss Drusilla Clack, the obsessively devout and cheerfully deluded religious busybody in *The Moonstone*, is a marvelously comic character with a blind, insidious side to her nature, but she is no match for the equally obsessive and insidious Mrs. Lecount of *No Name*: the latter being a far more richly developed individual. Whereas *The Moonstone* is the steady crawl of the tortoise, *No Name* is the frenzied dash of the hare. Indeed, *No Name* is the work that Kenneth Robinson has called "the most unjustly neglected of all Wilkie Collins' novels."[1] And this neglect is unfortunate, for in this novel Collins has created one of the most complex, credible women in Victorian fiction. As such, Magdalen Vanstone represents a time and place when a woman's sense of her own self worth and her very identity rested on a shaky foundation: a base that was likely to crumble, carrying her into the ground and burying her beneath the concrete of society's Draconian dictates.

In the course of this excellent novel, Magdalen assumes many identities and disguises, most of which are intended to further her schemes to reclaim from her father's family the inheritance that she feels rightly belongs to her and her sister. This is an inheritance that would have gone to these girls had they not been forced to pay for their father's rash, youthful indiscretion in marrying a "bad" woman who subsequently refused to grant him a divorce.

Additionally, their father compounded his error by living for over twenty-five years with another woman to whom he could not be legally bound while his legitimate wife lived. This second partner subsequently bore his children, but without benefit of that vital marriage document. In depicting the circumstances surrounding the girls' illegitimate status, Collins knew that he was in danger of strong criticism from the leading moralists of the day. And indeed, it was not a surprise "that one of the louder protests should appear in the pages of the *Quarterly Review*, by whose standards even Dickens was deemed vulgar."[2] Collins allows two of these vulgar Vanstone children to survive: Norah and Magdalen, who grow up cheerfully ignorant of the illegal status of their parents' living arrangement. They are eighteen and twenty-six, respectively, when, through an unfortunate series of events, they are suddenly orphaned: first, through their father's death in a railway accident and then, through their mother's death in childbirth. This awareness of their shaky position in an upper class British family occurs almost simultaneously with the loss of their parents.

His own private lifestyle reveals to what extent Wilkie Collins took a personal, if biased, view of the social stigma attached to such unconventional living arrangements. Collins never married, but he lived with two women. The first was Caroline Graves, whom Collins met around 1854.

Caroline had married George Robert Graves on March 30, 1850; less than one year later, on February 3, 1851, she bore one daughter, Harriet Elizabeth.[3] Some scholars have speculated that it is possible that her husband was dead by the time she began living with Collins.[4] However, another biographer has uncovered solid evidence that George Robert Graves died of tuberculosis on January 30, 1852, leaving his young widow with a child not yet one year old.[5]

In any event, the widow Graves entered into a long period of cohabitation with the novelist. Their relationship was discreet yet open. Despite Caroline's devotion to Collins, and in spite of Collins's loyalty to both Caroline and her daughter Harriet, Caroline eventually married again, the wedding notable for one curious fact: Collins was present at the ceremony. Almost immediately following Caroline's marriage to Joseph Charles Clow, Collins began a relationship with Martha Rudd. Their affair was a particularly fruitful one, for within the next five years, Collins and Martha had three children, the oldest of whom was born just nine months after Caroline's marriage.[6] Despite the obvious intimacy between Collins and Martha Rudd, Caroline returned to live with Collins in the 1870s, approximately five years after her union with the mysterious Mr. Clow. She resumed the name associated with her widowhood and, as Mrs. Graves, continued to live with Collins until his death about twenty years later.[7]

Thus, Collins wrote *No Name* from the viewpoint of someone who had lived for many decades on the fringes of respectability. Collins's personal perspective on Victorian morality contributes to the novel's verisimilitude and makes the ironies of the narrative quite compelling. The first of many such ironic twists appears shortly before Mr. Vanstone's death, when the long-gone-by-the-wayside Mrs. Vanstone fortuitously dies in her New Orleans home, thus allowing Mr. Vanstone to marry the mother of his daughters. But he dies before he can make another will and thereby legitimize his daughters' claims to his estate. Then, in another neat twist, his wife dies before she can sign the paper authorizing her late husband's estate to go to Norah and Magdalen. Furthermore, shortly before her demise, the newly legalized Mrs. Vanstone, who doubtless was surprised to find herself pregnant with a change-of-life baby, in due time gives birth to a legitimate child. This infant might then have been the lawful heiress, but Collins keeps turning the ironies of fate, so that the newborn dies as well, leaving the Vanstone daughters with no immediate family. Consequently, these two children born out of wedlock with no provisions made for them prior to their parents' deaths have no name and therefore no hope. The family fortune passes to Mr. Vanstone's ne'er-do-well brother, Michael, who has no intention of sharing any of it with his illegitimate nieces.

It is Magdalen, the more determined and aggressive of the sisters, who vows to get revenge on the evil uncle and to regain what she sees as their birthright. Uncertain of just how to proceed, Magdalen nonetheless deserts her sister. Then, writing to Norah from an undisclosed location, Magdalen realistically summarizes their present dilemma and, in so doing, speaks for all women of that time in similar circumstances, cast adrift by the Civil Law of Europe and by their place as the second sex. After asking Norah's forgiveness for abandoning the family, Magdalen admonishes her:

> Pray don't send and seek after me; I will write and relieve all your anxieties. You know, Norah, we must get our living for ourselves; I have only gone to get mine in the manner which is fittest for me. Whether I succeed, or whether I fail, I can do myself no harm, either way. I have no position to lose, and no name to degrade.[8]

Indeed, the Vanstone lawyer, Mr. Pendril, had previously presented the situation to the girls' governess, Miss Garth, clearly reiterating his knowledge of the cage into which the Vanstone daughters were boxed: "we must look facts as they are resolutely in the face. Mr. Vanstone's daughters are Nobody's Children; and the law leaves them helpless at their uncle's mercy."[9] Outcast in name, Magdalen also becomes an outcast in fact, resolving to use her wits as well as her talent for disguises in order to devise a means by which she might overcome the social and legal stigma accompanying her very existence.

Early in the novel, Collins has prepared us for Magdalen's metamorphic abilities when he depicts her talent for acting and for mimicry. Performing in an amateur production of Sheridan's *The Rivals*, she reveals a skill that, in another time and place, would have served her well as a vocation. But this is England in 1846, and well-bred ladies did not make a career of painting their faces, subsuming their identities, and going on the stage, thereby tempting their souls to everlasting damnation in the name of Art.

But Magdalen, as yet unaware of the horrible fate in store for her, cannot look beyond the thrill of the moment as she hears the applause of the audience at her theatrical debut. Collins's choice of *The Rivals* for Magdalen's debut offers the reader a forceful foreshadowing. The plot of *No Name* involves Magdalen in a rivalry of her own, as she enters into a series of adversarial, duplicitous relationships with everyone whom she sees as blocking her path to the money that she is convinced she deserves.

So too, in a reversal of what the tragic Magdalen attempts to accomplish, *The Rivals* portrays a man who adopts a disguise in order to convince someone to marry him. Finally, to add to the ironic twist — one of many such reversals that Collins gives to his plot throughout — *The Rivals* is a comedy where all ends happily, whereas *No Name* is ultimately a bitter tragedy of a foundering and — in the end — a lost lady.

In the interim, Magdalen assumes many identities as she wanders down the path to ruin. The first of these disguises is occasioned when she joins forces with a cunning schemer named Horatio Wragge, "the one really successful comic character in the pages of Wilkie Collins."[10] Captain Wragge has tenuous ties to the family of Magdalen's mother and, when he first recognizes Magdalen herself on the streets of York where she has gone to seek work from a theatrical producer, he figures that she is rich and an easy touch. Upon learning, first, of her true financial situation and, next, of her natural acting ability, Wragge proposes that they form a team to make money, with Magdalen as performer and Wragge as business manager, the keeper of the books and, incidentally, of most of Magdalen's earnings. Their partnership is a strange one: Magdalen is wary enough to know that she is being taken advantage of, yet she also appreciates Wragge's shrewd manipulative talents, as he does hers. So they stay together, ultimately involving themselves in exceedingly involved stratagems to gain back Magdalen's birthright.

But before they embark upon their theatrical enterprise, they must first give Magdalen a new name. In a journal, the captain tells of his efforts to determine what name Magdalen would prefer. Her response is revealing, as it evidences Magdalen's awareness that, her identity having been lost anyway, such a negligible topic as a name is no longer important to her. Wragge reports on their conversation:

> The trifling responsibility of finding a name for our talented Magdalen to perform under, has been cast on my shoulders. She feels no interest whatever in this part of the subject. "Give me any name you like," she said; "I have as much right to one as to another. Make it yourself." I have readily consented to gratify her wishes. The resources of my commercial library include a list of useful names to assume; and we can choose one at five minutes' notice.[11]

About one month later, Wragge writes another entry. This time, he has thought of another identity to give Magdalen, an archetypal one that even an old sinner like Wragge is afraid to mention by name: "She has shown the cloven foot already. I begin to be a little afraid of her."[12]

In spite of his growing apprehension, Wragge enjoys a challenge, and he sees in Magdalen a woman the likes of whom he has never previously encountered. For her part, she realizes that she needs Wragge's experience with the ways of the world. So, chameleon-like, these two thread their way through some complicated labyrinths of deception and disguise.

Not only do Magdalen and Wragge try on various identities in their efforts to better their lot, but this curious duo also involve Wragge's wife in their schemes. Mrs. Wragge is a pitiful woman who is as clueless with respect to her place in the world as is Magdalen, but who lacks Magdalen's innate intelligence and sense of righteous indignation. In fact, Mrs. Wragge is a browbeaten, simple woman whose head constantly buzzes, whose shoes are forever coming off—thus prompting her husband to reprimand her for being "down at the heels"—and whose mental capacities are always challenged to the limit.

Yet despite some superficial differences, we always sense camaraderie between Magdalen Vanstone and Matilda Wragge. Both characters represent a woman's dilemma in her search for self in England of the mid-nineteenth century. Magdalen gives to her efforts all the crafty intelligence she possesses; Mrs. Wragge possesses no artful intelligence at all, and so she simply gives up. As unlikely a pair as might be imagined, these women form a fast bond that outlasts the most terrible events that occur to them both.

Yet, ironically, Mrs. Wragge also represents resistance to her husband's ironclad efforts to run the world according to military order and efficiency. For instance, when she tries to puzzle through the recipe for an omelette, she becomes thoroughly befuddled; however, her confusion is both an unconscious recognition and a rejection of the male-dominated society represented by her husband. Deirdre David offers the following deconstructionist theory of Matilda Wragge as a disruptive burr lodged just inside the Captain's trousers leg:

> On the level of narrative, her contention with the cookery book implies female subversion of male-authorized texts or laws (the cookery book written by a woman for the instruction of other women in filling male orders); on the level of story, her resistance to accepted interpretation intimates the larger battle in this novel between legitimacy and illegitimacy, between male governance and female revenge. And she doesn't let up.... If her husband's attitudes, despite his raffish demeanor and picaresque career, represent conformity and conservatism, then Mrs. Wragge's attitudes represent resistance and interrogation.[13]

How much of Mrs. Wragge's resistance Magdalen actually recognizes is not clear, but Magdalen is astute enough to detect a troubled woman when she meets one. As she studies the cover of Mrs. Wragge's cookbook, Magdalen observes, more to herself than to Matilda Wragge: "'If this was anything but a cookery-book, I should say somebody had been crying over it.'" To this, Matilda admits to having moistened the pages with her tears of frustration, even as she chimes in with her complaints about the confusion generated by the book's language. She tells Magdalen that the Captain has "ordered" an omelette for his breakfast the following day. Reading from the cookbook, she points out to her new friend the reason that her head is constantly buzzing. Though Matilda is trying to please her husband, the tasks he has set upon her are too trying for her to master. She thus points out to Magdalen the fatally mixed up messages in her reading material:

> "Omelette with Herbs. Beat up two eggs with a little water or milk, salt, pepper, chives and parsley. Mince small."—There! mince small! How am I to mince small, when it's all mixed up and running? "Put a piece of butter the size of your thumb into the frying-pan."—Look at my thumb, and look at yours! whose size does she mean? "Boil, but not brown."—If it mustn't be brown, what colour must it be? She won't tell me; she expects me to know, and I don't.... "Keep it soft; put the dish on the frying-pan, and turn it over." Which am I to turn over — oh mercy ... tell me which — the dish or the frying-pan?[14]

When Magdalen helpfully suggests the correct antecedent for the pronoun *it* by responding that the *dish* needs to be placed on the frying pan and the *frying pan* turned over, Mrs. Wragge is so grateful that she asks Magdalen to repeat her instructions so that they will coalesce in her brain. She also confesses to Magdalen that the Captain has ordered her to do many things, but that "I've forgotten them all!"[15] To this desperate admission, Magdalen has a practical answer, one that reveals her penchant for subverting the dictates of a male-dominated society. Empathizing with Matilda, Magdalen simply advises her to say that she has done all of these things.

One similarity that these two women share is the fact that both are pariahs: Magdalen because she is not only nameless because she is illegitimate but also because she compounds her social ostracism by becoming an actress. So Magdalen has no name on two accounts. Likewise, Mrs. Wragge is a de facto nameless person, largely because her husband's constant browbeating has robbed her of any positive, definite feelings that she might once have had about who she is. Our first sight of Mrs. Wragge conveys the impression that here is a woman whose life consists of minutiae too tremendous for her to understand. Having divined that Miss Vanstone will be the ideal complement to him in his efforts to con his way across England, Captain Wragge escorts Magdalen to his lodgings, where she encounters for the first time the captain's dithering wife. Collins's use of the neuter pronoun "it" to refer to Mrs. Wragge speaks eloquently to this lady's treatment as a brainless, castaway piece of furniture, an object of scorn and ridicule on the part of her husband:

> The captain threw open the door of the front room on the first floor; and disclosed a female figure, arrayed in a gown of tarnished amber-coloured satin, seated solitary on a small chair, with dingy old gloves on its hands, with a tattered old book on its knees, and with one little bedroom candle by its side. The figure terminated at its upper extremity, in a large, smooth, white round face — like a moon — encircled by a cap and green ribbons; and dimly irradiated by eyes of mild and faded blue, which looked straightforward into vacancy, and took not the smallest notice of Magdalen's appearance, on the opening of the door.[16]

Indeed, poor Mrs. Wragge is so vacant and fuzzy minded that her confusion at first stuns Magdalen, but such bewilderment soon generates sympathy for this benighted and bewitched lady, a woman as incapable of doing anyone deliberate harm as she is unable to fathom the world in which she is tossed about. In truth, the deeper Magdalen dives into the muddy waters of the dirty world she has submerged herself in, the more frantic she becomes to hold fast to Mrs. Wragge.

At one point, the captain and Magdalen plot to keep Magdalen hidden in their house for two weeks. When Magdalen informs the captain that she wishes to take Mrs. Wragge into her own room for the duration of this exile, the captain is thunderstruck. Here is a man who has devoted his married life to belittling the human being who lives with him, treating his wife as though she were a large, ungainly lizard — slow, unattractive, shuffling her way through the maze of lies and traps set out to ensnare those whom he would con. So when Magdalen tells him, "I wish to remove Mrs Wragge from the miserable room she is in now, and to take her upstairs with me," he at first misunderstands, for he replies:

> "For the evening?"
> "For the whole fortnight."
> Captain Wragge followed her into the dining-room and wisely closed the door before he spoke again.
> "Do you seriously mean to inflict my wife's society on yourself, for a fortnight?" he asked, in great surprise.

"Your wife is the only innocent creature in this guilty house," she burst out vehemently. "I must and will have her with me!"[17]

Yet, unlike Mrs. Wragge, Magdalen vows that she will most emphatically not be tossed about by the vagaries of fortune. When her uncle, old Michael Vanstone, dies, thus leaving his ill-gotten inheritance to his weak-willed son Noel, a young man with a bad heart and the personality of a pimple, Magdalen adroitly shifts gears. Convinced that her acting skills and her talent for disguise will serve her well, she dons the attire of an old lady, paints her face with the appropriate wrinkles, and poses as her old governess, Miss Garth. In this guise, she pays a visit to Noel and his astute, nosy housekeeper, Mrs. Lecount. This woman will prove to be a formidable foe, one who penetrates Magdalen's various personae and who will come close to being Magdalen's complete undoing. Though Magdalen has cultivated the art of adroit dissimulation and is able to fool the cement-brained Noel, Mrs. Lecount sizes her up and figures her out, guessing correctly that "Miss Garth" is really Magdalen come to plead her own case for her father's money. But Mrs. Lecount does not give her hand away — not yet. She reveals to Noel her suspicions about the mysterious stranger's identity only after Magdalen has left, the imposter knowing only that her quest has been so far unsuccessful.

But Magdalen is not about to concede the fight, even as her mission turns dangerous. Still an adolescent, this shrewd conniver is described as a slender, alluring woman, one who is fully aware of her physical attractions and who decides to use her sex appeal to envelop Noel Vanstone in a web made from the fibers of his own pride and manifest obtuseness. Having exhausted her various reserves of duplicity and knowing of no other way to grab hold of her inheritance, Magdalen vows to marry Noel Vanstone, her first cousin. It is this duplicitous plan to trap Noel that the good-natured, honest Matilda Wragge comes close to unwittingly sabotaging.

But long before Magdalen has hooked up with the Wragges, she has suffered through an experience that has prompted her to take revenge on men and to use her manifold talents to subvert in her own way the patriarchal chain that enslaves women and leaves them helplessly bound, at the mercy of their captors. Before the collapse of the family fortunes subsequent to the collapse of the family name, Magdalen had fancied herself in love with another youth, one as worthless in his own way as Noel Vanstone, though her first love is healthier and poorer. But, shortly before her resolve to marry Noel, she receives a self-serving farewell letter from her erstwhile fiancé in China, where he has gone in a futile attempt to earn a living, his efforts occasioned by the fact that Magdalen no longer has the auspicious monetary prospects that she formerly had. Ironically, his letter contains the sort of posturing that is becoming so natural to Magdalen herself. But while Magdalen is only too aware of her need to deceive, to hide her own self in order to preserve herself, her young betrothed, Francis Clare, is too thick skulled to understand that he is not only lying to her but also lying to himself, though he does demonstrate that he has mastered the art of the simile. But one of the major motifs of his letter involves his rationalizations, his justification accompanying his loss of employment. In point of fact, Francis Clare has been fired:

> My prospects in China are all at an end. The Firm, to which I was brutally consigned as if I was a bale of merchandise, has worn out my patience by a series of petty insults; and I have felt compelled from motives of self-respect, to withdraw my services, which were undervalued from the first. My returning to England, under these circumstances, is out of the question. I have been too cruelly used in my own country to wish to go back to it — even if I could.[18]

When Magdalen receives this letter, she is initially so stupefied that she withdraws from reality, seemingly giving up, not only on her plans for revenge against Noel Vanstone but also on life itself. In this connection, Captain Wragge, temporarily separated from both Magdalen and his wife, receives a letter from a doctor who has been summoned to the Wragge lodgings in order to examine Magdalen. It is not the first time, nor will it be the last, that she will undergo a life-threatening depression. As a woman with no identity and therefore no future, she often verges on the edge of madness. Here, Dr. Jarvis writes to advise Captain Wragge:

> I recovered her [Magdalen] with great difficulty from one of the most obstinate fainting fits I ever remember to have met with. Since that time she has had no relapse, but there is apparently some heavy distress weighing on her mind, which it has hitherto been found impossible to remove. She sits, as I am informed, perfectly silent, and perfectly unconscious of what goes on about her, for hours together, with a letter in her hand, which she will allow nobody to take from her. If this state of depression continues, very distressing mental consequences may follow; and I only do my duty in suggesting that some relative or friend should interfere who has influence enough to rouse her.[19]

Magdalen's paralysis does not last long, however, for once she is reunited with Captain Wragge, she informs him of her latest scheme: she is going to marry Noel. Since Francis Clare has demonstrated his true nature as a crass opportunist, Magdalen feels that she might as well throw herself in the direction of cousin Noel, all the while gambling that she will be too tempting not to be caught.

In order to carry out these plans, however, she cannot allow Noel to discover who she really is. Accordingly, she and Captain Wragge devise a plan to pose as niece and uncle by the name of Bygrave. In addition, not knowing precisely what to do with the eternally disconcerting Mrs. Wragge, they agree to give her a new identity as well; she is to become Mrs. Bygrave, wife of Mr. Bygrave (Captain Wragge). Though her relationship to the captain naturally has not altered, her name has; consequently, the ever-vigilant captain fears that his wife will give the game away if she is allowed any direct contact with either Noel Vanstone or his sharply perceptive and exceedingly jealous housekeeper, Mrs. Lecount.

Once Magdalen has committed to a form of harlotry by plotting to sell herself to Noel, she is torn by a number of conflicting emotions — feelings that come within inches of tempting her to suicide just prior to her fateful wedding. For one, she knows what kind of stultifying life she will lead with this proud, prissy, stingy man. For another, she is aware of the dangers inherent in tying herself to a man while at the same time pretending to be someone else. Then there is Mrs. Lecount to contend with. This shrewd lady sees through Magdalen's pose as Miss Bygrave, just as she had earlier seen through her disguise as Miss Garth. In both of these instances, Mrs. Lecount correctly guesses Magdalen's true identity. But she is unable to convince her employer of the hoax about to be perpetrated upon him. Had she done so, and had the marriage between cousins never taken place, much grief could have been spared for both husband and wife.

In truth, the closer Magdalen comes to snatching the notably unconscious Noel, the more desperate she becomes to escape the fate that she herself has orchestrated. The nearer Magdalen approaches her long-sought-after success, the more distraught she becomes: less and less sure that she wants to identify herself as Mrs. Vanstone after all. Magdalen's language in the following scene demonstrates her mounting hysteria, her words connoting relentless terror, suggestive of her captivity as the prisoner of an apocalyptic vision. In this mental condition, she confronts Captain Wragge:

> "Take me away!" she exclaimed, tossing her hair back wildly from her face.
> "Take me away before he comes. I can't get over the horror of marrying him, while I am in this hateful place — take me somewhere where I can forget it,

or I shall go mad! Give me two days' rest — two days out of sight of that horrible sea — two days out of prison in this horrible house — two days anywhere
in the wide world, away from Aldborough. I'll come back with you! I'll go
through with it to the end! Only give me two days' escape from that man
and everything belonging to him! Do you hear, you villain?" she cried, seiz-
ing his arm and shaking it in a frenzy of passion — "I have been tortured
enough — I can bear it no longer!"[20]

As the day of her wedding approaches, she becomes ever more fearful. Even that old sinner Wragge observes her with alarm. Having informed
her that the marriage for which she had concocted such elaborate plans is
only three days away, he notes with amazement her apparent stupor, her
disassociation from her own feelings:

> He was prepared to quiet her if she burst into a frenzy of passion; to reason
> with her if she begged for time; to sympathize with her, if she melted into
> tears. To his inexpressible surprise, results falsified all his calculations. She
> heard him without uttering a word, without shedding a tear. When he had
> done, she dropped into a chair. Her large grey eyes stared at him vacantly. In
> one mysterious instant, all her beauty left her; her face stiffened awfully, like
> the face of a corpse. For the first time in the captain's experience of her,
> fear — all-mastering fear — had taken possession of her, body and soul.[21]

Shortly thereafter, this fear of the noose that she is about to tie around
her own neck leads Magdalen to purchase laudanum; her intention is to
ingest enough of the brown liquid poison to cause her demise. Here, it is
significant to recall that Wilkie Collins himself was becoming increasingly
dependent on laudanum, specifically on opium, the essential ingredient of
laudanum at this time.[22] In fact, for more than twenty years, with escalating frequency and in increasingly larger amounts, Collins took laudanum as a painkiller. A number of his friends observed that, in no time
flat, he could drink a wineglass filled with this liquid. Indeed, Collins once
told his guest Hall Caine that he indulged his laudanum requirement many
times a day. Collins also referred to his fellow author de Quincey as a man
who "used to drink the stuff out of a jug. He then told his visitor a long
and gruesome story of a man-servant of his who had killed himself through
taking less than half one of Wilkie's normal doses."[23] In short, when Collins
writes of Magdalen's vacillation between the choice of life and death, he
fully understands the sensations accompanying an immoderate dose of
laudanum.

Such first-hand experiential reference doubtless enabled Collins to
build suspense; we wonder if Magdalen will in fact succumb to the

inevitably dire outcome of her own dreadful plot. She even writes a farewell letter to her sister Norah, appending to it a note of instruction to Captain Wragge concerning the disposition of her corpse. In both of these melodramatic letters, a self-pitying Magdalen takes the blame for her own awful misfortune.

But Magdalen Vanstone is no Emma Bovary, so she opts for life and a dismal marriage to Noel rather than death and the legacy of a disgraceful memory. In addition, just as Magdalen's life has become a series of poses with no basis in reality, so her efforts to bring off the marriage are filled with deceit. In a series of serpentine maneuvers designed to thwart the canny, possessive Mrs. Lecount and involving Mrs. Lecount's brother, who is supposedly dying in Switzerland, Magdalen and Captain Wragge manage to get Mrs. Lecount packed off to Zurich — at best, a long, arduous trip in the mid-nineteenth century. So the wedding takes place as scheduled.

But there is no honeymoon, since both parties to this ill-fated match conceived in hell have their own agendas, each of which is designed to keep the other at a distance. To illustrate, Noel is as stingy in his husband role as he was in his bachelor mode, though he does make a will leaving his fortune to Magdalen, probably figuring that he can't take it with him. For her part, Magdalen apparently spends a good deal of time away from the family home as well as from her husband's bed. Collins suggests that the marriage is never consummated, perhaps because Noel has put Magdalen on such a fairy-tale-like pedestal that he sees her as unapproachable; or perhaps because he fears that excessive excitement coupled with frantic exercise will cause his already fragile heart to collapse. Even more significant are Magdalen's reasons for dodging her mate. Given her ulterior motives for the marriage, and considering her physical disgust whenever she contemplates the quality of her present existence, we may assume that she would just as soon eat ant paste as engage in conjugal relations with Noel. Whatever the reason, their brief marriage remains, at best, Platonic, and, at worst, downright antagonistic.

What is certain is that, after only about two and one half months of life with Magdalen, Noel's appearance, never especially attractive, has already altered for the worse. He is described as a man who looks tremendously old and all dried up, raisin-like:

> His wizen little cheeks were beginning to shrink into hollows; his frail little figure had already contracted a slight stoop. The former delicacy of his complexion had gone — the sickly paleness of it was all that remained. His thin

flaxen moustachios were no longer pragmatically waxed and twisted into a curl: their weak feathery ends hung meekly pendent over the querulous corners of his mouth. If the ten or twelve weeks since his marriage had been counted by his looks, they might have reckoned as ten or twelve years.[24]

Not only is Noel reaping the rewards of his oblivious journey through his short and formerly uneventful life, but he is also as yet unaware of the grim joke that Magdalen has played on him. He is simply facing the prospect of eating another morning meal by himself. So he asks the servant at what time his "bride" had left the cottage. Learning that she had escaped about an hour previously, he then inquires of another servant if the mistress had anything of particular importance to say before she left:

> "No message in particular, sir. My mistress only said she would be too late if she waited breakfast any longer."
> "Did she say nothing else?"
> "She told me at the carriage-door, sir, that she would most likely be back in a week."[25]

Though Magdalen is not running off to meet another lover, she nonetheless has nothing but disgust for the man she has trapped into marriage through falsifying both her age as well as her identity. In a letter she writes to her former governess Miss Garth, Magdalen speaks of her bittersweet triumph:

> Do you know who I am? I am a respectable married woman, accountable for my actions to nobody under Heaven but my husband. I have got a place in the world, and a name in the world, at last. Even the law, which is the friend of all you respectable people, has recognized my existence, and has become *my* friend too! The Archbishop of Canterbury gave me his licence to be married, and the vicar of Aldborough performed the service. If I found your spies following me in the street, and if I chose to claim protection from them, the law would acknowledge my claim. You forget what wonders my wickedness has done for me. It has made Nobody's Child, Somebody's Wife.[26]

But Mrs. Lecount finally convinces Noel of Magdalen's true identity. Ironically, in their search through Magdalen's belongings, trying to find visual evidence of her treachery, they discover the laudanum, which Magdalen has safely nestled away, no doubt in case she has another urge to end it all. However, unaware of Magdalen's former plans to quit this life lest she be stuck with the cloddish Noel forever, Noel and Mrs. Lecount assume that Magdalen has bought the poison in order to quickly dispatch Noel, thereby gaining the loot which she has felt was hers all along. Mistaking her intentions, they also misapprehend a key quality of Magdalen's character: her essentially decent instincts. Magdalen is no killer. So, in another ironic twist, Magdalen's true identity is indeed hidden to Noel and Mrs. Lecount, but in ways that they never suspect.

In any event, Noel has seen enough to be convinced of Magdalen's baseness and to be fearful for his own puny self. However, with his snail-like perception, he does need a few moments to consider the implications of the bottle that Mrs. Lecount has discovered:

> "Poison!" he said to himself slowly, "Poison locked up by my wife, in the cupboard in her own room." He stopped, and looked at Mrs. Lecount once more. "For *me?*" he asked, in a vacant, inquiring tone.[27]

As a consequence of her awful discovery, Mrs. Lecount persuades Noel to make a new will, cutting out Magdalen altogether and thus giving her no incentive to serve him a laudanum drink with his evening meal. In due course, Magdalen learns of Mrs. Lecount's success in opening Noel's dimly perceiving mind to the real name of his wife. But she does not have much time to ponder her most recent fate, for Noel soon dies of a heart attack. This fatality is not really unexpected when one considers his history of heart trouble as well as the recent storms and stresses put upon that organ by Captain Wragge and Magdalen. However, his death is greeted with ambivalence by Magdalen; on the one hand, she is decidedly glad to be rid of his offensive presence; on the other, she is even more fervently appalled at his effrontery in cutting her adrift through a hasty revision of his will.

In addition to being a financial castaway, Magdalen has also lost her partner in theatrical enterprises, Captain Wragge, a man who has been a sometime counselor and soulmate, for she and the Captain had agreed to part immediately following her marriage. So once again she is a woman alone, a lost lady with No Name. But she has no intention of giving up. Having come this far, she hardens her resolve and adopts another identity, as she takes the name of a former servant whom she has just dismissed in order that the young lady may be reunited with her lover. Under this new name, then, Magdalen becomes a maid in the home of Admiral Bartram, a cousin of her late father's and the new heir of Noel Vanstone. She reasons that if only she can get inside his spacious home, she will have plenty of time as well as excuses to prowl around the house, poke into drawers, and look for clues that might lead to any loopholes in Noel's will: loopholes large enough for her to crawl through and come out the other end with a large settlement from Noel's estate.

But one night she is caught on the prowl and is banished from the home, assumed name and all. From there, her downfall is swift and assured. Collins sets up his reader to believe that Magdalen will ultimately die alone, a victim to the poverty she had so feared and abjured for so long. Indeed, toward the end of the novel, we find Magdalen only one or two steps from the edge, her life poised and ready to slip over the rim into the ruins she has dug for herself. In one of the novel's final scenes, Magdalen, residing in a London slum, is discovered by Captain Kirke, a man who had once seen her when she was still hauntingly beautiful; a man who has never forgotten her face. This time, Magdalen has been evicted from these squalid surroundings and is in the apartment entrance, awaiting someone to take her to the hospital or, if she is turned away from there, to the workhouse. Thus, what Captain Kirke sees now as he enters the passageway to her dwelling is a picture that is nearly impossible for his mind to process properly:

> The sight that met his eyes should have been shielded in pity from the observation of the street. He saw a slatternly girl, with a frightened face, standing by an old chair placed in the middle of the passage, and holding a woman on the chair, too weak and helpless to support herself—a woman apparently in the last stage of illness, who was about to be removed ... Her head was drooping, when he first saw her, and an old shawl which covered it, had fallen forward so as to hide the upper part of her face.[28]

Not only is Magdalen's body ravaged, but her mind is gone as well. Having spent so much time during the past few years posing as someone else, she now truly has blocked out reality, descending into confusion and the madness born of her inability to find a firm footing in the slippery soil of nineteenth century moral and legal dictates. So when her newfound savior, Captain Kirke, insists on returning her to her room, she retreats into a safer time, a more secure former existence, one devoid of pretense and disguise:

> He stooped, and lifted Magdalen in his arms. Her head rested gently on the sailor's breast; her eyes looked up wonderingly into the sailor's face. She smiled and whispered to him vacantly. Her mind had wandered back to old days at home; and her few broken words showed that she fancied herself a child again in her father's arms. "Poor papa!" she said softly. "Why do you look so sorry? Poor papa!"[29]

In spite of Magdalen's precarious physical and mental condition, Captain Kirke soon rescues her from imminent death. And, learning of her sordid, spotted past, he forgives her anyway. And so Kirke and Magdalen agree to marry; indeed, the final scene might have been lifted from a typical sentimental romance novel of the period. Magdalen's self-abnegation verges on the cloying as she pleads with Kirke for a reaffirmation of her worthiness to be his wife, to at last have a Name that she can hold onto for her very own:

> "Tell me if you have any shadow of a misgiving! Tell me if you doubt that the one dear object of all my life to come, is to live worthy of you! I asked you to wait and see me; I asked you, if there was any hard truth to be told, to tell it me here, with your own lips. Tell it, my love, my husband!— tell it me now!"
>
> She looked up, still clinging to him as she clung to the hope of her better life to come.
>
> "Tell me the truth!" she repeated.
>
> "With my own lips?"
>
> "Yes!" she answered eagerly. "Say what you think of me, with your own lips."
>
> He stooped, and kissed her.[30]

And so on that final, happy note, Magdalen Vanstone becomes Magdalen Vanstone Kirke and they live happily every after — or perhaps not. In point of fact, *No Name* has more similarities to Dickens than it does to Flaubert.[31] Moreover, Collins brings his heroine back from the point of suicide, thus allowing Magdalen the opportunity for reflection on her actions. Whereas Emma Bovary fails to understand what has gone wrong with her cheerless life, Magdalen knows only too well and, in good Dickensian fashion, leads us to a conclusion where all the plot strands are tied together.

Yet Collins undercuts many of the actions of his characters with the sharp edge of cosmic irony. For instance, in a neat plot twist, Norah ultimately marries George Bartram, the nephew of Admiral Bartram, the old man in whose house Magdalen had reached the nadir of her disguised snooping when, posing as a maid under a false name, she is nabbed and sent away. Furthermore, as a result of this fortuitous marriage to a man she loves, Norah comes into the Vanstone fortune following the death of the old Admiral. So all of Magdalen's plots and counterplots have not yielded such luck as Norah has managed to grab for herself, with shillings and pounds falling on her, as it were, from Heaven.

Nor does Norah let slip the opportunity to remind Magdalen that her nearly fatal efforts have been in vain. Life sometimes deals us arbitrary hands, counsels Norah to her sister, as she tells Magdalen that the Secret Trust for which Magdalen had been searching and therefore creeping about

Admiral Bartram's house in the darkness of night had just come her way by accident. It was this Trust that told of Noel Vanstone's desire that cousin George Bartram be given the responsibility for Noel's fortune following his death. As a consequence of Noel's desperate attempts to eliminate altogether the feared and despised Magdalen from his life and his fortune, Noel has ironically not only given Magdalen's sister the Vanstone inheritance but also opened the door for Magdalen to receive at least a part of this bequest through Norah's generosity and continued love for her sister.

Nonetheless, Norah cannot let slip the chance to remind Magdalen that sometimes our efforts in this world represent nothing more than absurd vanity, that those things we strive the hardest for are those things that elude us the most. On a visit to Admiral Bartram's house — a visit, by the way, in which she has had no need to go in disguise, for Norah Vanstone is welcome in any of the homes of her family — Norah has been mechanically sifting through the ashes left in a tripod and has come across the much-sought-after document. As she describes the way in which she had accidentally discovered the paper setting forth the Secret Trust, Norah places it into Magdalen's hands, even as Magdalen responds with the proper awe and comprehension: "'You!' she said, looking at her sister with the remembrance of all that she had vainly ventured, of all that she had vainly suffered, at St. Crux. '*You* have found it!'" At this juncture, Norah is only too delighted to hammer in the lesson, as she responds cheerfully:

> "Yes," said Norah gaily; "the Trust has proved no exception to the general perversity of all lost things. Look for them, and they remain invisible. Leave them alone, and they reveal themselves! You and your lawyer, Magdalen, were both justified in supposing that your interest in this discovery was an interest of no common kind. I spare you all our consultations after I had produced the crumpled paper from the ashes. It ended in George's lawyer being written to, and in George himself being recalled from the Continent."[32]

A final noteworthy point concerns the shifting waves of Magdalen's identities throughout; she changes names to suit her purpose just as another woman might change her shoes or her hairstyle to match the occasion. Yet herein lies another irony. When Magdalen marries cousin Noel, she does so in the guise of a phony last name — Bygrave — even though her new married name is identical to the one she has carried since birth — Vanstone. So even in her long-coveted but brief sojourn as Mrs. Noel Vanstone, Magdalen is still as lost as she had been when she was the illegitimate outcast from the family home.

Moreover, Collins further twists the irony by reminding us that Magdalen has never been legally entitled to that last name, either by birth or by marriage. In the first instance, the circumstances of her illegitimacy preclude her legal right to be a Vanstone; in the second, her falsifying of her true identity negates the legality of her marriage. Magdalen is trapped from all sides, seemingly forever doomed to be branded both Nobody's Child and Nobody's Wife. Only when Captain Kirke provides the deus ex machina and legitimizes her is Magdalen given the right to be Somebody at last.

Nonetheless, lest we be misled by the "they-lived-happily-ever-after" ending, Collins provides enough realistic, graphic detail to propel us into a quasi-naturalistic realm whereby we are witness to the dreadful actions that humans are wont take against each other. We see the verbal abuse that Captain Wragge hurls upon his wife. We watch the pitiful condition of Mrs. Wragge as she drags herself through her days, measuring out her life by inches, each inch representing the tiny bit of progress she makes as she forever tries to decipher the riddles inherent in everyday tasks.

Despite all of the sympathy generated for Mrs. Wragge, however, a crucial note is sounded toward the end of the novel, one involving Matilda Wragge and her husband's latest moneymaking scheme. The Wragges reenter Magdalen's life at the point where she is at her most desperate, before Kirke's rescue. If Magdalen looks ready to expire, however, not so Captain Wragge, who peers into her dismal room and cheerily announces that he is now happily well situated in life. The reason for this happy situation is that Wragge has concocted a new recipe for success — one as easy for him to follow as that omelette recipe had been difficult for his beleaguered wife: the Captain now peddles pills. Moreover, his advertising slogans would do credit to the most creative Madison Avenue executive. In addition, the Captain boasts to Magdalen of the various forms of media that he has invaded in his quest for fame and fortune:

> There is not a single form of appeal in the whole range of human advertisement, which I am not making to the unfortunate public at this moment. Hire the last new novel — there I am, inside the boards of the book. Send for the last new Song — the instant you open the leaves, I drop out of it. Take a cab — I fly in at the window, in red. Buy a box of moth-powder at the chemist's — I wrap it up for you, in blue.... The mere titles of my advertisements are quite irresistible.... "A Pill in Time, saves Nine." ... "Excuse me, how is your stomach?" ... "Where are the three characteristics of a stubborn Englishman? His Hearth, his Home, and his Pill."[33]

In his most recent role as physician cum salesman, Captain Wragge has at last found a proper place for Matilda. His motto, "Down with Doctors!" is visibly validated by Mrs. Wragge, who has become an aging poster child for the Captain's nostrums, her physical progress displayed on banners throughout the countryside and documented with *Before* and *After* pictures. As Wragge boasts to Magdalen:

> She is the celebrated woman whom I have cured of indescribable agonies from every complaint under the sun. Her portrait is engraved on all the wrappers, with the following inscription beneath it: "Before she took the Pill, you might have blown this patient away with a feather. Look at her now!!!"[34]

Wragge's portrait of Mrs. Wragge's previously delicate condition seems peculiar, but nonetheless blissfully fantastic, especially when we recall that she has formerly been described as approximately six feet three inches tall, a "giantess" who, when she arises from a seated position, moves slowly upward to "an apparently interminable height."[35] It would have taken a very large, very weighty feather to have blown her away. Having been disguised by her husband as Mrs. Bygrave in order to further the scheming plans of Magdalen and the Captain, now Matilda Wragge once more assumes a new identity, compliments of her husband. But whereas Matilda had been most uncomfortable as Mrs. Bygrave and, in her trusting straightforwardness, had indeed given the disguise away to Mrs. Lecount, she can no longer be subversive in her new guise as an illustrated advertising figure. She has truly become the icon, the living symbol of what her husband has molded her into — immutable, frozen, lifeless. No longer able to act, she can therefore no longer act upon her husband's schemes by unwittingly thwarting them.

Referring to the parallels between Magdalen and Matilda as the novel approaches its conclusion, Deirdre David theorizes:

> Just as Magdalen's story of return to legitimate social identity in marriage assumes conventional narrative form, so Mrs Wragge's story of respectable celebrity puts an end to her disruption of parodic omnipotence. No longer the resisting reader of a recipe, like the Captain she becomes the thing itself and is read by others, engraved and inscribed as she is on all the wrappers for "The Pill." Mrs Wragge is in custody, just as, one might venture, Collins's interrogations of narrative form, patriarchal law, misogynistic sexual politics are (must be) eventually placed in the demanding custody of his serialised novel.[36]

Yet unlike Matilda Wragge, the Captain has the male advantage of becoming *more* than "the thing itself." As a man, Captain Wragge is able to identify himself beyond the boundaries of marriage. After all, he is the one who has instigated the profitable pill-pushing business, just as earlier he had orchestrated Magdalen's stage performances and had appropriated Magdalen's earnings.

Moreover, Matilda and Magdalen are not the only women whose problems Collins depicts realistically; these are quandaries that are only too typical of those shared by the majority of nineteenth century women. We also observe the circuitous plots of Mrs. Lecount, an aging but extremely clever widow, who owns nothing in her life but a desire to maintain her power as the servant cum confidante of Noel Vanstone. She is extremely jealous of his longing for Magdalen, not necessarily because she covets some of the Vanstone fortune for herself nor because she herself would like to marry Noel, even supposing that social class and age differences did not exist. What eats away at Mrs. Lecount is her possessive drive to be in charge, to be the sole caretaker of the lumpish Noel. Nor can we be certain that there is not a sexual element in this jealousy. As a childless middle-aged widow, supposedly devoted to her late husband's memory, we can see that Mrs. Lecount would find the attentions of a much younger man flattering, even those of a fool like Noel.

A further realistic element of *No Name* lies in the various settings that Collins uses to establish a sense of place and time. He takes us from the comfortable upper middle class home of the Vanstones to the working class streets of York to a seaside resort town and finally to the squalor of a London tenement.

In fact, Collins depicts the London that Henry James wrote about when he lived there in the mid–1870s. Though James was clearly more at home in the salon than in Hogarthian surroundings, he had seen London squalor when he had visited there as a child. By 1876, he was still observing that "there were too many gin shops, 'too many miserable women at their doorsteps; too many, far too many, dirty-faced children sprawling between one's legs.'"[37] James also witnessed with a squeamish horror the desperate straits into which women like Magdalen and Mrs. Wragge might fall. Edel describes James's revulsion as he views one such scene:

And one dark night, against the dismal background of fog and sleet, Henry came upon "a horrible old woman, in a smoky bonnet, lying prone in a puddle of whiskey!"[38]

So too, Collins's handling of the imagery associated with rural England at this time is just as skillfully drawn as is his portrait of the

London poor. Collins's description of the York neighborhood where Captain Wragge is living when he first teams with Magdalen is a good representative illustration of the author's skillful use of descriptive detail. He freezes the moment in a still-life painting, making the reader see this time and this place:

> In that part of the city of York, which is situated on the western bank of the Ouse, there is a narrow street, called Skeldergate, running nearly north and south, parallel with the course of the river.... Shops of the smaller and poorer order, intermixed here and there with dingy warehouses and joyless private residences of red brick, compose the present aspect of Skeldergate.... Here, where the street ends, and on the side of it farthest from the river, a narrow little lane leads up to the paved footway surmounting the ancient Walls of York. The one small row of buildings, which is all that the lane possesses, is composed of cheap lodging-houses, with an opposite view, at the distance of a few feet, of a portion of the massive city wall. This place is called Rosemary Lane. Very little light enters it; very few people live in it; the floating population of Skeldergate passes it by; and visitors to the Walk on the Walls, who use it as the way up or the way down, get out of the dreary little passage as fast as they can.[39]

Unlike the descriptive efforts of Stephen Crane in *Maggie: A Girl of the Streets*, a novel written some thirty years later, here there is no straining for metaphors, no hyperbolic attempts to recreate the dismal backdrop for character development. Collins simply paints the ugly desperation of this particular world. And against such a background are Captain Wragge and Magdalen, two equally desperate people, who will soon meet. Yet Magdalen is spared the fate of her successor, Maggie, just as she avoids the horrible finish of her predecessor, Emma Bovary. Though Magdalen toys with the idea of suicide through poison, she is neither a romantic dreamer like Emma nor a wretched prostitute like Maggie. Unlike the first character, she has no illusions about a romantic, easy slide from existence into non-existence; unlike the second, she is not facing the certainty of following a disgusting man into a squalid slum tenement for a few wretched, wrenching moments of sex.

So, though Magdalen comes precariously close to self-destruction when she contemplates a future with Noel Vanstone, and though she subsequently plays a childish game of chance — bargaining with herself that she will do the deed if a certain number of ships pass by her window — we feel that she would not have gone through with her plan in any event, even had her idiosyncratic type of Russian roulette not gone in her favor. Magdalen is too strong, too of this earth; she will never willingly allow the other side to win.

Not only is *No Name* a finely crafted novel, but it is also an excellent illustration of Collins's devotion to scrupulously accurate detail. According to Collins's biographer Kenneth Robinson, Collins wrote *No Name* while he was suffering from the stress of recurrent bouts of ill health and working frantically to meet the deadlines of his publishers:

> Writing against time, separated from books of reference, he is constantly importuning his friends to supply topographical details and information on a variety of subjects needed for *No Name*. Charles Ward is bombarded with requests to discover and report how long a letter took to reach Zurich in 1847; what is the average length of a round voyage to Hong Kong; what day of the week was March 4th, 1846; whether a letter posted in Dumbries can reach London the following morning; how many days' notice are required for a marriage by licence; and how often the mail leaves for Shanghai.[40]

In addition, Collins struggled as much with the problem of what to title his novel as he did with the research required to give his story an atmosphere of verisimilitude. As his work on *No Name* progressed and as he was preparing it for serialization in *All the Year Round*, he still had no title. He did, however, have at least two helpful friends: Charles Dickens and W.H. Wills, who was Dickens's business manager for *All the Year Round*. In fact, Dickens had written a letter to Collins on January 24, 1862, in which he suggested to his fellow novelist no fewer than twenty-seven possible titles, none of which especially interested Collins.[41] Some examples of these titles will illustrate why Collins ignored Dickens's less than inspired suggestions. Read today, these Dickensian titles sound more like the titles for pornographic movies than like the names of Victorian novels. In his Collins biography, Robinson lists some of these possibilities offered by Dickens to his good friend: *Through Thick and Thin, Changed, or Developed? Play out the Play, Nature's Own Daughter,* and *Which is Which?*[42] Evidently, W.H. Wills had a less titillating suggestion, *Under a Cloud*. But Collins also rejected this title, for Frederick Greenwood had chosen this identical title in 1860, only a few years earlier. Greenwood and his brother James had written a three-volume novel called *Under a Cloud*, and on January 27, 1862, in a letter to Wills, Collins alludes to this recent, previous use.[43]

While it is not entirely clear just whose idea it was to settle on the title *No Name*, a comparison between Collins's early draft and the published version of the story reveals that Collins subsequently modified passages in his manuscript so as to have his characters use the title phrase in the most appropriate places. As Virginia Blain concludes about these revisions:

The idea for the novel's title, while it certainly germinated from seeds contained within the story, did not spring fully formed from a verbal cue in the text. Rather, what we have uncovered here is one of Collins's craftier secrets: we glimpse the novelist, taking off his shoes, as it were, when he thinks no-one is looking, and carefully placing footprints in the midst of his existing text so cleverly that it could never be guessed that the clue was planted after the event.[44]

Yet it ultimately does not matter to what extent Collins molded occasional passages to fit the pattern imposed by the title. What remains is a careful, compassionate look into the fantastic territory of our minds as we might recreate ourselves in our own imaginations. And so Wilkie Collins enables us to join with Magdalen Vanstone in finding that the world has become, in Wordsworthian fashion, "too much with us."

Hide and Seek: *In the Name of Ambition and Honor*

For Henry James, who was of a generation that came just after Wilkie Collins, English society and customs were a constant source of entertainment, amusement, and curiosity. The customs and conventions followed by the leisure classes on a Sunday morning were especially fascinating to James:

In the sight of the English people getting up from its tea and toast of a Sunday morning and brushing its hat, and drawing on its gloves, and taking its wife on its arm, and making its offspring walk before, and so, for decency's, respectability's, propriety's sake, taking its way to a place of worship appointed by the State, in which it repeats the formulas of a creed to which it attaches no positive sense, and listens to a sermon over the length of which it explicitly haggles and grumbles — in this exhibition there is something very striking to a stranger, something which he hardly knows whether to regard as a great force or a great infirmity.[45]

The opening scenes of Wilkie Collins's 1854 novel *Hide and Seek* portray just such a domestic scene, with a comfortable middle class London family emerging from church on a rainy afternoon and being met at the church entrance by their servant, who carries three umbrellas. In keeping with the stratification so prevalent in English society at this time, a characteristic noted by Henry James some forty years after the events of this novel occur, these umbrellas are to be meted out according to a strict pecking order dictated by the family chain of command:

Snoxell [the servant] had been specially directed by the housemaid to distribute his three umbrellas in the following manner: the new silk umbrella was to be given to Mrs. and Mrs. Thorpe; the old silk umbrella was to be handed to Mr. Goodworth, Mrs. Thorpe's father; and the heavy gingham was to be kept by Snoxell himself, for the special protection of "Master Zack," aged six years, and the only child of Mr. Thorpe. Furnished with these instructions, the page set forth on his way to the church.[46]

Despite the placid tone on which the novel opens, suggesting an orderly, tidy series of events about to unfold, *Hide and Seek* is not really a novel of manners. It is, however, as aptly named as *No Name*, for *Hide and Seek* alludes to the child's game of search and find. The original deception on the part of Mr. Thorpe begins as a childish prank but quickly descends into tragedy for the woman he seduces. Therefore, paradoxically, what is hidden, what is sought, and what is ultimately found, go beyond child's play to reveal what lies beneath the games adults play. Moreover, though *Hide and Seek* contains clever satire and displays Collins's tendency to develop hard-edged wit, it too, like *No Name*, explores the darkness always lying concealed just under the bright surface: a surface that typically illuminates a deceptively ordinary world. Such darkness is foreshadowed in the phrase that introduces "Master Zack" as "the only child of Mr. Thorpe." Though we don't know it yet, Master Zack is *not* Mr. Thorpe's only child, but rather is his only legitimate child. Some years prior to the events chronicled at the outset, Mr. Thorpe had assumed a false identity and seduced a young woman, leaving her pregnant. But because Wilkie Collins's forte is the tale of mystery, we are unaware of these facts till late in the novel.

Moreover, the motif of slippery identities is one that concerns Collins here. Further, as he does in *No Name*, Collins couples his portrayal of the nameless, the disguised, and the people of assumed identities, with social commentary on the nature of shame, on the pitfalls of hypocrisy, and on the untenable positions of the "ruined" woman and her consequent illegitimate child, both of whom suffer from the mother's sin.

Though various scholars have criticized Collins for his inability to deal successfully with social issues, especially in his later novels, works such as *No Name* and *Hide and Seek* nonetheless portray quite accurately the social strictures of Victorian England. *Hide and Seek* explores four characters of a shadowy nature: two men and two women. The women's lack of a definite identity is tied to the moral decrees of the time. For the first half of the novel, we do not know the name of the luckless woman who bore the illegitimate child and then died when her infant was about two months old. Nor do we know the real identity of that infant, who lives with a cruel circus owner till she is ten, and then has the good fortune to be adopted by a kind-hearted artist named Valentine Blyth. Collins ordinarily depicts such artists/painters in a favorable light, doubtless as a tribute to his father, William Collins, a famous landscape painter and an early influence on his son's development. In this instance, Valentine, a thoroughly decent man, at last gives her a permanent name, calling her *Madonna*. So these two ladies, unlike Magdalen of *No Name*, do not willingly set out to lose themselves, to become the individuals that they are not. Both simply struggle to survive, the mother losing her life and the daughter losing her hearing at the age of seven, while simultaneously giving up the effort to speak when she realizes how cut off from the world she has become.

In *Hide and Seek* it is two men, both of whom are directly involved in the lives of these women, who willfully try to hide who they are. The first one we meet is the aforementioned Mr. Thorpe who, some ten years before the events described in the first scene, had fathered the illegitimate child that came to be known as *Madonna*. This illicit encounter had ironically come about because of Thorpe's desire for privacy. So, in seeking a retreat, he had escaped to the country and adopted the persona of a man named Arthur Carr, convinced that this pseudonym would allow him to pursue, undisturbed, his interest in botany. He also allows himself to pursue undisturbed a young milliner named Mary Grice. In spite of the prying eyes and ears of her hawk-like aunt, who thinks she has her frisky niece tied to a short rope, Mary becomes pregnant. Shortly after the deed is done, Arthur Carr (a.k.a. Zachary Thorpe) leaves, ignorant of Mary's growing girth.

Nonetheless, although he tries to contact Mary via letters, he remains unaware that the vindictive aunt, Joanna Grice, is systematically intercepting these letters. When it finally becomes clear to the grim maiden aunt that the alteration in her niece's mode of dress is owing to an alteration in her niece's body chemistry, the old girl has paroxysms of righteous indignation. She even has the temerity to write a lengthy journal about her woes, a sort of apologia of her behavior toward her "ruined" niece. Into this self-pitying screed she vents her venomous feelings of bitterness and jealousy: jealousy born in part from her own sexual frustration and repression, and in part from her knowledge that her brother Joshua, Mary's father, is only too willing to forgive Mary her transgression.

As he has done with his characters in *No Name*, Collins here exposes the hypocrisy of those who would pass judgment on such sins of the flesh. He also satirizes Aunt Joanna, who is apparently suffering from either mental deficiency or incredible myopia, as she demonstrates an inborn inability to see the reasons for Mary's gradually changing demeanor. In this journal, Aunt Joanna solemnly reports on her slowly dawning awakening:

> "At last, as the winter drew on, she altered so much, and got such a strange look in her face, which never seemed to leave it, that Joshua became alarmed, and said he must send for the doctor. She seemed to be frightened out of her wits at the mere thought of it; and declared, quite passionately, all of a sudden, that she had no want of a doctor, and would see one and answer the questions of none — no! not even if her father himself insisted on it.
>
> "This astonished me as well as Joshua; and when he asked me privately what I thought was the matter with her, I was obliged of course to tell him the truth, and say I believed that she was almost out of her mind with love for Mr. Carr."[47]

That Joanna Grice does not see the irony involved in this self-revelation of her own ignorant, arrogant blindness is a sign of one of her many character flaws. Determined that an evil woman will not dishonor the honorable family name of Grice, Joanna is pleased that Mary has chosen to leave rather than stay in the respectable family home and bear a bastard child — an infant with no legal name and therefore no proper identity.

In due course, Mary Grice becomes a woman with no name and no home. Disgraced, she flees the family home in the country town of Dibbledean and gives birth to her daughter among strangers, none of whom know her name. Naturally, her hapless infant is also nameless, until she is given the name *Mary* and then later becomes *Madonna*. Being illegitimate, she naturally cannot have a proper, authentic last name.

Whereas the mother and daughter in *Hide and Seek* become nonpersons because they do not conform to society's strict standards relative to moral uplift, the two disguised males, who freely choose to hide their true identities, have no such compunctions placed upon them. Though Zachary Thorpe/Arthur Carr possibly would have done the right thing by Mary Grice, had he been able to find her, he nonetheless is spared the humiliation and pain which accompany the disgrace of being an unwed mother.

Similarly, the other man in *Hide and Seek* who deliberately hides his true identity is Mary Grice's brother Matthew. Under the pseudonym of Mat Marksman, he has roamed from country to country, unable to settle for long in any one place, forever wondering about the fate of his sister. Furthermore, the two duplicitous males in this novel are temperamentally opposite — Thorpe originally hiding his identity as a sort of joke, concocted among his pals in the spirit of camaraderie; Mat hiding his identity as a consequence of his need to keep moving on, to escape from himself and from the past. Whereas Thorpe is an intellectual, a studious lover of botany — delicate, and even effeminate in appearance, Mat is rough, strong, devil-may-care. He has lived in the wilds of the American frontier and has survived a scalping. He is a fighter, a nomad, one who has been accustomed to living anywhere the mood strikes him. He is not particularly religious.

Alternatively, about two years after his brief but fruitful dalliance with Mary Grice, Zachary Thorpe resumes his own family name, and, in keeping with this newfound spirit of correctness, settles into a comfortable, bourgeois existence. He marries, fathers one son, and prides himself on his ability to govern his household according to his own stern, religious, ritualized principles. These principles are, in fact, the result of a sturdy, rigorous penitence. Though the stalwart Mr. Thorpe remains unaware throughout most of the novel that Zachary, Jr. is not his only child, his memory does extend as far as back to those halcyon days which he spent romping with Mary Grice and taking advantage of the ignorance of a young country girl.

As a consequence of the indiscreet behavior of his youth, Thorpe treats his namesake, Zachary, Jr., like a truculent servant, abusing his son both physically and emotionally, pounding into the small boy the desirability of remaining motionless in church during an interminable service, which has culminated with a forty-minute sermon. When the six-year-old disgraces his unbending parent by misbehaving during the service, Thorpe, Sr. locks up his heir in his own room and orders him to memorize verses from Select Bible Texts for Children. Having buried a few years previously the morally unfit Arthur Carr, Zachary Thorpe has resurfaced as a changed man, vowing to bury any trace of moral laxity in his young son. Nor does the elder Thorpe's penance end with the end of Zack, Jr.'s childhood. As a young adult, Zachary the younger continues to be subjected to the same sort of rigorous discipline. His father even chooses the young man's career for him. However, Zachary, Sr.'s efforts backfire. He tries unsuccessfully to make his son over in the image that the father fervently wishes he had not strayed from years earlier: a time when he had lied to a young woman about who he was and what he stood for. But

Zachary, Sr. will soon learn that it is as impossible for an outsider to mold another person into a new identity as it is for this same individual to change the shape of that person's skull by pretending a human head is a lump of clay.

> Among other unlucky results of Mr. Thorpe's conscientious imprisonment of his son in a merchant's office, was the vast increase which Zack's commercial penance produced in his natural appetite for the amusements and dissipations of the town. After nine hours of the most ungrateful daily labour that could well have been inflicted on him, the sight of play-bills and other wayside advertisements of places of public recreation appealed to him on his way home, with irresistible fascination.[48]

Moreover, since the elder Zachary insists on holding an 11 p.m. curfew over the head of his son, as though the young man were still a teenager, Zachary, Jr., devises a trick whereby he can sneak in and out of the family dwelling without being detected. As a consequence, then, of the father's misplaced sense of atonement for the devious trick of his youth, the son is even more tempted to haunt places of un–Christian amusement. It is in one of these places, perpetually inhabited by down-and-outers, that Zack meets the other man in this novel who has elected to carry a false name: Mat Marksman, a.k.a. Matthew Grice. Both Mat and Zack have blood ties to the not-as-yet-truly-identified Madonna. And because Wilkie Collins is writing a mystery novel, he keeps his readers in suspense as to the connections between Mat and Madonna, Zack and Madonna. Not till the end of the story do we learn that Mat and Madonna are uncle and niece and that Zack and Madonna are half brother and sister, their shared relative being their father: none other than the morally correct Zachary Thorpe, Sr.

Yet the elder Thorpe ultimately pays for the sins of his youth in a more substantial way than by emotionally garroting his adult son. One of the most effective and affecting scenes in the novel comes at the end, when the distraught and vengeance-driven Mat confronts Thorpe with the revelation that not only did Thorpe commit the ultimate horror upon Mat's sister, but that Thorpe also left the unfortunate girl pregnant and consequently abandoned by her virtuous family. We know that for twenty-four years Thorpe has hidden his guilty knowledge of the seduction away under a mattress of devoted family respectability and stern religious ritual. But now the sheer madness of his attempt to hide from the truth, even as he had attempted to hide his true identity from Mary Grice, erupts in an anguished outburst of grief, despair, and the pain of Mat's revelation that Mary's child — his own daughter — "lives within gunshot of you."[49]

When Mat threatens to expose Thorpe's deception as well as his arrogant hypocrisy, and to disgrace Thorpe within his own family and among his circle of friends and admirers, when he announces that he will bring Mary's child — Thorpe's illegitimate daughter — to clinch this disgrace, Thorpe's frenzied appearance briefly halts the aggrieved brother's attack:

> The cowering figure was struggling upward from the chair: one of the withered hands, slowly raised, was stretching itself out towards him; the panic-stricken eyes were growing less vacant, and were staring straight into his with a fearful meaning in their look; the pale lips were muttering rapidly — at first he could not tell what; then he succeeded in catching the two words, "Mary's child?" quickly, faintly, incessantly reiterated.[50]

Later that same evening, Thorpe has sufficiently recovered his self-possession to write an explanatory letter to Mat, an apologia wherein he expresses great grief and remorse for his early transgressions. He even volunteers an explanation of why he had adopted a phony name, the only name that Mary Grice had known him by. He admits to Mat that his adoption of a new identity had been originally conceived as a joke:

> "It is fit you should first be told that the assumed name by which I was known at Dibbledean, merely originated in a foolish jest — in a wager that certain companions of my own age, who were accustomed to ridicule my fondness for botanical pursuits, and often to follow and disturb me when I went in search of botanical specimens, would not be able to trace and discover me in my country retreat.[51]

Yet there is something ennobling in Thorpe's acknowledgement of this other, earlier self. He dies a man at peace with himself and with his family, finally aware of the wrongs that he has done his wife and son. And, incidentally, he also regrets his treatment of Mary Grice, the innocent whom he had left behind. And what of the daughter, another innocent, whose existence he learns of shortly before his death? The young woman does finally learn of her heritage, but this fact does not gain for her a comparable peace of mind: Magdalen/Mary necessarily remains illegitimate and therefore as nameless as the cunning Magdalen of *No Name*. In the world of such misbegotten identity, it is only the women who continue to float, rudderless, in the muddy waters of masculine definitions.

The New Magdalen *and the Tangled Webs*

A Tale of Two Women

When these definitions become too burdensome for a woman to handle, when society condemns her for the circumstances of her birth, sometimes she is sorely tempted to take desperate measures to ensure that her world will be a secure one. Such means are tried by Mercy Merrick in Collins's 1873 novel, *The New Magdalen*. Though this work is considered by most critics to be one of Collins's minor efforts, it still had a great success on the New York stage when it was presented at the Broadway Theatre in November 1873. Collins, who was visiting New York at the time, was even called upon to speak on stage at the conclusion of the performance, which he did — briefly and reluctantly.[52]

It is not surprising that New York audiences were so enthusiastic about *The New Magdalen*. The plot contains much exciting melodrama that undoubtedly is more effective when it is dramatized than when it is read. For one, the novel itself is static, lacking the speed-of-light movement that readers had come to expect from Collins's fiction. In fact, Collins formats the text much like a play: one intended for public performance. So too, the deliberate identity switch, which is central to the story's major conflict and is the story's main source of suspense, would naturally lend itself to a live, visual presentation. And the story's protagonist, a lower class woman who early on had been forced into prostitution, would have provided the middle to upper class New York crowds with some distinct titillation at the sight of this character on stage. Indeed, the woman of the title, a woman with many names but with no legal, legitimate one, leads a life which most in that Broadway audience of 1873 could have hardly imagined.

Indeed, Mercy Merrick of the original novel is a lady of great resourcefulness. When she is given the opportunity to change names and places with a woman of higher social status, she seizes the moment. Unfortunately, the moment is a transitory one: a momentary choice that she will have cause to regret. But at the time she executes the switch, Mercy feels as though she has nothing to lose — even more, that she has no choice if she wants to have any life at all. Unlike the two preceding Magdalens — the one of *No Name* and the one of *Hide and Seek* — Mercy Merrick is neither addressed as Magdalen anywhere in the novel nor is her real name ever revealed. Like Mary/Magdalen in *Hide and Seek*, she actually has no legitimate last name. And further, as is the case of the unfortunate child in *Hide and Seek*, Mercy is the product of an illegal liaison, her father abandoning her mother and her mother subsequently dying while Mercy is only a girl of ten.

If the plot of *The New Magdalen* sounds melodramatic, it is indeed one that skirts the edges of sentimentality and occasionally falls over into the territory of the overwrought. Nonetheless, the novel had its advocates, notably among them Matthew Arnold, "who said it was his favorite sensation-novel."[53]

Additionally, as with the two previous Collins's novels, social class, sex, beauty, and the law come together to predestine a woman to arrive at a dead end when she is luckless enough to take a wrong turn. We learn from Mercy that her mother had once been married, but that the union had been her ruin: she had wed a servant of her father's and, shortly there-after, had been separated from both him and her fortune, having given him what little she had possessed in her own name. Like Magdalen Van-stone, Mercy's mother is desperate for money, so she becomes a performer, joining a group of strolling players. It is from these performers that she is "rescued" by an upper class man who will become Mercy's father. Though this nameless rescuer moves her into a luxurious house, and though he appears hypnotized by the beauty of his new housemate, the relationship between an elegant roué and a woman already bound to a husband float-ing somewhere in her past quickly goes bad. Toward the end of the novel, Mercy relates this story of her sordid and dubious heritage to those whom she has earlier tried to deceive by slipping into another woman's clothing and consequently into another woman's identity:

> "I don't know how long they lived together. I only know that my father, at the time of my first recollections, had abandoned her. She had excited his suspicions of her fidelity — suspicions which cruelly wronged her, as she declared to her dying day. I believed her, because she was my mother. But I cannot expect others to do as I did — I can only repeat what she said. My father left her absolutely penniless. He never saw her again; and he refused to go to her when she sent to him in her last moments on earth."[54]

Following her mother's death, Mercy is left at the mercy of a heart-less social system that has no place for destitute girls. Mercy is only ten when she begins living on the edge, begging on the streets when she is at her most desperate. Though a respectable middle class husband and wife are good enough to take her in, she is forced out after a few years by the wife's jealousy. Mercy sees a foreordained tragedy in her quandary, which has been brought on by the middle-aged husband's lust for his adolescent boarder: "I was between fifteen and sixteen years of age when the fatal inheritance from my mother cast its first shadow on my life."[55] This shadow is, of course, her youthful beauty. So, although Mercy is innocent of any deliberate, sexual provocativeness, she becomes the cause of violence between husband and wife when the wife vows that "she would turn me out of the house with her own hand."[56] The husband, in turn, in a fit of priapic fury, "lost all self-control on his side."[57] The enraged, would-be lover next threatens his wife with his resolution to leave the house with Mercy, whom he swears he can no longer live without. To be accompanied throughout life with an aging fool is a thought too horrifying for Mercy to contemplate. She does not remain long enough to see the result of the couple's quarrel: "The maddened woman seized him by the arm — I saw that and saw no more. I ran out into the street, panic-stricken. A cab was passing. I got into it, before he could open the house door, and drove to the only place of refuge I could think of—a small shop, kept by the widowed sister of one of our servants."[58]

Yet Mercy's streetwise common sense and her inherent decency are not enough to save her from the capriciousness of life among the English underclass. She eventually ends up in a dwelling known as The Refuge where, as Mercy discreetly puts it, "fallen women" find shelter. The phrase itself contains much connotative meaning for the nineteenth century reader: a woman who had "fallen" was a woman who had been unfortunate enough not only to be hurled into a sexual liaison but also to get caught on the way down. Moreover, the other half of this liaison would clearly never be forced to suffer the same moral consequences. So the pregnant woman, deserted by her child's father, would hide herself away, bearing both her shame and her child in secret. Though Mercy mentions neither her pregnancy nor the nameless child that she is forced to give away, her implied message with respect to the price she has had to pay for her fatal beauty is tragically clear. And her efforts to completely erase all of the horrors of her past — as though her whole life has been one devastating error — drive her nearly to madness.

But at first, the temptation to shed her old skin and instead attach one belonging to a woman who is in somewhat better circumstances is too great for Mercy to allow to slip away. Mercy's slide into deceit begins at the outset of the novel, when she and an Englishwoman named Grace Roseberry, a lady in straitened circumstances, are thrown together in a battlefield hospital in France at the height of the 1870 war between France and Germany. Mercy has obtained a fairly respectable job as a nurse, while Grace is a traveler. During their brief meeting, they share stories related to their pasts. Significantly, Grace tells Mercy that she is headed for a new home in England, where she hopes to be welcomed by an elderly, aristocratic lady — connected by marriage to Grace's late father. Since Grace has been left no financial resources, her only option is to try to reach England in time to offer herself as a companion to this lady — before someone else snatches the job.

Mercy listens attentively to her fellow countrywoman's story, but cannot stretch her sympathy very far in Grace's direction: Mercy — the nameless, the destitute, the fallen — knows that there are worse fates than being a companion to a rich old lady. And she knows what these fates are, for when Grace pauses in the telling of her brief history to ask, "'Mine is a sad story, is it not?'"[59] Mercy responds prophetically, "'There are sadder stories than yours. There are thousands of miserable women who would ask for no greater blessing than to change places with you.'"[60] Much of Collins's work is tinged with bitter cosmic irony. Such irony is nowhere more evident than in the unraveling of Mercy's life once she becomes Grace Roseberry, trading her miserable existence for the "greater blessing" of living as the companion to the wealthy English lady, whose home had been the desired destination of the real Grace Roseberry. So too, though Mercy trades her existence, she does not actually trade her name, for Collins carefully leaves an ambiguous shadow around the figure of Mercy Merrick. Whatever name she might have been given at birth by her ill-fated mother, the name has long been lost in Mercy's journey through her life's squalid streets, layered with the grime of wayward impulses and tragic indiscretions. Mercy herself equivocates upon her initial meeting with Grace in the French hospital, for when Grace asks Mercy her name, she replies, reluctantly and wistfully, "'Not a pretty name, like yours.... Call me Mercy Merrick.'"[61]

For Wilkie Collins, our names are inextricably linked with our pasts. If this past has been a productive, prosperous, noteworthy one, then the names we call ourselves are also proper and respectable. If this past is stained a permanent dark color, whether by bad fortune or bad moral choices, then, in Keatsian fashion, our names are written in water and carried off by the tides. Such is the case with Mercy: Grace catches the hesitation in Mercy's voice when Mercy advises Grace about what name it is that she calls herself. Suspicious of the uncertainty with which Mercy responds, Grace immediately wonders, "Had she given an assumed name?

Was there some unhappy celebrity attached to her own name? Miss Roseberry did not wait to ask herself those questions."[62]

Yet in still another of Collins's fitting reversals of circumstance, Grace Roseberry finally does have many questions about Mercy's name when, back from the dead, she finds that she must try to establish herself as the authentic Grace Roseberry in the English home that Mercy has been occupying for many months. Mercy, under the erroneous impression that Grace has been killed and thus will not be appearing to establish her claim on the elderly, aristocratic English lady, and having adopted the name of the presumed-dead Grace Roseberry, has presented herself to this woman, Lady Janet Roy. But when Grace resurfaces as a living person, having been improbably resurrected by a German doctor, Mercy discovers that the road to wealth is strewn with the thorny bushes of uncertainty and fear.

Moreover, in a further plot twist, when the real Grace Roseberry appears at Lady Janet Roy's home to take on her duties as a companion, she has no idea that Mercy has planted herself firmly in the place where the real Grace should be. But who *is* the real Grace? Collins makes it clear that Mercy's Grace is far more graceful than Grace's Grace. In truth, the authentic Miss Roseberry is anything but a beautiful rose; rather, she is cruel, blunt, vindictive, and completely lacking in the social amenities, especially when she discovers that no one believes her story.

Yet, to be fair to the "real" Grace Roseberry, almost anyone would have been put out of temper when confronted with a pretender like Mercy Merrick. Even so, it appears that the lesson here is that our identities do not necessarily have to be at the mercy of social conventions and class rules governing behavioral expectations. Put a decent lady into a genteel setting, though the lady be just inches away from the streets, and she will show her moral worth. Put a boorish lady into the same genteel setting, though the lady be trained to act with a refined dignity, and she will show her sluttish side. Consequently, Mercy does, in fact, become Grace Roseberry, whereas Grace Roseberry becomes a crude, nameless object of scorn and derision to the people in Lady Janet's circle: that is, to those who see her as a fraud and an imposter.

Adding to the complexities of Grace's stolen identity is the fact that Lady Janet has become so attached to Mercy that this good-hearted but deliberately shortsighted Englishwoman does not want to know the truth. Therefore, she demands that Mercy tell her nothing that might compromise Mercy's place in the household. So although Mercy regrets her foolish decision to become someone else, and although she wants to confess her manifold transgressions, Lady Janet will have none of that and constantly dodges whatever opportunities come her way that might allow Mercy to come clean. In keeping with this self-inflicted blindness, Lady Janet refuses to listen to the real Grace Roseberry's indignant and arrogant protestations and threats; instead, she turns Grace away, threatening to have the authorities haul her off to an asylum. Though Grace manages to avoid such a dire fate, she is never able to force Lady Janet into an admission that she has finally learned which woman is really Grace Roseberry.

Meanwhile, poor Mercy Merrick comes close to being afflicted by the same awful marital disease suffered by Magdalen Vanstone. Whereas Magdalen cons into marriage the weak, effeminate toad Noel Vanstone, Mercy is courted by an equally weak mama's boy named Horace Holmcroft. Both Noel and Horace become smitten not only by the physical attractions of these ladies but also by their own incorrect assumptions that the objects of their adoration are high class, genteel, and well bred. In addition, these benighted lovers have no idea that they are courting women who have assigned themselves phony names while simultaneously giving themselves elevated social standings. By the same token, Collins signals to his readers that these two disgustingly priggish males are blind both to the enormity of their own character flaws and also to the values that matter when we come to evaluate the characters of others. Collins makes clear that identity is bound with our behavior toward one another. So if we define ourselves, for good or ill, by our actions, then Mercy Merrick has a far more positive moral identity than Grace Roseberry, for Mercy has tried to live according to principles of selflessness. And the fact that she succumbs to a weak impulse when she grabs Grace's name and her clothing does not negate Mercy's essential goodness, for at that time and in that place she does genuinely believe that Grace has been killed.

Yet it is Grace who is the mean-spirited one, who wants total revenge when she discovers who has usurped her rightful place. Finally confronting her imposter in the library of Lady Janet's house and sounding like a stock character from a melodrama, Grace threatens her: "'Mercy Merrick, I have got you at last. Thank God, my turn has come! You can't escape me now!'"

On the other hand, Mercy responds in a calm, patient tone, apologetic yet placating:

> "I have not avoided you," she said. "I would have gone to you of my own accord if I had known that you were here. It is my heart-felt wish to own that I have sinned against you, and to make all the atonement that I can. I am too anxious to deserve your forgiveness, to have any fear of seeing you."[63]

Yet Grace will not be appeased. She turns on Mercy in a fury, her inflexible sense of class-consciousness invaded and violated by Mercy's physical presence:

> "How dare you speak to me as if you were my equal!" she burst out. "You stand there, and answer me, as if you had your right and your place in this house. You audacious woman! *I* have my right and my place here — and what am I obliged to do? I am obliged to hang about in the grounds, and fly from the sight of the servants, and hide like a thief, and wait like a beggar; and all for what? For the chance of having a word with *you*. Yes! you, madam! with the air of the Refuge and the dirt of the streets on you!"[64]

Yet such uncouth, unforgiving behavior does not go unpunished, for Grace is at last forced to give up the quest for upper class comfort and respectability as she returns, humiliated, to her home in Canada. And Mercy is rewarded for her honesty and her humility by getting the love of a decent fellow, a minister named Julian Gray. He rescues her, much as Captain Kirke had rescued Magdalen Vanstone in *No Name*. So Julian gives Mercy a respectable name at last, and takes her to America, where there is a more egalitarian society awaiting them.

The New Magdalen suffers from weaknesses of plot and characterization; failings that the younger Wilkie Collins had usually avoided. Biographer Kenneth Robinson summarizes a few of the major flaws in this short novel:

> He was more interested in the propaganda aspect of his story, in upbraiding society for its hypocrisy and inhumanity, and in preaching tolerance toward human frailty. Unfortunately, he insisted on weighting the scales so heavily in favour of the reformed prostitute as to destroy any illusion of impartiality, and his plea thus loses much of its effectiveness. The crude melodrama and sentimentality of the book were perhaps more acceptable on the stage, but *The New Magdalen* must be numbered among his least satisfactory novels.[65]

Yet for all of its "crude melodrama and sentimentality," *The New Magdalen* remains an intriguing study of a world gone upside down, of individuals who refuse to see those truths that they don't want to recognize. It is a tale that reminds us of life's little ironies, a story of two women, thrown together by war and separated by chance. It is a work that probes the omnipresent absurdity of the human condition: an unpredictable world in which one's assumptions are forever being turned around with such a force as to leave one dizzy and looking for a place to settle down in order that one might discover where one fits into the anarchy of existence. In addition, the hateful exchanges and confrontations between Grace

Roseberry and Mercy Merrick, the pretender to legitimacy, are realistic. These two beleaguered ladies go at one another with all of the vitriolic passion they can muster, and their dialogue, despite being occasionally overblown, sounds authentic, even to the modern reader. Moreover, Collins ultimately makes us care about Mercy because her efforts to survive seem so logical, so orderly, and so completely at variance with her otherwise chaotic, uncaring universe. We want her to win, to make a "name" for herself, and we are relieved when she finally does so.

The New Magdalen is one of Collins's lesser works of fiction, one with which he seems to be losing control. Though he continued writing till the end of his life in 1889, many of his later works are marred by weak, sentimental plots and inadequate character development. Such waning of his prodigious talent may be attributed to the befuddling of his brain due to the debilitating nature of various ailments, which increasingly plagued him as he aged, and which subsequently forced him into an ever-escalating dependence on opium.

Alethea Hayter, in her book Opium and the Romantic Imagination, has studied the effects of laudanum on various writers, among them Collins and Coleridge. She has concluded that one of the negative effects of opium use is that it weakens the author's ability to picture realistic landscapes; rather, the landscapes often appear more symbolic than visually accurate. In addition, she maintains that Collins's storytelling abilities were considerably diminished by opium: "The most obvious damage to his literary achievement which the opium habit inflicted was its impairment of the power of sustained concentration needed for the tightly-constructed plots which were his greatest excellence."[66]

An Unwitting and Coerced Identity Shift

Yet when Wilkie Collins wrote The Woman in White (1861), he still had full control of his vast imaginative powers and could sustain compelling narratives. With this work, one of the best, most complex mystery novels ever written in English, Collins presents a rare achievement, one filled with sublime moments of suspense, apprehension, confusion, dread, sympathy, anticipation, and even satirical humor. In the latter case, Collins often provides such amusement through his portraits of a number of the more benighted personalities inhabiting England in the mid-nineteenth century. But not until we are about eighty-five percent through the novel are we confronted with an identity switch — this one involuntary, the result of a conspiracy between two aristocratic "gentlemen" who are trying to have the wife of one of these nefarious men — Sir Percival Glyde — declared dead so that Sir Percival might claim his "late" wife's inheritance as his own. Furthermore, this successful substitution results in Lady Glyde's imprisonment in an insane asylum, where she is nearly driven to madness in her efforts to prove to a disbelieving staff that she is Lady Glyde and not the Woman in White, who is also known as Anne Catherick. Anne herself had spent many years in this same asylum, thus the credibility of the switch. In addition, as with so many of his other novels, here Collins explores the extent to which the women inhabiting this particular world are horribly used and abused by powerful men who have the wherewithal to exploit a system in which gender matters. In short, though Anne Catherick and Laura Fairlie, who has the misfortune to marry Sir Percival Glyde — an aristocratic thug and bully — come from different social classes, both are easily manipulated into asylums. Such was the fate awaiting many women of this time whose relatives wanted them out of the way for various reasons, most of which were at best specious.

It is Anne Catherick who is the initial victim here, the one imprisoned behind the walls of an institution created in order to remove the out-of-the-ordinary person from contact with normal, civilized society. Such institutions continued to be maintained in order to house the unhappy individual who has become either a nuisance or a downright threat. This mysterious title character continues to float in and out of the narrative from time to time, appearing and disappearing like some kind of apocalyptic white angel. With each glimpse of her, we learn something more about her role in the narrative's developing events, until she eventually dies, a victim of heart disease and of her times. Among other facts about her past, we learn that she has been an asylum inmate who has had the ill luck to believe that she might successfully escape from the asylum and suffer no consequences as a result. And, since nothing that occurs in the typical Collins's plot happens by accident, we are also reminded many times during the first three quarters of the novel about the strong resemblance between Anne Catherick and Lady Glyde, who look so much alike that, at a cursory glance, one of these women might be mistaken for the other. And, because Collins always pursues probability within the extremely labyrinthine plot that he builds here, he ultimately reveals the credible reason for the resemblance between Anne and Laura Fairlie Glyde: they are half-sisters.

Moreover, this revelation becomes an important corollary to the matter of identity switches in this novel. In this connection, Collins interjects another of his favorite themes: the legal complications attendant upon the issue of illegitimacy. By the conclusion of *The Woman in White*, we have learned of the births of two children who, years before the events of the major narrative, were conceived out-of-wedlock: Sir Percival Glyde and Anne Catherick. In the case of Sir Percival, this crafty baronet uses any underhanded means at his disposal to keep the fact of his illegitimacy safely hidden. Again, as with other Collins's novels, class determines fate, and so it is with Sir Percival. It is in keeping with his monetary interests to protect his secret from becoming a well-known fact. Had the circumstances of his conception as a bastard son been generally known, he would have been unable to legally claim his aristocratic title and the accompanying fortune that he has subsequently squandered. So too, in his attempts to keep his shameful heritage a private matter, he has Anne Catherick committed to a lunatic asylum, convinced that she knows his awful secret and that she will reveal it if she is left free to wander in the outside world.

Many years later, after he has married Laura Fairlie, a woman who he knows stands to gain an inheritance that will alleviate his various financial embarrassments, Sir Percival tries to force her to sign a document that will accomplish that very thing. Failing in this attempt, he listens to his friend Count Fosco, who is wilier and more dangerous than Sir Percival. Fosco devises a complicated scheme whereby he dupes the half sisters Laura and Anne, placing Anne in Laura's position in a household of servants, none of whom knows Laura very well, and tossing Laura away into the asylum, where he tells the administrators that Sir Percival's erstwhile bride is the runaway inmate Anne. All of these machinations are accomplished by Count Fosco and Sir Percival, both of whom are ready to take advantage of the convergence of opportune circumstances.

Furthermore, Collins again probes the social conditions that have enabled Sir Percival and Count Fosco to carry out their reprehensible — and horrifyingly sexist — schemes without fear of interference or retribution. It was a common occurrence for men to dump women — wives, sisters, daughters, mothers, grandmothers, cousins — into prisons for the insane. Their victims included anyone who had become an obstruction or a threat to them as they pursued their ordinary occupations. In consequence, such women were likely to be driven insane by the icy cruelty of their captors. Often deprived of their homes, their personal belongings, their children, and their self-respect, they sometimes lingered for years.

Many died from disease, self-starvation, physical abuse, or overdoses of drugs administered by unscrupulous hospital personnel.[67] Collins was all too aware of such conditions that existed within these ironically and inappropriately named "asylums." Thus he depicts both Anne Catherick and Laura Fairlie Glyde nearly succumbing to the rigors of life among the mentally dispossessed. When Anne Catherick first appears to Walter Hartright — the Woman in White escaped from her asylum and accosting him on his solitary walk through the countryside — she seems paranoid and speaks in conundrums. Later, we are told in the narrative written by Anne's greedy, opportunistic, emotionally distant mother, that Anne was always a slow-witted, dull child. This expert, motherly opinion, however, is made suspect by our knowledge of the circumstances of Anne's birth: Anne had been born seven months after Mrs. Catherick's marriage to the convenient, but apparently unfertile, Mr. Catherick.

Yet with the explanation of Mrs. Catherick's background, Collins once more injects social commentary into his description of the circumstances attending Mrs. Catherick's untimely pregnancy. Like so many working class women of the time, she had gone into service in a respectable, upper middle class home. Like so many other women in that position, she had discovered that one perk associated with her household responsibilities was the opportunity given her to receive regular seductions by the master. In this instance, the soon-to-be Mrs. Catherick had been given the biological attention of Philip Fairlie, Laura's father. The result, of course, was an out of wedlock conception; the remedy, equally obvious, was the necessity of finding a husband — and quickly. This she does in the person of Mr. Catherick, who had obligingly given his last name to their "seven-month" baby girl, Anne.

In any event, what is important to remember about the unlucky circumstances of Anne's conception is that she and Laura Fairlie have the same father and that the evil Count Fosco has the wherewithal to use this family resemblance against them. Also fortunate for the scheming Italian count is the death of Anne in the house where she has been introduced as Laura Fairlie Glyde. For with Anne's death and burial under Laura's name, Laura's husband, Sir Percival Glyde, can now cast aside certain pecuniary dilemmas that have plagued him for years, the result of his spendthrift habits.

That men had complete legal dominance over women is a fact constantly reiterated by Collins. Not only does Count Fosco know that he is free to return the false Anne Catherick to her place in the asylum, but he also confidently realizes that he can with impunity hasten the demise of the gravely ill woman who is unwittingly passing as Laura Glyde. He admits that he would have readily dispatched the real Anne Catherick, in the event that nature had proved to be too slow in taking its course.

Among the various narratives and consequent shifting points of view in this novel, Count Fosco writes one of the most fascinating accounts. It appears toward the end of the story; in this high-handed, preening confession, he pulls together many of the loose strands of the carefully woven plot. In his formal, overly polite, metaphorically clichéd, and hyperbolic way, he calmly relates how he had prepared for contingencies, such as the possibility that Anne, already debilitated with a serious heart disease, might have a longer life expectancy than convenient for the furtherance of his plot:

> If Anne Catherick had not died when she did, what should I have done? I should, in that case, have assisted worn-out Nature in finding permanent repose. I should have opened the doors of the Prison of Life, and have extended to the captive (incurably afflicted in mind and body both) a happy release.[68]

Fosco takes further pride in his self-control, as he completely vindicates himself of all blame that might be forthcoming as a result of his schemes to aid his dilettante friend Sir Pervical. Toward the end of his narrative, Fosco offers this apologia:

> On a calm revision of all the circumstances — Is my conduct worthy of any serious blame? Most emphatically, No! Have I not carefully avoided exposing myself to the odium of committing unnecessary crime? With my vast resources in chemistry, I might have taken Lady Glyde's life. At immense personal sacrifice, I followed the dictates of my own ingenuity, my own humanity, my own caution, and took her identity, instead.[69]

It is no accident that both Anne Catherick and Laura Glyde are driven nearly to madness by their incarceration in the asylum since both fit the paradigm of the Unwanted Woman. Laura's case poses special problems because not only has Count Fosco thrown her into the madhouse, but he has also told the administrators that "Anne," the long sought-after escaped inmate, is delusional, that she thinks she is really Laura Glyde. Thus Laura, who is already in a fragile physical and mental condition due to her husband's constant threats and abuse, is faced with another horror: no one believes her when she reveals who she *really* is. And by this point in the novel, she has been so systematically browbeaten, threatened, deceived, and drugged as Lady Glyde that, when she enters the asylum in a semi stupor, she has lived for so long in the twilight nightmares of the nether world dominated by her husband that she has been easily led away from her true identity.

Unlike the sad and abused Anne, however, who dies and is buried under the name of Laura Glyde, the real Laura survives, regains her identity, learns that her husband has died in a fire — justly set through his own carelessness — and finally marries the right man, a painter whom she has loved all along and who has been instrumental in solving much of the mystery and undoing most of the damage that has originated with the villainous duo of Sir Percival Glyde and Count Fosco. And, as in *Hide and Seek*, the artist/painter is one of the more sympathetic characters in a work sorely lacking in estimable individuals. Again, an artist — this time Walter Hartright — is probably modeled after William Collins, Wilkie's well respected and well known artist father. Because Laura finds happiness with this artist, she presumably lives a contented, stress-free life thereafter, never again having to worry about a man robbing her of her existence.

Four

The Strange Cases
of Robert Louis Stevenson

Instantly the spirit of hell awoke in me and raged. With a transport of glee, I mauled the unresisting body, tasting delight from every blow; and it was not till weariness had begun to succeed that I was suddenly, in the top fit of my delirium, struck through the heart by a cold thrill of terror.

Robert Louis Stevenson,
The Strange Case of Dr. Jekyll and Mr. Hyde (1886)

Whose Body Is It?

One of the major characters in Robert Louis Stevenson's story "The Body Snatcher" is a haunted man named Fettes. He is a well educated old man from Scotland, an alcoholic, and a man of some wealth, since he has for many years had the opportunity to spend his days in idle drinking. He is also an extremely woeful man, his sorrow verging on madness. The story's narrator has come to know Fettes through their mutual participation in and satisfaction with the comradeship available at an inn called the George. Additionally, from the outset of the story, the narrator builds suspense through his description of Fettes's preoccupation with liquor as well as with his portrayal of Fettes's obscure past. It is this murky background that will finally resurface and reveal just what it is that has driven Fettes to his current, tortured psychological state. The narrator describes Fettes's dissipated demeanor:

He drank rum—five glasses regularly every evening; and for the greater portion of his nightly visit to the George sat, with his glass in his right hand, in a state of melancholy alcoholic saturation. We called him the Doctor, for he was supposed to have some special knowledge of medicine, and had been known, upon a pinch, to set a fracture or reduce a dislocation; but, beyond these slight particulars, we had no knowledge of his character and antecedents.[1]

But we are soon to learn more about Fettes's character when we are introduced to another physician, Dr. Wolfe Macfarlane, who has been called upon to treat an ailing man at the George. Years before, Dr. Macfarlane had been especially well known to Fettes when the latter was a medical student and Dr. Macfarlane his immediate supervisor, a class assistant. Since medical training involves the study of the human body, and since the best way to study the human anatomy in the nineteenth century was to examine the insides of actual bodies, Fettes and Dr. Macfarlane had developed a firm friendship, their bond stemming from their mutual understanding of a practical way to obtain these cadavers. The narrator describes the personal similarities between Fettes and Macfarlane:

> With Fettes he was on terms of intimacy; indeed, their relative positions called for some community of life; and when subjects were scarce the pair would drive far into the country in Macfarlane's gig, visit and desecrate some lonely graveyard, and return before dawn with their booty to the door of the dissecting-room.[2]

Though grave robbing is an efficient method of grabbing bodies for the purposes of medical inquiry, both Fettes and Macfarlane are aware of another way in which such subjects for experiment may be obtained. Various local thugs take care of this business by providing bodies in a more basic manner. The bodies thus provided do not even have the chance for burial, for they come to the medical students more directly, having been murdered and, shortly after, materializing in the aforementioned dissecting room. But we learn that Fettes had been a young student with a sort of conscience, though he had not been too scrupulous in his studies nor had he protested too vehemently against the manner of procuring individuals for dissection.

At one point, however, Fettes is clearly taken aback when he sees brought into the room a young girl whom he recognizes as his companion of the evening before — a girl who, only twenty-four hours earlier, had been enjoying good health. Fettes had previously harbored some reservations about the ragged looking men who were engaged in fetching the bodies for the students; indeed, he had even suspected foul play. These suspicions were lurking just outside of his consciousness:

The supply of subjects was a continual trouble to him as well as to his master. In that large and busy class, the raw material of the anatomists kept perpetually running out; and the business thus rendered necessary was not only unpleasant in itself, but threatened dangerous consequences to all who were concerned.... There was no understanding that the subjects were provided by the crime of murder. Had that idea been broached to him in words, he would have recoiled in horror ... Fettes ... had often remarked to himself upon the singular freshness of the bodies. He had been struck again and again by the hang-dog, abominable looks of the ruffians who came to him before the dawn; and, putting things together clearly in his private thoughts, he perhaps attributed a meaning too immoral and too categorical to the unguarded counsels of his master.[3]

Thus, when Fettes observes the "singular freshness" of the body of this girl with whom he had only recently held a quite mirthful conversation, he fears that her corpse is an omen he can no longer push aside. Yet Dr. Macfarlane warns his assistant not to be too concerned with the niceties of such body acquisition. He reminds Fettes that the two of them have been chosen by their supervisor, an anatomy instructor known only as Mr. K, because both of them are hardened men of the world, because Mr. K "'didn't want old wives."[4] So in the normal course of events, Fettes's young female acquaintance "was duly dissected, and no one remarked or appeared to recognise her."[5]

So far, Fettes's sense of the propriety of events has remained on a fairly level course. But it will soon take a tumble down the hill, as Fettes's fall and his ensuing madness begin with the introduction of a "coarse, vulgar, and stupid"[6] man into the picture. This "vulgar" individual is first seen at the tavern in the company of the morally deficient Macfarlane. Not only is this offensive person lacking in manners, but he also exercises some sort of control over Macfarlane, a control that the stranger will have reason to regret, for it is clear that Macfarlane has nothing but loathing for his companion. When Macfarlane warns the man not to call him "Toddy," the stranger's response is unwittingly prescient: "'Hear him! Did you ever see the lads play knife? He would like to do that all over my body.'"[7] At this juncture, Fettes's rejoinder is also tinged with unconscious irony: "'We medicals have a better way than that ... When we dislike a dead friend of ours, we dissect him.'"[8] This exchange gives Macfarlane a thought, for he "looked up sharply, as though this jest was scarcely to his mind."[9] Macfarlane, however, is not in a jesting mood; he is, rather, in dead earnest, especially after the stranger, who the narrator learns goes by the name of Gray, orders an immense feast to be served at the tavern and then "commanded Macfarlane to settle the bill."[10] Obviously, the humor here escapes Macfarlane: the next occasion on which Fettes sees Gray occurs about twenty-four hours later, at which time the stranger's appearance has altered considerably, though Fettes at once recognizes the deceased man. After Macfarlane has deposited Gray's body on the dissecting table, Fettes has one of those ephemeral moments of self-examination: "He had almost expected the sight that met his eyes, and yet the shock was cruel. To see, fixed in the rigidity of death and naked on that coarse layer of sack-cloth, the man whom he had left well-clad and full of meat and sin upon the threshold of a tavern, awoke, even in the thoughtless Fettes, some of the terrors of the conscience."[11]

Even so, the terrors that Fettes feels are also partly the result not only of his horror at seeing the formerly living Gray now laid out in the vulnerability of death, but also of his desperate awareness that we are at best a fragile speck drifting in the vast realms of the earthly. So now Gray is doomed to be cut up on the medical students' butcher's block, just as the young girl had been dispatched some days before. Gray as a sentient being is no more, his reality killed by the vengeful Macfarlane. The matter-of-fact way in which the narrator describes the resultant dispersal of Gray's remains is especially chilling and provides insight into the causes of Fettes's benumbed state: "Hours passed; the class began to arrive; the members of the unhappy Gray were dealt out to one and to another, and received without remark. Richardson was made happy with the head; and before the hour of freedom rang Fettes trembled with exultation to perceive how far they had already gone toward safety."[12]

The "they" just alluded to refers, of course, to Macfarlane and his inadvertent accomplice, the unfortunate Fettes. Indeed, as days pass and it begins to look as though no one either suspects or cares about the disappearance of the dishonorable, drunken Mr. Gray, Fettes becomes even more confident, beginning "to plume himself upon his courage, and had so arranged the story in his mind that he could look back on these events with an unhealthy pride. Of his accomplice he saw but little."[13] However, Fettes is about to see Macfarlane one more fateful time, and what the two of them will see together is enough to send Fettes over the edge.

The serendipitous event that brings this pair back into action is the chance to exhume a body from an isolated, country cemetery. The subject for such upending had been a sixty-year-old woman, recently deceased and now about to be disturbed. In keeping with the darkly humorous tone of much of this tale, Stevenson guides his narrator's voice in a macabre way. We are told, for instance, that this woman, who had "been known for nothing but good butter and a godly conversation, was to be rooted from her grave at midnight and carried, dead and naked, to that far-away city that she had always honoured with her Sunday best; the place beside her family was to be empty till the crack of doom; her innocent and almost venerable members to be exposed to that last curiosity of the anatomist."[14]

But before these two medical specialists can carry out their ghoulish deed, they stop at an inn where they enjoy a good dinner and, more important, drink glass after glass of wine. Having paused earlier that day at another inn, where they relished a good deal of whisky and ale, both are feeling pretty mellow by the time they are ready to greet the farmer's wife: "With every glass their cordiality increased."[15] To add to the mood of the intense, feverish impetus of the body snatchers, there is a pounding rainstorm serving as a backdrop to the scene about to be played out on this grim, ironic, dimly lit stage. And the stage becomes even more dimly lit when these two nighttime adventurers lose their lantern in the midst of their rain-soaked quest. This loss of a light source is a significant one, because added to this disaster is the mental darkness resulting from their alcohol soaked brains, which has become coupled to the physical darkness resulting from the forceful rainstorm. But they are in a hurry, so they ignore the dark: "The coffin was exhumed and broken open; the body inserted in the dripping sack and carried between them to the gig."[16]

Here it is significant to note that the narrator uses the passive voice ("coffin was exhumed") to describe the actions of Fettes and Macfarlane as they proceed to disinter the body. The use of the weaker verb voice serves two purposes stylistically: first, it suggests that these nighttime wanderers are so besotted that they are no longer acting on their own volition but that they are being acted upon by some outside, supernatural forces; second, it reinforces the passivity of these two, which has been exacerbated by the alcoholic, convivial stupor that they have achieved over the past several hours. Moreover, the passive construction serves a thematic purpose as well. It foreshadows the horrifying vision that they witness at the end of the tale, a vision resulting from a major theme of this work. What Stevenson is trying to demonstrate throughout is that when a person loses his moral center, he loses not only his own sense of self but also his ability to discriminate among individual personalities. That is, he can no longer see people as distinctive human beings. Such lack of perspicacity has come to pass with Fettes and Macfarlane and, furthermore, this limited perception on Fettes's part will at last destroy him.

The beginning of Fettes's final deterioration occurs as these merry two journey forward, rain-soaked but pleased to have their booty at last. As the shrouded corpse veers from one of them to the other, both have an eerie feeling that something is amiss, that something is not quite right with respect to this body:

> A creeping chill began to possess the soul of Fettes. He peered at the bundle, and it seemed somehow larger than at first. All over the countryside, and from every degree of distance, the farm dogs accompanied their passage with tragic ululations; and it grew and grew upon his mind that some unnatural miracle had been accomplished, that some nameless change had befallen the dead body, and that it was in fear of their unholy burden that the dogs were howling.[17]

What is not right about this body becomes obvious at the story's conclusion, when both Fettes and Macfarlane sagely observe that the person wrapped in the drenched sack is not the person whom they had grabbed from the grave. For one, opines Macfarlane, the body is decidedly not a woman's. To which Fettes whispers confidently to his cohort, as though he were considering the not-too-surprising possibility that the corpse has undergone a hasty sex-change operation: "'It was a woman when we put her in.'" At last, they shine a lamp upon the face of the one whose sexual identity is now in question. What they see sends both into a terrified frenzy as they leap away from the wagon. The horse, equally spooked by the commotion caused by human noise, runs off, carrying with him his only passenger: the body of the dissected, dismembered, murdered Gray.

Here the tale of The Body Snatcher ends, but like so many narratives that deal with identity switching and confusion, this one raises many provocative questions. So too, it is a story that offers more questions than answers. For instance, we are left to wonder whose body it is that our two gentlemen of the evening see through the mist of the rain and the haze of the wine and whisky. Has some prankster learned of their plans to visit the late wife of the good country farmer and made a death mask of Gray, superimposing it upon the head of the deceased lady? Or is it possible that both are instead hallucinating from a sense of guilt over their recent nefarious activities? Perhaps the rain has so soaked and distorted the features of the farmer's wife that she indeed resembles a dead male. But then how are we to account for the fact that the body appears to have grown taller since it was first placed in the wagon? Has the despicable Gray such a strong will that, like Poe's Ligeia, he has returned to take over the body of another? Perhaps that is Gray's ultimate colossal joke on his two erstwhile adversaries; maybe his spirit has returned to frighten to death Fettes and Macfarlane, who thought that Gray was safely dead, his body dispersed in many different directions.

The answer to all of these various puzzling aspects of "The Body Snatcher" undoubtedly lies in the minds of Fettes and Macfarlane themselves. Having created a monster when they sacrificed another human upon the altar of scientific expediency and medical acquisitiveness, they find that the monster has subsumed the will of its creators to its own selfish ends. If the living Gray, a whole person occupying an earthly space, was a threat to Macfarlane's power and autonomy, the dead Gray is even more of a menace, as he returns, once again a whole creature, to taunt his tormenters. It is almost as if he is saying, "Aha! I've got you this time!"

But Macfarlane appears not to have been one to reflect too deeply nor care too much that he is, after all, a murderer. Indeed, we have already seen Macfarlane in the present when he is reunited with the dissolute Fettes. The two could not have neared the end of their days in a more dissimilar manner, for Macfarlane has become a great London physician: rich, respected, famous, arrogant — a man who still maintains "a dangerous glitter in his spectacles."[18] The great doctor has defeated the monster, after all. Unlike Fettes, he has not been haunted in the least by the memory of the changeling corpse. Though he is initially startled when he reencounters Fettes after so long a time, and though he hastily flees from Fettes's presence, breaking those glittering spectacles in his retreat, we gather that Macfarlane will quickly regain his composure and continue to minister to the London elite.

But Fettes, as we have seen, is not destined to be so fortunate. He has never been able to let go of the vision of that rain-splattered night, when he and Macfarlane saw — or thought they saw — an identity switch between corpses, the first of which was presumed to have been cut up, examined, and then flung out like the day's supply of garbage. "'Have you seen it again?'" he cries out to the noted physician upon first seeing him after so long. The question itself presupposes the answer, for Fettes has obviously seen "it" again and again and again. He has learned a hard lesson; he has discovered that when we disturb the sanctity of other people's identities, we lose sight of our own as well. Moreover, in so doing, we forego what little self-respect we have left for ourselves. This last consequence has been the fate of Macfarlane as well, though its manifestation has taken a different form. Macfarlane has sublimated his darkness by hiding behind a façade of efficient respectability; Fettes has obliterated his darkness with booze. In so doing, however, Fettes has simply replaced one darkness with another. Unlike the restored body of Gray, neither Macfarlane nor Fettes will ever be perfectly whole again. Their punishment is somehow fitting.

Although "The Body Snatcher" is considered by some critics to be one of Stevenson's minor works, it is nonetheless a suspenseful story, told with a modicum of tongue-in-cheek. So too, the concept of corpse grabbing is one that would have been familiar to readers of Stevenson's day, for such an activity was quite common during the nineteenth century in both England and America, as physicians-in-training and physicians-in-fact desperately sought actual human bodies upon which to practice their art. Sometimes the bodies were stolen from freshly dug graves; some were obtained through less natural means. The latter method would be used in Chicago in the early 1890s by a physician who went by various aliases but who often called himself Dr. Holmes. This unscrupulous medicine man enticed young women into a hotel he owned and operated in Chicago, made promises to them, made love to them, sometimes married them, killed them, skinned and burned their bodies, scraped their bones clean, and sold their precisely restored skeletons to medical schools.[19] In fact, since Stevenson himself drew on an actual case in England, "The Body Snatcher" is a tribute to its author's ever-restless imagination, for Stevenson adapted his fiction from the bare facts of the life of Robert Knox, a man who did indeed receive bodies that had been snatched for the purposes of dissection.[20] But Stevenson transforms these facts into an eerie study of the morally weird; in so doing, he creates order from the mundane incoherence of everyday existence.

Science Run Amok: Fiction, Stage, and Film

In January 1886, the British publisher Longman's printed the first edition of *The Strange Case of Dr. Jekyll and Mr. Hyde*. The book was relatively inexpensive, costing a mere shilling, for the publisher felt that this story should receive a wide audience and accordingly priced it inexpensively. The British reception of this work was enthusiastic and the book was subsequently pirated in America, where British copyrights were not protected.[21] Yet despite its wide readership by the end of the nineteenth century, some early twentieth century critics, notably Frank Swinnerton, saw *Dr. Jekyll and Mr. Hyde* as being of "a distinct second class,"[22] especially when compared to other Stevenson works. On the other hand, Swinnerton praises an important quality of Stevenson's style: a technique that he alludes to as "Stevenson's boyish love of the picturesquely terrible."[23] Certainly Stevenson's depiction of the ill-fated Jekyll/Hyde could be categorized in such a paradoxical way.

Yet modern popular culture has not been respectful of Robert Louis Stevenson's best-known novel. As is the situation with Edgar Allan Poe, Stevenson's reputation today has been distorted and truncated by playwrights and filmmakers, who have long stressed the terrible over the picturesque; and who, as a consequence, want nothing better than to cash in on the more ghoulish, supernatural aspects of Stevenson's finely crafted, often subtle work about the divided soul. What readers of later decades know about Stevenson is largely based upon their hearsay knowledge of this, arguably the most memorable of his stories. And this knowledge ordinarily comes, not from the actual text itself, but from the multitude of dramatizations that have been inspired by it. As early as 1887 in the United States, Richard Mansfield had performed on the New York stage in a very successful adaptation of the work, this one a version written by T. R. Sullivan.[24] Likewise, by 1888, a London production of *Dr. Jekyll and Mr. Hyde* was drawing in large audiences at the Lyceum. At the same time, a parody called *Hide and Seekyll* was playing at the nearby Royalty Theater.[25]

By the early twentieth century, the story had become an integral part of popular culture in both Great Britain and America, and its title had come into the language as a synonym for the dual manifestation of both good and evil in an individual. Indeed, in addition to its popularity as a stage play, Stevenson's creepy description of the crazed, obsessive man who undergoes numerous self-induced transformations has been filmed worldwide at least forty times: one of the first a silent movie in 1911, made by Thanhouser studio with James Cruze as the mad protagonist. It is not surprising, however, that filmmakers have adapted so many of Stevenson's stories for the screen, for much of his work does in fact have a cinematic quality to it. One critic has observed that Stevenson "unconsciously employed ... an excellent film technique" and that he himself was reported to have "visualized his novels in a series of small, bright, restless pictures."[26] In short, Stevenson, who would naturally have been familiar with still photography, saw the words that he was creating on paper as photographs constantly in motion.

Yet Stevenson would doubtless have been quite chagrined to see what the twentieth century was to make of his vision of such "small, bright, restless pictures." The titles of some of these loose adaptations onto film, produced over a period of about ninety-five years, reveal the degree to which Stevenson's story has been so distorted by filmmakers as to make the original unrecognizable. Many of the title themselves sound like parodies, so ridiculous as to induce a chuckle or two in individuals who are able to appreciate the absurdity underlying the story's contemporary fame: *Dr. Pyckle and Mr. Pride* (Film Booking Office, 1925); *Dr. Jekyll and Mr. Mouse* (MGM, 1947); *Abbott & Costello Meet Dr. Jekyll and Mr. Hyde* (Universal, 1953); *Dr. Jekyll's Hyde* (Warner Bros., 1958); *Man with Two Heads* (Great Britain, 1971); *Adult Version of Jekyll and Hyde* (Independent, 1972); and *Dr. Black and Mr. Hyde* (Independent, 1976).[27]

But to watch these various motion picture incarnations is to do a tremendous disservice to Stevenson, the artist and careful storyteller. To begin, Stevenson's Mr. Hyde is not the stalking, menacing lecher of filmdom, the man on the make who pursues the slatternly barmaid. Nor is Stevenson's Dr. Jekyll engaged to an elegant, sophisticated, respectable woman, as he is in many film adaptations. Furthermore, Stevenson's story is not told in the straightforward, chronological order seen in the movies. Rather, we learn about Jekyll/Hyde from various characters and from various perspectives, in an apparently random order, until we are able to piece the whole together. In addition, Stevenson's narrative covers several years, whereas in the movies, only about ninety minutes are needed for Jekyll to move quickly from a kindly, selfless doctor to a raving lunatic. From that first fateful drink to his inevitable death, Dr.Jekyll of the cinema ordinarily requires less than two hours' worth of disintegration. On the other hand, when we first meet Dr. Jekyll in Stevenson's work, he has been at his tubes, potions, burners, and flames for a long time, and has already performed many nefarious deeds as Mr. Hyde.

In short, people who are followers of good literature should reread Stevenson's original work from time to time in order to better appreciate its fine qualities. For example, Stevenson's use of setting in the story is especially skillful, so closely intertwined with his narrative as to be like the heart is to the body. Cut out the dizzying, claustrophobic, sense of place — where night reigns eternal — and the story would perish. In addition, although Stevenson points out a number of times from the outset that the story is set in London, many critics have correctly observed that it is Stevenson's native Edinburgh which he is actually describing. J. C. Furnas, in his splendid critical biography of Stevenson, describes the Edinburgh of both the nineteenth and twentieth centuries:

The Old Town retains many "closes"—steep, squeezed alleys, often overbuilt into mere tunnels, falling left and right from the High Street as reminder of what the nobility and gentry of Scotland once considered fit to live in ... Even in the New Town ... Edinburgh is devious and surprising. Streets dip and twist into sudden intimacy with the ravine of the Water of Leith or fly over it on lofty bridges. Solemnly stone-lined avenues drop, lengthen, and open to frame views of Fife or the Pentlands in a fashion that only San Francisco can equal.... Any reasonably comprehensive view of this city is unique. No two elements are ever on the same level, none is horizontal, the composition has the planes of a junk heap and the skyline of a smutty fairyland.[28]

It is this "reminder of what the nobility and gentry of Scotland once considered fit to live in" that Stevenson pictures so well in *The Strange Case of Dr. Jekyll and Mr. Hyde*. For instance, here in the description of Mr. Utterson's approach to the house of his good friend Dr. Jekyll, we can see the dislocating quality of Stevenson's native city:

Round the corner from the by-street there was a square of ancient, handsome houses, now for the most part decayed from their high estate, and let in flats and chambers to all sorts and conditions of men: map-engravers, architects, shady lawyers, and the agents of obscure enterprises.[29]

Just as Ambrose Bierce uses the fractured, distorted landscape of San Francisco in "A Watcher by the Dead," so Stevenson pictures in "Dr. Jekyll and Mr. Hyde" a city whose parts never really come together.

But the symbolism of *setting* is not the only aspect altered for the worse by stage and film adaptations. Raw feminine sexuality is also bypassed in the story, for in the original world of Robert Louis Stevenson, there is no love interest for Jekyll/Hyde. Perhaps this lack of feminine pulchritude was the result of Stevenson's real-life reluctance to become romantically involved, though he did eventually marry Fanny Osbourne, a divorced woman ten years older than he: a woman who was to become as much a nurse to her chronically ailing spouse as she was a wife.[30]

Moreover, the beginning of Stevenson's relationship with Fanny evolved in a way that demonstrated anything but a placid, ordinary boy-meets-girl romance. Rather, it involved their living together prior to marriage as well as the complications resulting from Fanny Osbourne's marital status at the time of Stevenson's courtship. When Stevenson began keeping company with Fanny, she still possessed a very demanding husband, who insisted that she return to him in California while Stevenson remained in England. In addition, Fanny's letters to Stevenson during this period of a six thousand-mile separation reveal a frequently incoherent, hysterical woman. In short, Stevenson had no romantic illusions about love and marriage. He even referred to marriage as "the one illogical adventure."[31] Perhaps these personal demons resurfaced when he wrote *The Strange Case of Dr. Jekyll and Mr. Hyde*. Stevenson probably surmised that his title character had enough complications to confront without the added burden of a bothersome, dreary, demanding female.

In contrast to Stevenson's creation of the relatively simple, all-male world of Jekyll/Hyde — a world without the complications that he naturally associated with the opposite sex — most of the movie versions require Jekyll to have at least two women in his life. In fact, in one of the filmed reincarnations of the story, a movie made in Great Britain in 1971 with the fetching title of *Dr. Jekyll and Sister Hyde*, the good doctor undergoes not just a transformation from devoted physician to demented London wayfarer, but also manages a sex change as well. Such a daring biological alteration was undoubtedly never dreamed of by Stevenson, who avoids any detailed depiction of women whatsoever in his story.

In addition, Stevenson's story builds suspense in a way that the film adaptations are unable to do. For instance, Stevenson's narrative technique does not at first give away the split identity, the connection between Jekyll/Hyde. Rather, it allows the reader to see events from the perspective of various friends and acquaintances of the clever scientist and experimenter. In fact, the narrative is so tightly constructed that it circles around the characters of Jekyll/Hyde. Moreover, as the circle closes in, it reveals more and more facts about the odd behaviors of each side, respectively, until, in the final section of the story, in the center of the circle, we have Henry Jekyll's own self-appraisal and confession. Then that centerpiece draws up within itself till it becomes a small dot and disappears altogether, at which point Dr. Jekyll ceases to exist, the final victim of the nefarious Mr. Hyde.

At this point, we should remember that modern readers already know, or think they know, the answer to the riddle of identity hidden within the twisted brain of Dr. Jekyll; they know from the outset that Jekyll and Hyde are one and the same. But it is also important to recall that a nineteenth century reader, coming to the story for the first time, would be led through the clever maze constructed by Stevenson, would be balancing precariously along the edge of suspense, turning those dark corners that, for Stevenson, forever signal the darkness of the human will.

What Stevenson Actually Wrote

The story opens before we even see Jekyll/Hyde; instead, we learn of Hyde's overweening brutality via a conversation between two friends, a lawyer named Utterson and his distant relative, a man named Enfield. The story's narrator is careful to point out that neither man is given to an excess of emotion: that, in fact, when they take walks together every Sunday, they look "singularly dull."[32] Their unexciting, undemonstrative personalities contribute a good deal to the tone of unrelenting horror that pervades this story, for when these two comment with awe upon the monstrous deeds and the equally subhuman appearance of Mr. Hyde, we are all the more convinced of the dark terrors attendant upon these visions. These are not men to engage in sentimental hyperbole.

For instance, when Enfield tells Utterson of the time he saw a small, ugly man almost fatally trample a little girl, we can appreciate how even this matter-of-fact witness, a capable lawyer, would have been deeply disturbed by the sight. As he reports his adventure to Utterson, he begins by describing how these two, the man and the small girl, chanced to collide with one another at "about three o'clock of a black winter morning."[33] It is a dark night, even for London, and Enfield confesses that, prior to his witnessing this atrocity, he has felt horribly isolated, cut off, alone. Indeed, *darkness* and the accompanying fear of the unknown are major motifs throughout. The only light on the street is an unnatural one: a luminous hue caused by the gaslights giving off a dim glow. Enfield defines this atmosphere to Utterson: "Street after street, and all the folks asleep — street after street, all lighted up as if for a procession, and all empty as a church — till at last I got into that state of mind when a man listens and listens and begins to long for the sight of a policeman."[34] What Enfield has the misfortune to see, however, is not a policeman but the collision of man and child, followed by "the horrible part of the thing; for the man trampled calmly over the child's body and left her screaming on the ground. It sounds nothing to hear, but it was hellish to see. It wasn't like a man; it was like some damned Juggernaut."[35] Furthermore, Utterson is particularly interested in hearing the name of the brutish, gnome-like man involved in this episode, for he is also familiar with the name of Mr. Hyde. As a friend of Dr. Henry Jekyll, Utterson has assisted the noble doctor in making out a curious will, whereby Dr. Jekyll has left all of his possessions to his friend Edward Hyde on one strange condition: that is, if Jekyll were to disappear for more than three months, Hyde would be entitled to all that was Jekyll's. Now that Utterson has a physical description to go with the name of this mysterious character, he is even more disturbed by the apparent mental lapse suffered by his friend when he wrote the will. So the suspense concerning the relationship between Dr. Jekyll and Mr. Hyde begins to build. But as yet, even the most careful reader — but one who is unfamiliar with the story — is unaware of the connection between the two.

In a story filled with reversals of expectations, one of the earliest of these occurs as Utterson thinks about what he has just learned from Enfield concerning the less-than-friendly demeanor of Mr. Hyde:

> And hitherto it was his ignorance of Mr. Hyde that had swelled his indignation; now, by a sudden turn, it was his knowledge. It was already bad enough when the name was but a name of which he could learn no more. It was worse when it began to be clothed upon with detestable attributes; and out of the shifting, insubstantial mists that had so long baffled his eye, there leaped up the sudden, definite presentment of a fiend.[36]

Another paradoxical aspect of this story is the ever-widening circle of characters who gradually offer their insights into the peculiar state of Dr. Jekyll. What is particularly ironic about these increasing perspectives is that, the wider the circle becomes, the more narrow its focus onto the specific activities of the Jekyll/Hyde duo, until finally we are allowed into the mind of Dr. Jekyll himself by means of his own written confession. The distinguished literary scholar David Daiches has commented on the recurring moral pattern of every one of the Stevenson novels; Daiches's analysis of this prominent motif could apply very well to the Jekyll/Hyde narrative and its shifting points of view. According to Daiches, Stevenson does not preach morality as such: his novels are not "didactic, or edifying, or orthodox in point of view. ... the design of the narrative, and the interplay of character which carries on the narrative, is keyed to some profound moral problem, or it might be better to say moral dilemma — for Stevenson shares with the great writers of tragedy the knowledge that there are no permanent solutions to the real human problems."[37]

One such individual who comes to learn of the impermanence of such solutions and who, moreover, provides early clues into the precarious mental condition of Dr. Jekyll is Dr. Lanyon, an old friend of both Jekyll and the increasingly perplexed and curious lawyer, Utterson. When Utterson pays a call on Dr. Lanyon in hopes of learning more about this odd hold that the dreadful Mr. Hyde has on the erudite Dr. Jekyll, he receives more details from Jekyll's old friend: details to arouse further suspicion concerning Jekyll's mental balance. In response to Utterson's comment that Jekyll and Lanyon had at one time shared "a bond of common interest," Lanyon is quite blunt in his judgment:

> "We had," was the reply. "But it is more than ten years since Henry Jekyll became too fanciful for me. He began to go wrong, wrong in mind; and though, of course, I continue to take an interest in him for old sake's sake as they say, I see and have seen devilish little of the man. Such unscientific balderdash," added the doctor, flushing suddenly purple, "would have estranged Damon and Pythias."[38]

So now we know that Mr. Hyde is a homicidal creep with the physical appearance of an ugly troll and that he furthermore holds some kind of sword over the increasingly disturbed head of Dr. Jekyll. We know this latter fact because we have learned through Utterson that Jekyll's will reveals the doctor's dread that he might soon disappear altogether. And from the time that Utterson actually meets the fearsome, distasteful Hyde and has a conversation with him, the lawyer is even more convinced that Jekyll is in need of protection. Indeed, Utterson fears that Hyde might "suspect the existence of the will"; in which case, thinks Utterson, "he may grow impatient to inherit."[39] Of course, Dr. Jekyll is in mortal danger from Mr. Hyde, but neither Utterson nor the reader knows as yet the real reason for Jekyll's perilous state, both mentally and physically.

Even so, Stevenson carefully plants clues throughout that lead us on to the inevitable conclusion. For instance, we never see Jekyll and Hyde occupying the same space. We are also provided with the intriguing information that Dr. Jekyll and Mr. Hyde share many similarities with respect to their handwriting. This fact is provided by Utterson's head clerk, Mr. Guest, a man widely respected for his trustworthiness and for "being a great critic and student of handwriting."[40] Upon his examination of the writing of both Dr. Jekyll and Mr. Hyde, Guest reports his conclusion to his employer when he tells Utterson that "there's a rather singular resemblance; the two hands are in many points identical: only differently sloped."[41]

We also witness a further mystery in the fast onset and the even faster deterioration and consequent death of Dr. Jekyll's former friend, Dr. Lanyon. Having already interviewed Lanyon about the peculiarities of Dr. Jekyll, and having dined with Lanyon and Jekyll somewhat later, Utterson goes to visit the doctor only a few evenings following this dinner and is astonished to find Lanyon a pitiably altered man. It has apparently taken only about six days for Lanyon to appear with a "death-warrant written legibly upon his face."[42] Moreover, Lanyon informs the incredulous Utterson of impending doom:

> "I have had a shock," he said, "and I shall never recover. It is a question of weeks. Well, life has been pleasant; I liked it; yes, sir, used to like it. I sometimes think if we knew all, we should be more glad to get away."[43]

Here Lanyon's cryptic statement makes the reader even more curious to know what has been transpiring between Lanyon and Dr. Jekyll. And, more to the point, we are becoming increasingly uneasy as we get closer to answering the riddle of Jekyll and Hyde. Like the doomed Dr. Lanyon, we suspect that we too will soon know "all."

What is destroying Dr. Lanyon is the awful vision that Henry Jekyll has just recently provided him. We learn about this vision later in the text through a letter from Lanyon that Utterson reads. According to Lanyon's account, Jekyll had earlier instructed Lanyon to break into Jekyll's laboratory, bring the contents of one drawer back to Lanyon's home, and wait for someone to show up to claim the contents. The individual who appears as claimant is, of course, Mr. Hyde, who gives a demonstration of the powers of transcendence inherent in the potions that Lanyon has carried back home with him. As Lanyon watches Hyde become Henry Jekyll, Lanyon knows that his own life and his own beliefs have been forever changed, and that he can no longer live in a world where men such as Hyde, who is at that moment being sought for the murder of Sir Danvers Carew, can continue to carry on with their abhorrent activities.

A Man's World

Following his description of the reappearance of Dr. Jekyll, who has sprung from the trappings of Mr. Hyde, Lanyon proceeds to relate vague hints concerning the kind of life led and the unspeakable acts performed by Hyde. Elaine Showalter has convincingly argued that one of the most prominent motifs of this story involves homosexual "images of forced penetration through locked doors into private cabinets, rooms and closets," images that "permeate Utterson's narrative."[44] And Lanyon had indeed been instructed by Jekyll's letter to force open, with the aid of a locksmith, Jekyll's laboratory cabinet; and thence, if the need arose, to break open the drawer containing all of Jekyll's precious vials and powders. So, in connection with such an interpretation of male dominance over other males, Lanyon's desperate words in the letter to Utterson take on added significance. Once Dr. Henry Jekyll has manifested himself before Lanyon's affrighted eyes, Jekyll proceeds with the story that Lanyon is too circumspect to pass on in any detail. Lanyon's reticence is seen notably at the end of his letter to Utterson:

> What he told me in the next hour I cannot bring my mind to set on paper. I saw what I saw, I heard what I heard, and my soul sickened at it.... My life is shaken to its roots; sleep has left me; the deadliest terror sits by me at all hours of the day and night; I feel that my days are numbered, and that I must die; and yet I die incredulous.... As for the moral turpitude that man unveiled to me, even with tears of penitence, I cannot, even in memory, dwell on it without a start of horror.[45]

The exact nature of this moral turpitude remains a matter for conjecture, since Stevenson does not fill in its outlines for us. Yet since this is indeed a story of men without women, we must assume that whatever horrible acts Jekyll has committed in the person of Hyde, these adventures have taken some unnatural turns. Furthermore, Lanyon is so distraught over what he has just seen and heard that, from this point on, he gives up entirely on life. His death comes just weeks after he learns Dr. Jekyll's terrible secret.

This pattern that involves these hints of homosexuality does not suggest, however, that Stevenson himself had homosexual leanings, despite the fact that one of his good friends was John Addington Symonds, a fairly open and vocal homosexual.[46] But the Symonds/Stevenson relationship appears to have been based solely on friendship and on admiration that each had for the other's work.[47] J.C. Furnas, in his comments on the friendships that Stevenson cultivated during his university days, offers the following caveat to the modern reader: "His times allowed *friend* a significant warmth greater than ours now permit. Our comradeship between young men may be equally close, but explicit acknowledgment is rarer."[48]

Moreover, as a young man, Stevenson had been sexually involved with any number of women, including prostitutes. When he was a student in Edinburgh, he rebelled against his strict Puritan upbringing with its emphasis on mankind's inherent wickedness. He asserted his freedom by cutting his college classes and by spending many hours in Edinburgh's more squalid places of recreation.[49] So too, he lived for a time with Fanny Osbourne who, when she initially began keeping company with Stevenson, already had a husband, Sam Osbourne: a man at first quite reluctant to give up his wife to a sickly, improvident writer. Furthermore,

Stevenson and Fanny eventually married, once the inconvenience of her first husband was resolved through divorce.

Despite Stevenson's attraction toward the opposite sex, the narrative of Jekyll and Hyde nonetheless remains a story of men and their relationships with one another — both professional and personal. And one of the most distinguished of these men is the loyal Lanyon, the man who has heard of such unspeakable "moral turpitude" from Dr. Jekyll that he reports having recoiled in horror at Jekyll's revelations. But what, precisely, does Lanyon die of? Stevenson leaves the exact cause in doubt. We know from the bits and pieces culled from the narrative that Lanyon and Jekyll are old friends. In fact, at one point, Utterson goes to see Lanyon and remarks to the doctor, "'...you and I must be the two oldest friends that Henry Jekyll has."[50] We also know that Lanyon had disapproved of Dr. Jekyll's experiments. In talking with Utterson, Jekyll himself tells the lawyer that Lanyon had referred to Jekyll's "scientific heresies." But Jekyll replies in kind, defining Lanyon as "a hide-bound pedant for all that; an ignorant, blatant pedant. I was never more disappointed in any man than Lanyon."[51] Perhaps, then, in light of the nature of the Jekyll/Lanyon disagreement over the limits of scientific inquiry, Lanyon dies of a broken mind and spirit, greatly disturbed over the fatal culmination of Jekyll's striving to go beyond what mortals should attempt. Some three weeks before his death, Lanyon unequivocally informs Utterson of his feelings regarding Dr. Jekyll: "'I am quite done with that person; and I beg that you will spare me any allusion to one whom I regard as dead.'"[52] The finality of Lanyon's judgment is clear. So too, when Utterson writes to Jekyll, asking for an explanation regarding the break with Lanyon, Jekyll's written reply is just as final and unequivocal. As Utterson thinks of the way in which Jekyll describes the breach, he comes to the following conclusion: "The quarrel with Lanyon was incurable."[53] The disease metaphor here is apt, for Jekyll seems to transmit to Lanyon his sickness in both mind and body.

In addition, Jekyll and Lanyon ultimately suffer the same fate: both withdraw from the world, Jekyll because he has no choice, his personality devoured by Hyde; Lanyon because he has been driven to self-annihilation by his glimpse of the unthinkable, by his vision of his good friend's obliteration. It is tempting to read some biography into Stevenson's preoccupation here with the twin entities of disease and withdrawal. As a boy, Stevenson, the only child of a frequently ill mother and a stern father who was often absent on business, suffered from precarious health, spending a good deal of time by himself playing indoors, creating his own stories and enacting his own dramas with the aid of cutout characters placed on the stage of a miniature theater.[54] He was also prone to nightmarish terrors, fostered by the lurid stories of ghosts and devils told to him by his nurse, Alison Cunningham, as well as by his own vivid imagination.[55]

It is further possible to surmise that *The Strange Case of Dr. Jekyll and Mr. Hyde* might have been a very different story had Stevenson not burned the first manuscript, which he wrote in a frazzled frenzy in three days. According to the most widely accepted version of the events surrounding the story's creation, Louis, emerging from his room after his three-day writing orgy, read the rough draft to Fanny and Fanny's son Lloyd. While Lloyd was spellbound by it, Fanny allegedly thought it awful. By some accounts, Fanny was appalled that Stevenson could have written such a superficial potboiler, one that neglected the allegorical possibilities while focusing only on the sensational aspects.[56] Stevenson was reportedly furious at his wife's carping criticism and subsequently burned the manuscript.

What kind of story *The Strange Case of Dr. Jekyll and Mr. Hyde* might have been had Stevenson not destroyed his initial effort in a fit of pique will always remain a mystery. However, perhaps Fanny's real motive in attacking her husband's work lay outside of any quarrels that she might have had with its supposed sensationalism. Perhaps what Stevenson had written contained scandalous descriptions of an explicitly heterosexual nature.[57] Some psychological interpretations suggest that Fanny disapproved of her husband's first draft because it depicted "a true female figure."[58] Moreover, it is just possible that this female figure was graphically depicted in ways that would have been offensive to Victorian sensibilities. If such was the case, Fanny need not have worried about Louis's revision, for there is no "true female" to be found anywhere in the finished work. Be that as it may, whatever the initial draft did contain, Stevenson completed its sequel in another astonishing burst of creativity; he was finished after another three days of frantic composition.

A Closer Look at the Imitators and Descendants of Dr. Jekyll and Mr. Hyde

It is a testament to the enduring quality of Stevenson's tale that Dr. Jekyll and Mr. Hyde have taken on metaphoric and iconic status over the decades. So we should possibly examine the imitators and descendants of Stevenson's immortal split personality in a positive way: as compliments to Stevenson's brilliant imagination. Never mind the curious changes wrought upon the story — and some have been curious indeed. To begin, why have filmmakers often considered it necessary to give Dr. Jekyll a female love interest? Elaine Showalter has pointed out that not one of the many movie and television versions of this story depicts the events the way Stevenson wrote them, for Stevenson's story is a story about men. Moreover, as we have seen, Showalter finds it to be a work with a decided homosexual motif.[59] Likewise, in looking for imitators and descendants, she also finds some similarities between the 1920 John Barrymore film and Oscar Wilde's darkly cynical look at identity and homoeroticism in *The Picture of Dorian Gray*.[60] The latter is a provocative comparison, suggesting that Wilde was influenced by his Scottish predecessor.

If it is true, as Showalter has suggested, that male bonding, forced entry from the rear through the locked doors of homes and laboratories, and unspeakable acts committed in darkness are prevalent throughout the Stevenson story, then we have the answer to our question about the inclusion of the female love interest in film versions made during the first half of the twentieth century. Any demonstration of sexual perversion would have been most unwelcome in early twentieth century American movie houses.

Yet, for all that, John Barrymore as the 1920 Jekyll/Hyde manifests a few interesting peculiarities; he is kin not only to Dorian Gray but also to Dracula in his desire to consume the woman he so hungrily pursues. In one particularly grotesque scene, Barrymore as Hyde grabs the virginal Milicent, the upper class lady to whom Dr. Jekyll is betrothed, and proceeds to embrace her while simultaneously biting her neck. It thus becomes evident at this point that Dr. Jekyll is not going to be betrothed to Milicent much longer. Barrymore's Hyde also lusts after a slatternly barmaid in a music hall, a woman more in keeping with the class to which Hyde obviously belongs. In addition, Barrymore undergoes his agonizing transformation in much the same manner as Stevenson describes this metamorphosis in the story. Here, Stevenson offers us Dr. Jekyll as the first person narrator, explaining his own transformation upon first drinking the chemicals he has boiled into a hellish mixture: "The most racking pangs succeeded: a grinding in the bones, deadly nausea, and a horror of the spirit that cannot be exceeded at the hour of birth or death.[61]

In fact, the 1920 onscreen mutation occurring when Dr. Jekyll becomes Mr. Hyde is probably the closest resemblance that we see between fiction and film. In the 1920 incarnation, through the use of some flawless cinematography involving the superposition of one image on top of another, Barrymore turns into a different person altogether, though we know that it is still Barrymore behind the Lon Chaneyesque makeup. But he gradually changes from the handsome, well-groomed Dr. Jekyll, complete with that famous, aristocratic, long-nosed Barrymore profile, into a creature with unkempt hair. These hairs insist on sprouting and sprawling at cross-angles across his head, like unruly tendrils of plants that have been long neglected. Furthermore, the clear, white complexion of Dr. Jekyll turns into a mass of pustules, doubtless a sign of the continuous flowering of some longstanding venereal disease. Here he resembles a potato with many tubers sticking up from the pocked and wrinkled skin. To complete his dreadful appearance, the teeth become hideously malformed, as though they belong to a creature of a reptilian species. In addition, as in the Stevenson story, by the climax, Dr. Jekyll is no longer able to control his metamorphosis and therefore is likewise unable to keep the personality and appearance of Mr. Hyde from taking over. Furthermore, the wrenching alteration ultimately takes place without benefit of the chemical concoction, which heretofore Jekyll/Hyde had been required to drink in order to assume a different identity.

In the 1932 story adaptation, when Fredric March turns into Hyde, the effect is not quite so stunning, though the physical pain remains evident — the type of pain accompanying the paroxysms of such contortions that are required to convey the shedding of skin. What makes this transformation less striking than the earlier Barrymore one is paradoxically related to the introduction of *sound* to the motion picture. The 1920 Jekyll/Hyde suggests the suffocation brought on by a silent, atmospheric darkness. By 1932, with the introduction of dialogue, the filmmakers have added an element of realism that, strangely enough, distances us from the horror. Though the cinematography and the superposition of images are still strikingly effective, once the characters talk, they no longer seem so supernaturally frightening. With the addition of *sound*, they become more ordinary: in short, more like us.

Nor does the appearance of Fredric March as Mr. Hyde generate the same kind of horror as Barrymore does as the dissipated reprobate. The filmmakers of 1932 try to give March's Mr. Hyde an ape-like bearing and countenance, but they give him protruding canine teeth, so that he resembles a hybrid of two species, a cloning experiment gone horribly awry. In addition, March has difficulty talking through these teeth; as a result, his diction is less insidiously threatening than just basically sloppy. Moreover, the unkempt hairstyle of Barrymore has been replaced by a crewcut, neatly plastered to March's head. Although March tries hard to look and act menacing, he instead resembles Jerry Lewis; that is, Lewis had he dressed in Halloween attire and headed off for a meeting of Rotarians.

There are a number of other significant differences as well between the films made in 1920 and in 1932 and Stevenson's story. Besides the injection of women into both movies, the movie plots are presented in a more straightforward manner, so that we are aware much sooner that Jekyll and Hyde are one. Moreover, both films make it seem as though Jekyll's destruction begins and ends within the time frame of about one hundred minutes. Whereas in the story, Dr. Jekyll is a philosopher who has pondered for years the riddle of good and evil dwelling within the same individual, in the 1920 version, Dr. Jekyll listens to an old friend, Sir George Carew, who goads him into a desire to taste the delights of life's sordid side. Seeming to have no mind or will of his own, Jekyll wastes no time whatsoever in taking Carew's advice. An intriguing paradox within the movie's plot involves Carew's daughter Milicent, who is engaged to Dr. Jekyll; as a consequence of this family connection, one would assume that Carew would have better sense than to send his future son-in-law out into the dark world of murky morality. But obviously he does not.

In the Stevenson story, on the other hand, while there is a character named Carew — this one called Sir Danvers Carew — he is murdered by Hyde and never figures prominently as a character as such. While Carew is also murdered by Hyde in the 1920 film, here the killing results from Carew's sanctimonious, insulting visit to Dr. Jekyll, at which time Carew informs the doctor that, due to Jekyll's recent peculiar behavior, he has concluded that perhaps Jekyll is not fit to marry his daughter. Angered beyond reason, Jekyll promptly changes into Hyde in front of the astonished Carew, the first such instance in which anyone has actually witnessed the awful event. Maddened even more now that his secret is out, Hyde brutally clubs to death the man who had ironically been the one to push Jekyll down that slide into hell.

This scene is reminiscent of one in the novel alluded to by Showalter, Oscar Wilde's *The Picture of Dorian Gray* (1898). This work, which also explores a soul gone mad, may have indeed been influenced by Stevenson's story. Like Stevenson, Wilde depicts the tragedy of a man's alter ego gone berserk when Dorian Gray murders Basil Hallward, the painter responsible for the portrait that has become Dorian's Mr. Hyde. For once Dorian has shown the portrait to Hallward and thus revealed his secret to another, Dorian knows that he must kill the only living person who now understands what has become of the painting. Looking at the monstrous image in disbelief, Hallward is desperate for reassurance that there is some trick involved, some sleight-of-hand that will disprove the reality of the hideous portrait. Therefore, he states matter-of-factly, "You told me you had destroyed it." But Dorian can offer Hallward no comfort, as he responds, equally matter-of-factly, "I was wrong. It has destroyed me."[62] It is a statement that could well have been made by Dr. Jekyll.

But again, the Stevenson story differs considerably from the 1920 movie depicting the misfortunes of Jekyll/Hyde. In the original, Hyde kills Sir Danvers Carew for no apparent reason, making the murder even more chilling. In fact, Stevenson's Edward Hyde exemplifies the "motive-less malignity" once ascribed to Iago by the English poet and sometime critic Samuel Taylor Coleridge. Though the distinguished Shakespeare scholar A.C. Bradley would later criticize Coleridge's interpretation, calling the poet "the author of that misleading phrase,"[63] the concept of pure evil for the sake of evil does, in fact, suit the character of Stevenson's Mr. Hyde, if not precisely that of Iago.

Nor does the Fredric March interpretation of Jekyll/Hyde fit the definition of "motiveless malignity." For instance, in his manifestation as Edward Hyde, he stalks a prostitute named Ivy Pearson (Miriam Hopkins), establishes a cozy living arrangement with her, and makes her his sexual slave. Clearly, then, in this 1932 movie, Hyde's most obvious motive in so assiduously pursuing evil involves his sexual drives.

In fact, this depiction of the sexual urgency of the protagonist is quite graphic for its time. Made before the strict enforcement of the Hollywood Production Code of 1930, the film portrays both Dr. Jekyll and Mr. Hyde as men who are hungry for sex: Dr. Jekyll makes it clear to his fiancée, Muriel Carew (Rose Hobart) that he cannot stand the thought of her father delaying their wedding. Furthermore, it is also apparent that what he really cannot stand is the forced delay of their sexual union: a necessary obstacle to his sensual fulfillment in light of the sexual mores of the time and the fact that his intended is a "lady." But Muriel's father, Danvers Carew (the name has reverted in this film to Stevenson's original) has insisted that the young couple wait. Muriel, being an obedient daughter, has unwillingly agreed. She is, after all, a "good" woman, one to whom Dr. Jekyll would naturally be attracted. His attraction, however, is definitely of a physical nature. He clearly is not interested in marrying her for the opportunity of discussing with her his scientific discoveries.

On the other hand, the other woman in Jekyll/Hyde's life is Ivy Pearson, the formulaic bad-girl-as-victim. It is with Jekyll/Hyde's behavior toward Ivy that the 1932 film differs not only from Stevenson's story but also from the 1920 Barrymore picture as well. No character by that name appears in either the story or the Barrymore version. But to Fredric March's Mr. Hyde, Ivy becomes the embodiment of this character's sexual hunger, whether he takes the form of Dr. Jekyll or Mr. Hyde. Ivy first encounters March in the person of Dr. Jekyll when he intervenes in a quarrel between Ivy and one of her low life associates, who is engaged in assaulting her on the street near the squalid flat where she lives. Dr. Jekyll rescues her, carries her into her dwelling, and examines her injuries in a somewhat unprofessional manner. And for her part, Ivy, unaware that her well-dressed gentleman visitor is a doctor, tries to seduce her caller by exposing her thighs, shoulders, and as much of her breasts as the censors would allow. But Dr. Lanyon, who has been waiting outside, interrupts this friendly encounter at the point where Jekyll and Ivy embrace and kiss. Embarrassed, convinced that Ivy is not seriously hurt, Jekyll rearranges both his coattails and his comforting, professional expression, and hastily exits with his friend.

But he remembers Ivy. And he comes back. And this time he is Mr. Hyde. Now as decidedly unattractive as Jekyll had been exceedingly handsome, he goes to the nightspot where Ivy is singing, and he forces her to notice him a second time. On this occasion, however, she cringes when she faces her would-be suitor, unmistakably oblivious to his relationship to the handsome doctor whom she had just recently treated so seductively. Eventually, Hyde forces her to live with him, where we assume she is repeatedly sexually victimized, doubtless in any number of unnatural ways, a fact given credibility largely through March's bestial appearance as Hyde. Finally, he beats her to death. None of this is to be found in Stevenson's *The Strange Case of Dr. Jekyll and Mr. Hyde.*

However, the symbol of the *mirror* or *looking glass* is one that is featured in both the story and in the 1932 film version. Traditionally, the mirror has symbolized in varying degrees the topic of identity, notably a character's validation of him/herself. Often, what this individual sees when s/he looks into a mirror is the image of what s/he wants to be or, contrarily, what this character fears s/he has become. In short, the mirror reflects the truth. According to vampire folklore, vampires, those creatures who are undead, do not cast mirror reflections, since they do not really exist in the same way that we mortals ordinarily define existence.

As a part of Stevenson's chronicle, Dr. Jekyll himself alludes to the mirror or looking glass in his description of his initial transformation. Prior to these experiments with chemicals and his consuming of this hellish mixture, Jekyll informs us that he had no mirror in his laboratory, so his first view of his New Self comes when he slinks back into his own house and his own room, there to gaze for the first time on his fascinating but abhorrent new creation. Yet he reports that he soon gets a mirror for that laboratory; this looking glass has one specific purpose. The "room" that he refers to here is his laboratory:

> There was no mirror, at that date, in my room; that which stands beside me as I write was brought there later on, and for the very purpose of those transformations.... I determined, flushed as I was with hope and triumph, to venture in my new shape as far as to my bedroom ... I stole through the corridors, a stranger in my own house; and coming to my room, I saw for the first time the appearance of Edward Hyde.[64]

Not only does Stevenson's protagonist see Hyde for the first time, but he also becomes supremely obsessed with that reflection in the glass. He is like a man with an abscessed tooth who wants the pain to stop but who nonetheless is driven to poke at the offending tooth and thus cause himself even more pain. Dr. Jekyll is especially intrigued by the fact that his new creation is smaller than Jekyll, and that he is, moreover, dissipated, ugly, and younger than his counterpart. After returning from his laboratory to his room at home, Jekyll fastens his attention on the mirror and reports on these changes with a certain amount of pride coupled with disgust. He becomes a type of perverted Narcissus, one whose reflection is just as enchanting in its own way as Narcissus had found his to be:

> Even as good shone upon the countenance of the one evil was written broadly and plainly on the face of the other. Evil besides (which I must still believe to be the lethal side of man) had left on that body an imprint of deformity and decay. And yet when I looked upon that ugly idol in the glass, I was conscious of no repugnance, rather of a leap of welcome. This, too, was myself. It seemed natural and human.[65]

Likewise, in the 1932 *Dr. Jekyll and Mr. Hyde*, the opening shots of March as Dr. Jekyll are deliberately discomfiting. We open with a point of view shot of March that enables us to hear his voice; further, we stay with him as he walks through his house. As the camera tracks March's movements from March's perspective, we are with the camera, tracking along with March. Then, when March pauses to look in a mirror, we see his face for the first time. It is a disorienting use of point of view, with some fine camera work by cinematographer Karl Struss.

And it is meant to be disturbing and jarring, just as the original story is unsettling. In fact, one of the major movements of the 1932 film entails a quandary faced by the protagonist, specifically March's ultimate inability to place or orient himself in the proper setting according to the identity that he has assumed at that particular time. Thus, at one point, he kisses the smitten Ivy, while he is formally dressed for the evening and also clad in his proper persona as Dr. Jekyll. Alternatively, at another point, this one toward the end of the film, he has been transformed without benefit of the magic potion; thus, as Mr. Hyde, he enters the sumptuous Carew home and tries to attack the horrified Muriel, who naturally does not recognize him as her beloved betrothed.

A memorable, symbolic cinematic touch used to good effect throughout the 1932 movie to show this dual personality is the diagonal split screen. This juxtaposition is often employed to highlight scenes featuring opposing characters, such as the picture of Ivy on one half of the screen and Muriel on the other. It is an effective use of the visual medium to convey the fluid movement between the protagonist's two identities. Since such a technique was obviously not available to Stevenson, he achieves much the same effect by crosscutting throughout the story from one point of view to another. But Stevenson also builds suspense through his manipulation of various points of view. We never get the full story behind the Jekyll/Hyde relationship until the final section, where we read Dr. Jekyll's own account of his gradual, inexorable self-destruction. Not until this moment in the story do we see for ourselves precisely where all of these diverse narratives have been heading.

The Final Complexity of Stevenson's Story

While many of the film and stage adaptations of *The Strange Case of Dr. Jekyll and Mr. Hyde* retain the obvious theme explored by Stevenson — the deleterious side effects resulting from unfettered science — all of these descendants and imitators lack the complexity of character and the tight narrative control that Stevenson achieves. His characters are eminently intriguing because they demonstrate realistic qualities that engage us from the outset. We want to know more about even the secondary characters:

their drives, their motives, their fears. For instance, the first sentence of the story introduces a man of apparent contradictions about whom we want to know more: "Mr Utterson the lawyer was a man of rugged countenance, that was never lighted by a smile; cold, scanty and embarrassed in discourse; backward in sentiment; lean, long, dusty, dreary, and yet somehow lovable."[66] Indeed, when Utterson becomes personally involved in the misfortunes of Jekyll and Hyde, we remember this early description, and we can subsequently better understand why he reacts with a rational, practical demeanor on the one hand, but with a genuine concern for Dr. Jekyll's mental state on the other.

Then there is Utterson's distant relative, Richard Enfield, a "well-known man about town," who immensely enjoys his Sunday walks with Utterson, though few people can see what these two have in common. It is Enfield's description of Hyde that gives us our first impression of Hyde's grotesque physical appearance as well as of his equally grotesque — indeed homicidal — character. Despite their outward differences, Utterson and Enfield share some common bonds. Both have some knowledge of Mr. Hyde; both are curious about his odd, sybaritic relationship to Dr. Jekyll; and both are afraid of what they will discover if they go too deeply into the secrets hidden within dark streets and within even darker, more enigmatic legal documents. Both pursue goals related to these puzzles; so too, neither is afraid to directly confront Mr. Hyde in an attempt to challenge him, to probe the nature of such a disquieting creature.

A further noteworthy character is Dr. Lanyon, a congenial, practical man of science and old friend of both Utterson and Dr. Jekyll. He has philosophically opposed everything that Dr. Jekyll has recently become: he sees Jekyll has an impractical, romantic, fanciful idealist, whose ideas are so much "unscientific balderdash."[67] Lanyon is, of course, ultimately driven to madness and death by the sight of Dr. Jekyll turning into Mr. Hyde. In his response to this horrifying spectacle, even the rational, humorous, ironic perspective that Lanyon has heretofore evinced at last fails him. He can no longer deny the reality of Dr. Jekyll's success, for Jekyll has indeed become the true physical embodiment of his own philosophical fancies and fantasies. He is every romantic transcendentalist who has ever wanted to go beyond the physical body in order to attain a higher, more perfect reality. Like Emerson's transparent eyeball, Jekyll becomes both everything and nothing.

And therein lies the terror for everyone, for *The Strange Case of Dr. Jekyll and Mr. Hyde* is not just a story about a scientist whose desire for knowledge goes beyond what God has ordained that man should know, nor is it solely a story about the dual nature of man, in whom both good and evil dwell. Rather it is both a cautionary work about the complexities of the human mind as well as a story of denial. All of Jekyll's friends and associates — even his long-time servant Poole — deny the irrefutable evidence of their senses. None of them are willing to concede that there is anything at all odd in the many coincidences involving the Jekyll/Hyde relationship.

In addition, *The Strange Case of Dr. Jekyll and Mr. Hyde* is a story of male camaraderie; as noted before, it depicts a world where women are excluded. Even those horrible excesses that Jekyll describes in his account of himself seem to involve forms of debauchery not dependent on women for their successful completion. As a young man, confesses Jekyll, he was not without sin: "...I stood already committed to a profound duplicity of life. Many a man would have blazoned such irregularities as I was guilty of; but from the high views that I had set before me, I regarded and hid them with an almost morbid sense of shame."[68] Is there a suggestion of homosexuality in these "irregularities" that Jekyll admits being "guilty of"? Perhaps. One does hesitate to draw this conclusion, however, especially in light of Jekyll's next observation concerning his manifold sins: "It was thus rather the exacting nature of my aspirations, than any particular degradation in my faults, that made me what I was."[69]

If Jekyll is not particularly degraded, he is nonetheless still ambitious, determined to discover how one might sever the connection between good and evil in the character of a single individual. But in his attempted amputation of one part of his total self, Dr. Jekyll goes mad, for he discovers that a person's identity cannot be halved, that an individual is a composite of all those fears, weaknesses, desires, and flaws that make him/her human. By mutilating his person, Dr. Jekyll forever destroys what he had made of himself through long years of study and sacrifice.

Five

Charles Chesnutt and the Despair of Blackness

At the time when I first broke into print seriously, no American colored writer had ever secured critical recognition except Paul Laurence Dunbar, who had won his laurels as a poet. Phyllis Wheatley, a Colonial poet, had gained recognition largely because she was a slave and born in Africa, but the short story, or the novel of life and manners, had not been attempted by any one of the group.

Charles W. Chesnutt,
"Post-Bellum, Pre-Harlem," 1931

Mandy's Denial

Mandy Oxendine (1896) is the first extant novel written by the talented, insightful, but largely forgotten black author Charles W. Chesnutt, who was both a social historian as well as a psychological realist. While some of Chesnutt's early twentieth century novels employ sentimental, melodramatic plot devices, he nonetheless eschewed the "self-deluding sentimentalism of romantic American fiction."[1] Indeed, as Chesnutt develops the character of Mandy Oxendine, we see the all-too-real effects of such self-delusion, for Mandy is a determined woman who not only tries to alter her identity by hiding her past as a Southern black but also comes to pay the price for such duplicity.

Charles Chesnutt was born in 1858 in Cleveland, Ohio, and thus was not a native southerner. But in 1866, he moved with his family to Fayetteville, North Carolina.[2] The move was an important one: Chesnutt's early life was to have a lasting effect on his perceptions of racism. As a child growing up in the South during Reconstruction, Chesnutt witnessed the turbulence of the times, notably the excessive violence that became the hallmark of Southern culture for decades. Such violence was aimed at curbing the effects of the Emancipation and at reinstituting a form of slavery on these Southern blacks.[3] Nor did the North intervene on behalf of the blacks' welfare. It was not in the best interests of Northern businessmen to interfere with internal Southern social policy, for these same businessmen had economic ties to the whites in the South. They were less concerned with the rights of Southern blacks than with the finances of Northern whites.[4]

Even though Chesnutt was greatly affected by such race prejudice and by the subsequent exploitation from both North and South, as well as by the efforts of the Southern white populace to break down organizations established to benefit freedmen, he wrote works of social protest that would eventually transcend the boundaries of race and time. Though Chesnutt has long been neglected, he was an important and influential writer. According to some sources, it was Chesnutt who first used the expression "jim crow" in one of his works: a phrase that originally meant a kind of crude comb.[5] In spite of his brief popularity in the late nineteenth and early twentieth centuries, both Chesnutt himself as well as his earliest novel, *Mandy Oxendine*, have been overlooked for decades. In fact, *Mandy* was not published until the end of the twentieth century, over one hundred years after it was written. As a result, critical commentary on *Mandy* is scarce; much analysis published on Chesnutt's writings was written before the 1997 publication of *Mandy Oxendine*.

In fact, there is convincing evidence that Chesnutt was working on the story of Mandy as early as 1889. Sometime in March of that year, Chesnutt wrote a letter to George W. Cable, a liberal, well-known Southern author who had praised Chesnutt's work. In this letter, Chesnutt alludes to the various literary genres in which he has been working: "I can turn my hand to several kinds of literary work, can write a story, a funny skit, can turn a verse, and write a serious essay. I have even written a novel, though it has never seen the light, nor been offered to a publisher."[6] It is probable that the novel to which Chesnutt refers here is *Mandy Oxendine*. It is further safe to infer from Chesnutt's letter that he had completed *Mandy* by the time he wrote to Cable. However, when Chesnutt finally sought a publisher for his novel in the late 1890s, he would discover that no one was willing to risk printing such daring, controversial material. It was far too audacious for late nineteenth century readers, especially rural white southerners, who are presented throughout as cruel, illiterate, lewd, and appallingly stupid opportunists. The novel could not find its audience until the end of the twentieth century. In his introduction to the 1997 edition of the work, Charles Hackenberry compares it to *The Marrow of Tradition*, a novel published by Chesnutt some twelve years after he had completed *Mandy Oxendine*. Hackenberry's explanation addresses the daring quality of this, Chesnutt's earlier novel:

> To a degree, Mandy Oxendine and Tom Lowrey prefigure Josh Green and Dr. Miller, two symbolic characters in *The Marrow of Tradition* (1901), a work that brought the wrath of the conservative white critical establishment down firmly on Chesnutt's tender ego and his even more fragile literary career. Mandy's means are as extreme as Josh Green's — less violent, but much more insidious and almost impossible for the dominant white culture to counter. One can only imagine the controversy *Mandy Oxendine* would have stirred up, and the consequent effects on Chesnutt's budding literary career, had the editors at Houghton Mifflin decided to publish this slim novel in 1897.[7]

Some of these more controversial aspects of *Mandy Oxendine* include an attempted rape, a murder, a near lynching, an allusion to sexual exploitation of female prisoners by their male jailers, and an exposé of the wretched condition of the few schoolhouses allotted to black children in the Reconstruction South — and of how pitifully little knowledge these same children received with respect to even the most basic aspects of reading.

In truth, it is impossible to read *Mandy Oxendine* today without feeling stunned by the sense of hopelessness that Chesnutt conveys, despite his somewhat qualified happy ending. The novel is nonetheless a daringly realistic work by a black writer trying to probe the problem of racial definition in the Reconstruction South. Moreover, the "notion of unstable or evolving identity not only pervades much of Chesnutt's fiction but also in many ways describes his own literary reputation."[8] Chesnutt was always searching for a style, even as he deliberated over the issue of whether or not he himself should try to pass for white. Finally deciding against making this daring attempt, Chesnutt strove to write for white as well as black audiences.[9]

In this connection, Chesnutt demonstrates in *Mandy Oxendine* that the issue of choosing an identity is not limited to race; the novel also explores the prejudices associated with sex and class. Mandy herself exemplifies the dilemma inherent in trying to define oneself within two of these categories, as she tries climbing above and beyond race and class, unencumbered by roots that might eventually be dug up and that would subsequently connect her to her past. These are roots that she hopes will remain undiscovered, for she knows that, once unearthed, they will inevitably lead to her being buried beneath that earth.

The character of Mandy Oxendine is probably based in part on the character of Charles Chesnutt's own mother, Ann Maria Sampson, who had left her native Fayetteville, North Carolina in 1856 and headed north in search of laws that were less prohibitive to blacks. Even though Ann Maria was a free black, she was a strong, rebellious young woman, and she despised the North Carolina restrictions that forbid anyone to educate blacks. These prohibitions resulted from the hard economic times in the 1830s in North Carolina. Whenever times are uncertain and a society is facing the probability of unwelcome change, no matter what the reason for such a change, what often follows is the persecution of the most helpless inhabitants by the most powerful. It was just such a society in a state of religious upheaval and dissension that fostered the Salem witchcraft trials in 1692; here in the pre–Civil War South, it was an economic depression that caused the whites to fear a black uprising. Consequently, in 1835, a Free Negro Code was enacted. This Code stripped even the free blacks of any basic citizenship rights.[10]

In the face of such injustice, Ann Maria had determined to defy the Code. As a young woman in North Carolina, she had demonstrated her teaching talent, even as "she had repeatedly risked fine, imprisonment, or from twenty to thirty-nine lashes on her bare back in order to instruct slave children secretly."[11]

Although it is probable that Ann Maria, a mulatto, was fair-skinned like Mandy, we have no indication that she ever tried to pass for white. The resemblance between Chesnutt's mother and his fictional creation lies within the strongly defiant spirit evidenced by both young women. But they differ in the form of their defiance; whereas Ann Maria believed that hard work, a good education, and a move northward would enable her race to overcome the all-pervasive barriers against the Negro, Mandy believes that such barriers will remain forever in place. Consequently, she obliterates her identity by climbing over to the white side, convinced that, once over this obstacle, she will find the opportunity which awaits on the proper side of the fence. Unlike Ann Maria, Mandy is not especially interested in either hard work or a good education. Indeed, Mandy Oxendine is not a particularly sympathetic character. As presented throughout the first three-fourths of the novel, she is opportunistic, arrogant, disloyal, and cruel. In short, she disgraces both the race that she has eschewed and the race that she has adopted.

One of the most prominent patterns in the novel is the contrast between Mandy's philosophy and that of her male counterpart, Tom Lowrey, who, like Mandy, could also redefine himself by passing for white if he so chose, but who opts instead for a life lived between two worlds: one white and one black. But these two characters pay a heavy, nearly fatal, price for the lifestyles that they do choose. Mandy resolves to uproot both herself and her mother in order to move to Sandy Run, North Carolina, a community some seventy-five miles from her birthplace. On the other hand, Tom elects to move from this same birthplace in order to attend "an institute in a distant part of the State, where Northern philanthropy had provided opportunity for the higher education of colored youth. There the gates of a new world were unlocked for him."[12] Moreover, because Tom has been in love with Mandy since they were children, he searches for her upon his return from this institute of higher learning and, once he discovers her hiding place, obtains a teaching position in the black school in the Sandy Run settlement. Though Tom is intelligent and sensible enough to realize that he dare not directly intrude himself into Mandy's newly created persona, he still hopes to win her over by rational persuasion.

But Mandy's ambitions have little to do with common sense. Chesnutt makes it clear that only a certain kind of person can relinquish his/her heritage in order to be reborn into a different color. Such a fair-skinned person knows that upward mobility for someone known by the dominant white race to have black blood is impossible. Therefore, the only alternative is a complete identity switch, the cost of which is incalculable and involves "a severance from one's former life almost as complete as that made by death; one must forsake home and relatives and friends, must cease to see them, to communicate with them, to inquire of them. It was a heroic remedy, and demanded either great courage or great meanness, according to the point of view."[13]

At first, it seems that Mandy qualifies in the second category, for she does indeed appear to be mean-spirited. In fact, Mandy's attempts to reinvent herself as a white woman manifest themselves in a number of self-serving, merciless ways. To begin, she convinces herself that a local aristocratic white man, Bob Utley, is a worthy goal for her to pursue. And to complicate her desires, Utley is a boorish clod, always in debt, contemptuous of both races, a conniver: in sum, a worthless human. Early in the novel, a black farmer named Deacon Pate succinctly informs Lowrey of Utley's less than attractive personality: "'dey say young Mistah Utley is fast as dey make 'em, drinkin', gamblin' and rakin'.'"[14] Another complicating factor likely to thwart the romantic attachment between Mandy and the hard living, hard drinking sexual predator Bob Utley is the fact that Utley is engaged to his cousin, Florence Brewington. But this engagement hardly represents a match made in heaven, for Florence is a snobbish Southern belle, who shares Utley's distaste for humanity and who has the decided advantage in Utley's eyes of being rich. Once again, the philosophical and perceptive Deacon Pate is on target in his analysis of the uppity Miss Brewington, as he advises Tom: "'Miss Flo'ence is a fine-lookin' gal, and proud as proud kin be. She doan look at common white folks ez much mo' d'n dirt, an' ez fer niggers, dey ain't no mo' ter her d'n dust, er smoke.'"[15]

Nor does the match intimidate Mandy. At one point, finding Utley in a romantic, ardent mood, she bluntly accuses him: "'I reckon you think it nice to have two girls, but I don't. I've heard that you're engaged to be married to your cousin.'"[16] To this challenge, Utley gives an equivocal answer; he neither promises to break his engagement to Florence nor agrees to marry Mandy. But Mandy has come too far, has rendered herself too blind to the actual ways of the world, to give up now. Even though she instinctively pulls back from a man who she knows might be very dangerous, Mandy nonetheless cannot resist the attraction of all the enticing dangers that Utley represents. It is for men such as this, for all the opportunities they represent, that Mandy has, at least in part, changed her identity. The following description shows just how much Chesnutt was aware of the desperation of people like Mandy, of the untenable position into which the white world had placed her:

> She had grasped by intuition the essential element of difference in the status of the two races she stood between; she felt that it was not learning or wealth, or even aspiration — but opportunity. And she saw that to have opportunity was to possess the road to all else in life. And so by becoming white she had stepped across the line of demarcation and into the freedom and light of opportunity.[17]

And the opportunity that beckons so alluringly to Mandy is associated with the exceedingly sinister yet exceedingly white Bob Utley. The imagery in the following passage alludes to Utley's serpent-like qualities, even as it reveals his hypnotic allure:

...there was a fascination in the glitter of his eye, a charm in his flattering tongue, a seduction in his smile, that few women could in the end resist. He was not popular among men. They held him to be cold, and selfish and treacherous, and his friends were few. But to Mandy he represented that great, rich, powerful white world of which she dreamed, and to enter which since meeting him she dared to aspire.[18]

Not only is Mandy determined to capture Utley for herself, but she is also equally convinced that she must treat Tom cruelly in order not to blow her cover. For his part, however, Tom tries every stratagem he can devise in order to grab the chance to meet Mandy, but only when she is alone. For Tom is also unwilling to compromise Mandy's position in the community, which knows that she is poor, but believes that she is white.

One afternoon, Tom does his best to arrange a meeting with Mandy following the dismissal of her school. But his plans are set back when he discovers that Mandy is accompanied by a girlfriend from school. Thus, when he sees Mandy, he makes no gestures that would indicate their acquaintance. However, to Mandy's horror, her white companion feels it necessary to comment upon him. In spite of Tom's efforts to remain unobtrusive, Mandy regrets that she is in no position to deny his presence altogether:

> On this occasion, as the two girls drew near, he stepped out into the road, met and passed them, going in the opposite direction to theirs. He looked at Mandy, but did not venture to speak, and she gave no sign of recognition.
> "Oh, Mandy," said her companion, when Lowrey was out of hearing, "who do you reckon that is? It's the nigger teacher down at Sandy Run. He looks like a white man, don't he, Mandy?"
> "Niggers is niggers," said Mandy, "and looks don't make 'em white."
> Mandy's own position was too uncertain to permit any latitude in regard to niggers. People who were born white and could prove it might afford to be liberal in their views on the matter of blood, but Mandy had the zeal of a proselyte.
> "My mammy won't let me speak to niggers," said the girl.
> "I should think not," said Mandy, emphatically.[19]

It is significant to our understanding of Mandy's character and of her subsequent dilemma that this conversation takes place after Tom has already passed by; he is therefore unable to hear Mandy's incredibly insulting tone and powerfully charged language. Mandy waits until Tom is out of hearing range, for Mandy would actually like the best of both worlds: she wants the gentle dependability of Tom Lowrey, but she also craves the white respectability of the dangerous Bob Utley. Chesnutt demonstrates that Mandy wants to string Tom along, keeping him in reserve, lest her plans to snare Utley fall through the net. She also occasionally admits to herself that she still has a few soft, sentimental feelings for Tom. Additionally, Mandy is enough of a realist to know that Tom could ruin her plans at any time by exposing her "real" race, by revealing her "true" identity: "And mingled with these tender thoughts came too the very obvious consideration, which had escaped her in the agitation of their first meeting, that, whatever her future course, it would be well to speak to Lowrey fair, since by a word, a breath, he could destroy the fragile fabric of her social standing."[20]

And Mandy will soon discover just how fragile her world truly is, but not in the way that she had feared. Her life breaks apart, not because her black blood is exposed, but because Bob Utley demands more than blood from her: he orders her to demonstrate physical proof of her love for him. By using a line that is probably as old as spoken language itself, Utley responds to Mandy's innocent question with regard to how she might demonstrate her love:

> "Give me the last, best proof," he whispered. "Be mine without reserve. Then I will know that you love me, and that you will not fail me."
> Then Mandy saw through his web of lies. She struggled to tear herself away from him, but he held her fast.
> "Let me go," she said, "or I'll scream. I hate you and despise you."
> "You shall not go," he said. "You shall not trifle with me."
> He placed his hand over her mouth, and, as she struggled with him, tried to draw her deeper into the wood.[21]

But Mandy is spared from the horror of what looks to be an inevitable rape, for at this moment, Chesnutt introduces a mysterious rescuer lurking in the shadows. This particular chapter ends on a suspenseful note, as Mandy struggles to preserve her virtue against the attack of the dangerous white man whom she has so vigorously pursued:

> What the result would have been is uncertain. Whether she would have been strong enough to resist him successfully, or whether weapons within herself would have come to his assistance and made his victory easy, can never be known, for she was not put to the test. He had scarcely seized her, when a dark form burst from the woods, crossed the road with a spring, and pulling them apart grappled with her assailant.[22]

Although Chesnutt emphasizes the rising action as he completes this chapter, most readers by this point know something of the way Chesnutt will handle the denouement; that is, they are fairly sure of her attacker's identity. There is, of course, the possibility that it might be Tom Lowrey himself, but the more logical choice is an itinerant preacher named Elder Gadson. Gadson is a white man, as well as a descendant of those emotionally charged, nomadic, born again, instant-salvation-for-all preachers who dominated the Great Awakening. He is also smitten by Mandy to the point of obsession; he cannot even preach a coherent sermon unless he knows that she is among the congregation. In short, by this moment in the narrative, we are aware that three men are courting Mandy, only one of whom is black. Tom Lowrey, Bob Utley, and Elder Gadson all have their own reasons for their devotion to her, but only the black man has the humanity and decency to plant his courtship on firm ground. Yet in her frenzied despair to forever alter her identity, Mandy has also caused two of these men, both mentally unbalanced, to covet her, to crave exclusive possession of her. Neither one of these ardent suitors, both men rigidly tied to the nineteenth century and its strictures against miscegenation, would have been so impassioned had either suspected her of carrying a few drops of black blood. Nor would she have placed herself in such danger from both of these men had she not so desperately wanted to join that white realm, the one which represented security, prosperity, and opportunity.

In the meantime, we are given clear insights into the characters of Utley and Gadson, and into the inevitability of the clash between them: Utley, the treacherous, and Gadson, the misguided. In addition, as Chesnutt develops his narrative from this moment of Utley's attempted sexual assault on Mandy, he continually points the reader in Gadson's direction. Moreover, we ultimately learn that Gadson is indeed not only Mandy's rescuer but also Utley's killer. But most of the characters in this novel are not as certain about the identity of the murderer as the readers are, so that when Mandy is arrested for the crime, none of the townspeople show any surprise at her imprisonment. Only Mandy is surprised: a fitting irony, since, in her attempt to redefine herself, Mandy has seemingly nailed her own coffin by lying to herself, by convincing herself that Utley can be hers exclusively if only she wills this conviction to be true.

A further irony associated with Mandy's arrest is reflected in the reason for Mandy's arrest in the first place. A pathetic little black girl named Rose Amelia, a ten-year-old child with an ominously sad home life and no future, has a crush on her teacher, Tom Lowrey. In the haze of her childish infatuation, she has been following Tom as he leaves the school; indeed, she has been stalking and spying on Tom and Mandy in their furtive meetings. Because she has seen Tom and Mandy together, she assumes that Tom has killed Utley so, in her foolhardy frenzy to protect the man she worships, she asks her father — who is temporarily out of jail, where he spends the majority of his dissolute life — to go to the authorities with the accusation. As a result of Rose Amelia's schemes, Mandy, who has been trying to avoid any connection whatsoever with the Man of the Wrong Color, is jailed for a crime that she did not commit because a sad, doomed child is jealous of Mandy's involvement with this very same man.

Another complication arising from Mandy's tormented, twisted values surfaces shortly after Mandy is jailed. In spite of her ambitions, one part of Mandy still loves Tom. Along with this love, long hidden even from herself, come Mandy's efforts to protect Tom, which she hopes to accomplish by way of her confession to Utley's murder. So ironically, Mandy Oxendine and Rose Amelia have two characteristics in common: both love Tom Lowrey, and both think that Tom is in actuality the guilty one.

A further irony lies in the fact that Rose Amelia's actions nearly lead to the execution of her hero, Tom Lowrey. When he learns of Mandy's arrest, Lowrey gallantly goes to the white authorities and admits to the fatal deed in order to spare Mandy a fate that he is certain awaits her in prison. Such a fate is one that he considers worse than death for a woman: it is the same fate that she had forestalled when she fought off Utley's advances. As a part of the social criticism that runs through the novel, Chesnutt includes a careful though oblique description of the sexual exploitation of women by their male jailers and visitors. When Lowrey overhears some of these white men making crude jokes about their past conquests of the incarcerated females, Lowrey is so indignant that he overlooks the inevitable consequences that will accrue to a black man who admits to killing a white man.

But Lowrey is presented throughout as too noble a character to allow Mandy to be so cruelly used. The dialogue that prompts Lowrey to take the bold step and make his confession is a fine illustration of Chesnutt's skill with dialect and understatement. It also reveals Chesnutt's conviction of the baseness of these rural southern whites and of their sexist attitudes. Standing in front of the sheriff's office, Lowrey overhears some of the locals discussing Mandy's manifold charms and the methods that jailers expect to use in order to become the recipients of such charms:

> "She's a mighty likely gal," said one of the group. "A fellow would almost
> risk the chance of bein' killed to be on good terms with her."
> "Bob Utley always did have luck with the women," said another. "I

remember—" and he went off into a story in which Utley figured as the prin-
cipal character, and played a despicable role. The story, however, seemed to
be greatly enjoyed by the group, who laughed immoderately.

"I wouldn't mind being jailer till court opens," said another of the party,
whom Lowrey had once had pointed out to him as a "man who had killed his
nigger." "Reckon I'll go over an offer to keep jail for Bill while he takes a
vacation."

"Bill air no fool," said a third, a long-haired individual, in a voice somewhat impeded by a huge quid of tobacco. "Bill takes good keer ter collect the
perq'isites er his office."[23]

As if this interesting bit of information about Bill's tenacity were not
enough to convince Lowrey that he must rescue Mandy, he becomes even
more determined as he continues to listen to this ragtag group; for their
subsequent dialog consists of the men's nostalgic reminiscences about the
heroic Bill and his exploitative activities with an earlier female inmate:

> "I remember," said the second speaker, "when Cindy Murchison wuz in jail
> fer shootin' Tom Miller—that wuz ten years ago. *She* wuz a fine lookin'
> woman. The sheriff thought so, the jailer thought so too, the prosecutin'
> attorney was of the same opinion. *She* got good treatment in jail, and wuz
> acquitted without the jury leaving the box. Bill wuz jailer then, an' yer can't
> break an old dog from suckin' aigs. Yer see—"[24]

Knowing that Mandy will assuredly suffer the same horrific abuse as
her predecessor, Tom resolves to take her place and confess to Utley's murder. His selfless behavior is all the more remarkable since he knows that
Mandy has brought her predicament upon herself. Had Mandy not thrown
herself at Utley: had she not, in fact, posed as a white woman, she would
not have lived so precariously and, consequently, would never have invited
Utley's attack. Furthermore, there is another complication attendant upon
Lowrey's determination to save Mandy: Tom believes that Mandy is indeed
Utley's killer. Moreover, he knows that his confession will doom him to
being summarily hanged, and he is tormented by the fact that he will be
at the mercy of white men, those very people whom he considers his social,
emotional, and educational inferiors. Nonetheless, at the risk of his own
life, Tom gathers the courage to spare Mandy's virtue. He is willing to die
to preserve the integrity of a woman who has already sacrificed her integrity
for the nebulous world of her own creation. But paradoxically, then, this
creation is nearly the destruction of both of them.

As Mandy sits in her jail cell and contemplates her probable fate of
death by hanging, she has a few moments unclouded by the fog of self-
delusion. Yet Mandy's realization of what she has wrought comes slowly:

wrung painfully from her subconscious, from her most primal fears. Her first night in jail is an especially difficult trial, for, as the darkness deepens, she has a vision of a hanging that she had seen as a child. This is the first time in the narrative that Mandy understands what consequences she must undergo as a result of her impulsive confession.

Chesnutt's depiction of this hanging is vivid and memorable. We know why Mandy has never been able to let go of the image, why it has been forever imprinted upon her memory. She still remembers *blackness* as the prevalent color: the evil of darkness surrounding her — then, as now. Chesnutt's description is painted with sarcasm as he depicts Mandy's recollection of the North Carolinians and their mixture of the murderous and the pious:

> In the dark hours of the night black dreams had come to her, and the terror of death had fallen upon her. She had once been taken, when a child, to see a man hanged for burglary, under the humane code of North Carolina. She recalled with the vividness of reality every event of that day: the old field, overgrown with weeds, and here and there a solitary persimmon tree or a short-leafed pine; the rude gallows, with the dangling noose; the surging crowd, not noisy and bandying ribald jests, but speaking in low tones and with solemn inflections; the death-cart, on which the condemned man sat between two jailers; the minister's prayer; the pinioning of the condemned man's arms, the black cap; the agony of suspense, the fatal drop, the thrill of horror, the black burden of the gallows swinging to and fro; the groans, the shudders, the sobs of hysterical women. She remembered how she had turned and run, far, far away from the scene of this judicial murder, and how for a week she had been afraid of the dark, had been frightened at shadows, and how slowly her mind had shaken off these dark impressions.[25]

No Easy Solutions

Ultimately, both Mandy and Tom are saved by the confession of the real killer: the white preacher, Elder Gadson — he who has been so overpowered with Mandy's physical presence that he would have risked everything to spirit her away with him into the nether world of his own psychological demons. So both Tom and Mandy are ultimately freed and they marry. Furthermore, because Elder Gadson is white, the humanitarian populace of this North Carolina community hastily acquits him of murder.

Yet the world of Charles Chesnutt is one in which such absurd, ironic conclusions are presented in a matter-of-fact way. This world nearly hangs the black Lowrey on no evidence but his confession, yet it acquits the white Gadson on the basis of this same evidence. And the white men fail to see this contradiction. In fact, Chesnutt returns again and again to a depiction of the discrepancy between what the arrogant, unlettered whites smugly think of themselves and what Lowrey knows about them and about the fool's paradise in which they dwell. Lowrey himself frequently broods bitterly about this discrepancy. At one point, he contemplates attending a revival meeting at which many whites will be present, hesitating to go because he abhors the idea of mingling with so many white people:

> He very rarely went among white people. He had never served them in any menial capacity, and he was so nearly one of them that it always aroused in him a sort of dull resentment at being treated as an inferior creature. He reasoned with himself to overcome this feeling, as unworthy of him, and showing a want of self-respect. He knew he was as white as they, he believed he was the superior of many of them, in intellect, in culture, in energy; and he tried to look down, with a fine philosophic scorn, upon the unworthy prejudice that condemned him to hopeless social inferiority.[26]

An excellent illustration of Tom's dilemma may be found in the conversation featuring Tom, his would-be hangmen, and Elder Gadson. Knowing that protest would be useless, Tom has allowed himself to be dragged from the jail by a vociferous lynching mob. Still convinced that Mandy is the murderer but equally certain that he is doing the right thing in saving her from the rope, Tom is forced into a conversation that reveals the stunning difference in dialect between the educated black man and the obtuse white mob. Chesnutt is adept at reproducing the crude, often peculiar, and sometimes unintentionally funny dialect of the lower class whites.[27] As Tom stands amidst this restless lump of men, he sees his unlikely rescuer, Elder Gadson. It is this itinerant fire-and-brimstone preacher who finally gives the first truthful confession to come forth from this jagged-edged puzzle surrounding Utley's murder. However, even after Gadson's confession, the lynching party members remain angry: disgruntled because they have come together to hang a black man, and now it appears that they have missed their chance for some recreation. The following dialogue illustrates just how adroit Chesnutt was at reproducing the speech of crude, unlettered whites: a speech pattern that he offers in contrast to the educated dialect of the white Gadson and the literate grammar and syntax of the black Tom Lowrey. Chesnutt handles all three types of speech equally well in this, a crucial scene coming toward the end of the novel.

It begins with Gadson's last-minute, nick-of-time confession to the supercharged white mob, as he silences them in his best, redundant, Old Testament preacher style, protesting that "'the prisoner whom you are about to hurry into the presence of God is innocent. I and I alone committed this crime; my hand, and mine alone, struck the blow that slew Robert Utley. I loved this woman. I saw him with her. I followed them. He assaulted her; I killed him. Most men in my place would have done the same.'"[28] But Gadson need not have pleaded justifiable homicide, for in this world of flesh and fantasy, he will not be held accountable, even though, like Lowrey and Mandy, he has confessed.

Following Gadson's timely admission, the unruly but now stupefied crowd turns to Lowrey, who, to their direct query as to whether he did indeed kill Utley, replies in the same perfectly standard English as Gadson has just used: "'I did not,' he said. 'I thought she did and I was willing to take her place.'"[29]

This unexpected, revolting situation is too much for the small mind of one mob member, an ideal representative citizen of this community, complete with dialect appropriate to his education and class:

> "Well," said Skinner in tones of impatience mingled with disgust, "what are we goin' to do? I come out here to do somethin'.
> "Shall we hang the nigger?"
> "Not if he didn't kill Utley," answered Peebles.
> "I dunno," said Skinner stubbornly. "'Pears like a pity ter buy this rope an' break our night's res' fer nuthin'. It's true the nigger didn' kill Utley, but he said he did, an' it kind er goes ag'in the grain fer me ter hear a nigger even *say* he killed a white man."
> Don't be so onpatient, Jeff," said Peebles. We ain't goin' ter hang the wrong man just to please you, even if he is a nigger. After all, he's a pretty white nigger. You kin save that rope; you may have a use fer it some other time."[30]

When another one of these vigilantes asks a very logical question, given the circumstances in which all participants now find themselves, "'What's the matter ... with hangin' the preacher?'" Peebles responds with an illogical reply, one that reveals the all-encompassing double racial standard that Chesnutt has been ridiculing throughout — and that Mandy has risked her life to dispute:

> "No, gentlemen ... I purtest ag'in the si'gestion. Every man should have a fair trial and have his guilt passed on by a jury before he is convicted of a crime. The right to trial by jury is one o' the bull-works of our libbutty. Mebbe the preacher wuz jestified in killin' him. We'll pos'pone the hangin' fer ternight, and lock 'em both up, an' let the officrs o' the law 'rastle with the problem, fer there's evidently some myst'ry somewhar."[31]

The matter-of-fact, absurd non sequitur of this conversation underscores one of the major ironies of fate underlying this story. Mandy, wanting desperately to guarantee her future as a white woman, is always presented against such an unjust background, for she has willfully vowed to alter her own ancestry in order to make it conform to the standards of white supremacy. Yet this very supremacy, which is, at first, Mandy's only goal, is soiled by the crude ignorance of not only the poor, illiterate whites — tidily exemplified by Skinner and White in the aforementioned scene — but also by the white ruling class. And Chesnutt argues that no matter *which* class you are born into, if you are white, you begin with distinct advantages that you never really forfeit. Mandy senses these advantages, and tries to grab onto what she feels should be her birthright, even though she and her mother must necessarily live as poor whites.

Likewise, Chesnutt compounds this cosmic irony by depicting an incontrovertible fact. As a member of the lower class, even though she has redefined herself as "white," Mandy can never rise to the level of Utley's plateau, to that summit at the top of which are those refined but ragged remnants of the old pre–Civil War South. But she tries: oh, how she tries. And in her efforts, she demonstrates not only boundless cruelty but also nearly incomprehensible, deliberate, and dangerous self-deception. The cruelty is most evident in the earlier exchange between Mandy and her white friend from school, when Mandy snubs Lowrey, and then, speaking of Lowrey, confides to this friend that "'Niggers is niggers ... and looks don't make 'em white.'"[32] The self-deception is evident in her fervent — but nearly fatal — belief in the power of her charms to lure Utley away from his cousin and into her arms as his wife.

Ultimately, then, Mandy's attempt to change her identity has a number of far-reaching, devastating results. First, little Rose Amelia dies of unknown causes, but these causes are directly linked to her horror at the thought that her idol Tom might be executed, and all because she had fingered Mandy as the true killer. Then Tom almost dies in order that he might protect the woman who has been trying to avoid him, to deny his very presence in order to protect her mask. The effects continue with Elder Gadson, who turns from preacher to killer, as he rescues his own ideal white woman from the loathsome sexual predator, Bob Utley. Finally, there is Mandy herself, who continually vacillates between her affection for the stable, secure, dependable Tom Lowrey and her fascination with the treacherous opportunities spread out before her in the figure of Bob Utley.

Charles Chesnutt believed that one way for blacks to gain equality of opportunity with whites was for a continual intermingling of the races to occur until the cruel blackness had been bleached out. But he also believed that this process would take at least five hundred years.[33] Mandy does not have five hundred years, however, so she nearly collapses the black portion of her heritage into a different ethnicity. Then, at the end of the novel, in a plot twist that might be construed as an unfair narrative device akin to a deus ex machina, Mandy's "true" color is revealed. Having been spared the gallows through the propitious timing of Gadson's confession, both Mandy — now once again a black person — and Tom are free to marry. But is this a truly happy ending? Chesnutt's commentary with respect to the causes of Mandy's black blood finally spilling forth is both rueful and trenchant; likewise, it underscores the overwhelming difficulty facing Mandy and Tom as they try to find secure footing in this slippery world:

> The next day the three prisoners were brought before a magistrate and a preliminary examination was held to ascertain the facts of Utley's murder. The whole story came out, and in order to explain the connection of Lowrey with the affair, his hitherto secret relations with Mandy became a matter of public knowledge, as did also the fact of her origin and her connection with the colored race. This cleared up many difficulties. The fact that Mandy was colored justified Lowrey's attentions; that she was supposed to be white explained the preacher's interest; and her youth, her sex and her beauty excused in Mandy what would ordinarily have been regarded as an almost unpardonable social crime — the breaking of caste and the intrusion of one tainted by base blood into the ranks of the white people.[34]

Moreover, Chesnutt refuses to allow Tom and Mandy an optimistic faith in the future, the promise of a brighter tomorrow. He denies them an unequivocally happy conclusion. He tells us that they return to their original home in order to be married, but he also observes that this world — still the segregated and often brutal post–Civil War South — the place in which they will now try to rebuild their battered and fragmented lives, is far from an ideal one. In fact, the final words of Chesnutt's narrator contain some of that same quality of fatalism as may be found in the commentary of the chorus at the end of a classical Greek tragedy. While Tom and Mandy can never reach the tragic stature of an Oedipus or an Antigone, they still come to represent the strivings of mere humans against the frequently unjust gods of fortune:

> Whether they went to the North, where there was larger opportunity and a more liberal environment, and remaining true to their own people, in spite

of some scorn and some isolation, found a measurable degree of contentment and happiness; or whether they chose to sink their past in the gulf of oblivion, and sought in the great white world such a place as their talents and their virtues merited, it is not for this chronicle to relate. They deserved to be happy; but we do not all get our deserts, as many a lucky rogue may congratulate himself, and as many an ill-used honest man can testify.[35]

• *Six* •

Lillie Devereux Blake
and the Perilous Web of Sex

> For all literary artists ... self-definition necessarily precedes self-
> assertion: the creative "I am" cannot be uttered if the "I" knows
> not what it is. But for the female artist the essential process of
> self-definition is complicated by all those patriarchal definitions
> that intervene between herself and herself.
>
> Sandra M. Gilbert and Susan Gubar,
> *The Madwoman in the Attic*, 1979

The Blighted Woman

As we have seen, Wilkie Collins was concerned with women's issues
and with the unfair treatment of women in his society. Yet he was not
nearly as determined to write about social injustice as was his American
contemporary, Lillie Devereux Blake. Where Collins smoothly and deftly
integrates into the narrative his concerns about the domestic and legal
injustices done to women, Lillie Blake, in her 1874 novel *Fettered for Life*,
frequently intrudes upon her story in order to have a character give a soap-
box oration on the horrible evils that men commit against women. Unlike
Collins, Blake is concerned with the political shenanigans of big city wards
run by corrupt politicians and the effect that their unstatesman-like conduct has on nineteenth century New York City. These ward bosses have a
great impact not only on the way the city is run but also on the women
who become tangled in the webs of disdain and cruelty that are displayed
by these bosses as they rise to political power.

Like Collins, Blake sets her work within an urban environment.
Against such a backdrop, both authors quite vividly demonstrate that

161

poverty and disease, cruel and unsafe working conditions, prostitution, rape, forced abortions, and wife abuse and murder, are the bitter, inevitable norm for many women. Likewise, both Collins and Blake show with piercing irony the false hope of those benighted ladies who believe that women of a higher social class are immune to the dreary, dangerous conditions that so often beset those of the lower class. In fact, scheming, calculating men trap the women of both the working class and the aristocratic social order; in neither category do these women have legal control of their own money or even of their own bodies. So too, the domineering male is just as much a fixture in rural settings as he is in urban environments. Whether a farmer, a businessman, a judge, a ward boss, or a school superintendent, the man typically beats down the woman — wife, mother, daughter, sister — and does it with impunity.

A double sexual standard is also a major issue for both authors, as they deplore the unconscionable behavior of men who exploit women, usually for sexual advantage, and then leave the women they have conquered. Such women are consequently soiled and ostracized by "respectable" society. Moreover, the man ordinarily continues on his arrogant, uncaring way, often as a distinguished member of the aristocratic or professional class, whereas the woman he has used is left behind, broken and often desperately ill. Likewise, even when couples marry and thus sex between men and women is made legitimate, both authors often portray marriage as a funeral pyre onto which the woman throws herself, thus opting for a self-immolation of the slowest and most painful kind. And, once again, whether the marriage involves lower class couples or upper class/aristocratic pairings, it remains an institution that traps women for life.

The Solution of the Crossdresser

While Collins probes the identity question by having many of his female protagonists take on the identity of another woman — usually for the purpose of gaining social advantage — Blake takes a daringly different approach. In *Fettered for Life*, she explores the character of Frank Heywood, a newspaper reporter who is presented sympathetically. And, although Blake is less adept at building suspense than her British contemporary, she weaves the identity question so skillfully throughout in her presentation of Heywood that most readers fail at first to discern the reason for Heywood's distinctive, peculiar behavior.

What Blake finally reveals at the novel's end is not that Heywood has disguised himself because he wants to be of a different class, race or occupation. He disguises himself because he was born the wrong sex, for Frank Heywood is really a woman — one who has gotten away for many years with her/his disguise and who has subsequently become a successful newspaper reporter, all as a result of her/his switching to the proper sex. Although much of *Fettered for Life* is didactic and heavy-handed —filled with long polemical speeches about the need for women's suffrage — nonetheless, for the first nine-tenths of the novel, the writer leaves her readers guessing as to the reason for Frank Heywood's melancholy behavior throughout. In fact, modern readers are tempted to guess incorrectly when they read of "Frank's" reticence to court Laura Stanley, the book's heroine. Frank becomes especially suspect when we read the work anachronistically and set him down in modern times, interpreting his character against the modern temper. In his gentle bearing and his circumspect behavior, he appears to be a closet homosexual. In spite of our modern presuppositions, we should not be surprised at the true identity of Frank Heywood. In order to pursue an active life of the body as well as the mind, Heywood has no choice but to switch his sex.

An examination of social conditions in large, nineteenth century American cities, such as the New York City of this novel, reveals just how fettered women were. For instance, women like Laura were discouraged from pursuing careers outside the home; indeed, they were discouraged from engaging in too much activity by such distinguished male bastions of authority as physicians and clergymen. It was thought that such strenuous exertion, whether physical or mental, would lead to those popular nineteenth century women's curses — neurasthenia and its cousin, hysteria. Contemporary newspapers took delight in touting the medical curiosities that surfaced as a result of such fettering of the female mind and body. One of the most notable of these true-life oddities was the case of Mollie Fancher. Mollie had been an active Brooklyn teenager, engaged to be married, until an 1865 horsecar accident changed the direction of her life. The debilitating injuries resulting from this accident precipitated the eighteen-year-old girl's decline into inaction and self-imposed exile within a house that would become a hermitage from which she never emerged for the next fifty-one years: the remainder of her life.[1]

It is quite possible that Lillie Blake was familiar with Mollie Fancher's strange state: an extreme example of self-immolation, but nonetheless understandable in light of the way in which nineteenth century society treated women as frail, tender, and weak; in sum, they were housebound intellectual zeros. Certainly there had been much sensational publicity about the case of Mollie Fancher by the time of the 1874 publication of *Fettered for Life*. And it was to avoid such a wasted, stupefying, paralyzing fate that Blake's Frank Heywood opts for life as a disguised man. So too, Lillie Blake has prepared us all along for Frank's final stunning revelation that he is a woman, for she has devoted many descriptive passages and many pages of dialogue to the demonstration of her major theme: that women have no chance to find fulfillment because men will give them no chance. And so, because she cannot defeat the enemy, a woman joins their forces and becomes one of their vast, overbearing army. But Frank is an extremely gentle member of this army, and this gentleness significantly sets him apart from the "other" men in this novel, even those few authentic males whom Blake presents sympathetically. In addition, Frank impresses us as differing from the men depicted by Blake in that he demonstrates clear evidence of tolerance toward women who at that time were often branded as "fallen."

Yet Frank Heywood's decision to become a "male" is fraught with distress. Only by denying biology, along with the drives and instincts that go with being female, can Frank Heywood find success in his chosen career as a newspaper reporter and escape the unwelcome sexual advances of men — offers that he endured as a woman. In one of the novel's final scenes, Frank confesses to the heroine, Laura Stanley, that, when he arrived in New York, undisguised, he discovered first hand the debilitation that accompanies women: the second — and inferior — sex:

> "I was insulted, refused work, unless I would comply with the disgraceful propositions of my employers; in short, I had the experience which so many young women have in the great city; poverty, temptation, cruelty. I was resolved not to sink where so many had fallen; but it was hard work sometimes. There was one man in particular who persecuted me so persistently, that at last I scarcely dared to go out, lest he should carry me off to some hopeless pit. Then I grew desperate, and as much to avoid him as for any other purpose, I pawned my last article of value — my father's watch — which I had kept securely till then, and which, by the way, I have since redeemed; and with the money thus obtained, bought a suit of boy's clothes. The change was delightful! ... My limbs were free; I could move untrammelled, and my actions were free. I could go about unquestioned. No man insulted me, and when I asked for work, I was not offered outrage."[2]

To give up one's sex, to keep secret from the world that which makes a person whole, requires even more cunning, courage, and self-inflicted isolation than that illustrated by Mandy in *Mandy Oxendine.* For Mandy did not have to adopt a disguise, did not have to fear that she might be exposed were anyone to get too close to her, did not have to relinquish her normal sexual desires. But Frank Heywood must do all of these things; as a result, he turns a sad face to the world, as though there were a part of him that was forever misplaced, forever irrecoverable.

Thus, from the outset, we recognize something different about Frank Heywood. When we first see him, he is acting in his professional capacity as a reporter for the New York *Trumpeter,* sitting in a courtroom and taking notes on the latest arrests of the unfortunate and downtrodden, the outcasts living in the New York underside. The name of Heywood's paper is significant, for we soon learn that Heywood "trumpets" in his reporting many of the most pressing social and political ills of the day. As Heywood watches the evening's progression of misfits as each is handed over to the judge — a man who is himself one of the most corrupt denizens of the city — Heywood's attention is caught by Laura Stanley. She does not fit the mold; and indeed, we are told that she has sought a policeman because, as a single woman in the city, she has been turned away from a hotel and knows that it is unsafe to be on the streets alone. Blake's initial description of Heywood suggests that there is something odd about him:

> He was a good-looking young man, apparently about twenty-five, with brown hair and chestnut moustache, shading a mouth that, but for this, would have been effeminate; dark earnest eyes, with a strange expression lurking in their depths, an indefinable something hard to interpret, yet felt by all who knew him; a look as of perpetual unrest; of yearning, almost of despair.[3]

The unrest, the yearning, and the despair arise from this young reporter's uncomfortable intimacy with the precariousness of his chosen lifestyle. Furthermore, though Blake leaves her reader in suspense about the cause of Heywood's curious demeanor, she nonetheless provides teasing hints to suggest that Heywood is an unsettled, uneasy person with a past, an individual always fearful that he might at any moment fall over the edge of a shifting precipice and destroy himself on the sharp rocks of duplicity and disguise.

For instance, the unique perceptions held by others concerning Frank's general appearance and manner are in evidence shortly after Frank first sees Laura. In an unselfish gesture that will come to represent a major pattern of the novel, he rescues her from a house where she is about to become the unwitting victim of the nefarious courtroom judge and his perpetual plots to snare women into a life of sordid sex. As Frank leads Laura away from this squalid dwelling, she takes the opportunity to look closely at her rescuer: "Laura regarded him keenly, the dark mournful eyes met hers with a look which she never forgot, there was in it so strange a mixture of earnest appeal, and yet of dumb hopeless sorrow."[4] A few moments later, those eyes again capture Laura's attention, as she notices that "the deep eyes were gazing away into space as if he saw some mournful picture, rather than as if he were thinking of her."[5] Shortly after Laura makes this mental observation, she tells her new friend that she still has a trunk at the depot. At this, Frank insists on going after it. In a comment that is indicative of revelations to come, he assures her, "'I know that young ladies like to make a change in their dress sometimes.' An odd smile crossing his face."[6] Occasionally, this smile is sometimes depicted as "inscrutable"[7] Moreover, this "odd smile" is often accompanied by "a fresh sweet voice"[8] and a "delicate face."[9]

Laura is not the only character to be puzzled by Frank's inherent strangeness: that indefinable, impalpable, and unexplored something in his nature. Significantly, there is something suggestive in the fact that Blake associates such intuitive insights with the feminine, for it is only the female characters who sense the unseen. To illustrate, at one point Rhoda, one of the many browbeaten, working class women in 1874 New York, visits Frank to plead with him to help keep their mutual friend Laura out of danger. Having persuaded him to accompany her in a carriage so that they might go to Laura's house and warn her, Rhoda takes a moment to look at the person who has just seated himself next to her in the conveyance. What she sees is something disquieting:

> At this moment the light from a lamp fell strongly on both faces. Rhoda's, pale, sad, with a strange wistfulness in her intense gaze. Frank's, handsome, careworn, and with a deep mysterious light in the eyes. As their glances met, the young journalist started visibly, and a flush colored his sensitive complexion. Rhoda did not turn away, her regard lingered a moment, and there was in its eloquent earnestness a mute question.[10]

Later, Frank accompanies Rhoda and her friend Maggie to Maggie's home in a southern state. He acts as a combination protector/traveling companion as they journey by train away from the squalor of the city and its accompanying sinful, masculine-dominated places. All of the friends who bid them goodbye are female. Furthermore, none of the women who see these three off on their trip think that there is anything at all compromising in this situation. Under ordinary circumstances, two unmarried ladies traveling with one unmarried man might have raised nineteenth century eyebrows. However, this is not the case with Frank Heywood, Rhoda, and Maggie. The farewells between this trio and those who care about them are tearful but not at all suspicious or apprehensive. Likewise, as Frank and his two charges approach the native place of both Frank and Maggie, Frank is again depicted in a definitely unromantic light in his approach toward these girls: "Frank, who had been as tenderly devoted as any brother to the two girls, drew up the sash, admitting the air that was soft with a peculiar balminess unknown to more frigid climes."[11] As the three travelers draw closer to their destinations, Blake provides a further description of Rhoda's response to that ephemeral uneasiness running deep under the surface of Frank's personality:

> Heywood, too, seemed to be strongly affected by the landscape that recalled so vividly the home of his childhood. His strange eyes had a deep yearning in their gaze, and there was a nameless shade on his delicate features. Rhoda, who had watched him whenever he had been with them during the journey, watched him now, with a singular intentness in her gaze.[12]

Finally, as the train reaches the station where Rhoda and Maggie must get off, leaving Frank to continue on a little longer, Rhoda makes a telling gesture: she says goodbye to Frank by "holding his fingers for a few seconds, hesitatingly, almost as if she would say a word to him beyond those of farewell; but there was no time for delay, and after a brief instant she passed him with some murmured expressions of adieu."[13]

What is it that Rhoda sees in Frank that leads her to guess his secret? Is it her close proximity to him on such a long trip? Does he give himself away through the movement of his head, a hand signal, a motion with his arms, a certain kind of body language as he sits? Whatever the reason, Rhoda discovers through her careful scrutiny the answer to her earlier "mute question."

That Rhoda has figured out the answer to the riddle of Frank's existence is shown later when she and Frank are reunited on an old steamer that is bringing them from Richmond, Virginia to Washington. The ancient boat breaks apart in a fierce storm, and Rhoda and Frank are tossed into the water. While they are clinging to a small remnant of the dismembered vessel, Rhoda offers the following tantalizing bit of dialogue:

> "Frank," she said, "I know your secret. Will you give me a kiss?"
> Even in that danger the young journalist started and a look of terror crossed his face.

"No," she whispered; "I shall never betray you. Only just once for friendship; one kiss, it may be the last, you know."

Her companion seemed unable to frame a word, and there was a moisture in his eyes that was not of the sea as he bent towards her, and their cold lips met in a strange despairing embrace.

There was a moment of silence: Rhoda had drawn away a little; she turned suddenly:

"Frank your life is better worth saving than mine, good-bye — good-bye!"[14]

And so poor Rhoda — driven to sin by the evil of men — releases the plank and eases herself into a symbolic conclusion, allowing herself to be engulfed by the water that subsequently washes away her transgressions. And what of Frank? He is picked up shortly thereafter, the worth of his existence validated by this timely rescue. By now, we are probably more than ever convinced that Frank is a homosexual and that Rhoda has ferreted out this truth. But we are, of course, wrong.

In yet another instance that implies Frank's choice of an alternative lifestyle, Frank confesses to Laura his career ambitions and his corresponding confidence that he will one day reach his goal, becoming an editor-in-chief of a great journal, Laura automatically responds by alluding to his recent career successes:

"But now that you are so well off," said Laura lightly; "you will be getting married."

Heywood smiled with that strange lightless smile that seemed to carry no joy, and regarded his companion with a singular questioning look.

"No," he said, "I shall not marry; my work must be father and mother, wife and children to me."[15]

Nowhere is such instinctive, distinctly feminine feeling about Frank as evident as it is in the scene that describes Laura's differing reactions to the appearance of the two men in her life: Frank Heywood and Guy Bradford. In fact, Laura is seriously attracted to Guy: an attraction that seems to contradict everything that she believes and that she very vocally and continually espouses, sometimes with enthusiastic sarcasm, on the subject of men's barbaric enslavement of women. But Laura's evenings with Frank suggest a bonding between a brother and sister or two girlfriends:

With Frank Heywood she had long confidential conversations, which she keenly enjoyed, so that they came after a time to be on terms of the closest intimacy. Sometimes he would read aloud, while she went on with her drawing; sometimes she went with him to some place of public amusement, for which he had always an unlimited amount of tickets; and it was to him that she owed a constant supply of papers and new books.[16]

Yet when Guy Bradford comes to call, Laura's behavior changes immeasurably: "When Laura was told that Mr. Bradford was in the parlor, she would take a sly peep in the glass, perhaps put on a bright ribbon, or another collar, and then going down to the sitting-room door, would knock softly."[17]

Much later, Laura becomes extremely distraught following a domestic quarrel between the Moulders, the couple with whom she boards: the man, an autocratic tyrant, and his wife, a kind, submissive, fluttery woman, whose pathetic qualities Laura most deeply pities. Yet when a servant girl announces the arrival of Guy Bradford, Laura's mood quickly shifts. She has convinced herself that this man is truly the one for her; as a consequence, upon hearing that he is waiting for her in the parlor, Laura acts less like the strong, reasonable woman that she prides herself on being and more like a foolish adolescent with her first starry-eyed crush: "Laura went slowly up stairs, her heart beating with quick swelling pulsations, her cheeks burning with a tell-tale blush."[18]

Likewise, Laura reacts differently to the gifts brought to her by these two men, even when these gifts are of essentially the same type. On one occasion, she receives bouquets of flowers from both Frank and Guy. But these bouquets do not carry equal meaning. Though Laura herself is unable to articulate this distinction, a marked disparity is nonetheless present:

> The early morning had brought to Laura two bouquets. A large and handsome one, with "Mr. Bradford's compliments," and a mere knot of choice flowers, "From your friend, F.H." Laura left these last in a vase at home; they were a valuable present, as a study for some small water-color pictures. The bouquet she carried in her hand.[19]

Although the cards attached to both bouquets are in keeping with the conventions of the day in that each one is quite formal, quite proper and discreet, Laura still attaches a different meaning to each present. If Guy's brief greeting carries at least a hint of admiration and the possibility of further intimacy, Frank's message offers nothing except what a businessman might offer to his associate. But beyond the words that Laura reads lie the fragile filaments of memory, moments recalled of days spent with members of one's own sex. Within Laura resides a hint of understanding that surpasses mere knowledge. And so she somehow knows that she can never love Frank in the same way that she thinks she loves Guy.

However, men and women do not see Frank in the same way. For instance, Guy Bradford is exceedingly jealous whenever he finds Laura in Frank's presence. One evening, Frank escorts Laura home, and, as they are about to part, he takes a bold action and "touched his lips to her cheek."[20] It is significant that Frank's move is not characterized as a *kiss*, a subtle point that might well be overlooked by the reader. But one who does not overlook this affectionate gesture is Guy Bradford. He has been lurking somewhere in the background like some sort of stalking presence; then, once Frank disappears into the darkness, Guy materializes, coming into Laura's line of vision:

> At this moment she caught sight of Guy Bradford. He stood at the foot of the steps, looking up at her with eyes that seemed burning with a somber light, and with a face that she could see even through the dimness, was desperately pale.[21]

Guy is angered and disappointed: jealous of Frank's attentions to Laura, though Laura at first tries to greet him with a smile, for her interpretation of the brief episode is far different from Guy's. Yet here, Guy is rendered as a typical male, with a typically masculine response, "as he raised his hat to her with a cold salutation, and turned away."[22] Following this abrupt rebuff, Laura realizes that Guy has misunderstood this incident, yet she also senses the futility of trying to explain the inexplicable, of trying to capture meaning from an ephemera:

> Then it came to her that he had witnessed the parting between her and Heywood, and that he had interpreted it by the dictates of his own jealous heart. For an instant she was tempted to run after him, and force him to listen to an explanation; then the conventional impropriety of such an action occurred to her, and she went slowly into the house; but as she closed the door, it seemed as if the darkness of the night was not shut out, but went gloomily upstairs with her.[23]

What this passage highlights is Laura's distress at Guy's insensitive response to an innocent signal from Frank. For all of her proto-feminist beliefs, Laura still has those primal yearnings that, in her case, manifest themselves as anxiety, nervousness, embarrassment, feverish excitement, and disappointment when she fears that Guy might be jealous of Frank. For his part, however, Guy shows some unattractive traits, which are all the more striking because he continues to hold favor with the independent-minded, spirited Laura. By the same token, Laura recognizes no such unattractive traits whatsoever in Frank.

Guy, however, continues for the first three-fourths of the novel to see Frank as a serious rival. When Guy next sees Laura, some time has passed since they have had an abrupt, chance meeting on the street. They exchange a few awkward words, and Guy admits that he has counted the days since they last saw each other. But he also confesses his reason for staying away from Laura: "'I thought until this afternoon that you were engaged to Frank Heywood.'"[24] The idea of marriage to Frank is one that has always been far removed from even the most fantastic of Laura's dreams and desires.

Furthermore, the misunderstandings and the corresponding feelings of jealousy are mutual. If Guy is jealous of Frank's attentions to Laura, Laura is equally resentful of Guy's obvious appeal to other women. Sometime following the incident in which Guy surprises Laura by springing upon her after he has witnessed Frank's less-than-ardent kiss, Laura happens to see Guy walking down Fifth Avenue; it is this chance encounter that they are alluding to when Guy confesses his previously-held but erroneous belief in Laura's engagement to Frank. Here, it is Laura who is jealous: "He had a very pretty and youthful lady beside him, and Laura's heart contracted with a spasm of agony that was a new revelation to her."[25] On the other hand, Laura — a moral, chaste, proper lady — has no such agonizing spasms when Frank accompanies those two young ladies, Rhoda and Maggie, on the long train ride south.

Nor is it only Laura who feels such safety in Frank's presence. A further curious indication of the differing, singular way in which those who consider themselves the arbiters of proper moral behavior perceive the conduct of these two men may be found in the fact that Frank Heywood requires no chaperone when he calls upon Laura, whereas Guy's appearance summons Minnie, the daughter of the house, into the same room as the young man and woman. Again, the two *women* with whom Laura is boarding are the ones to make the distinction between Frank and Guy. Both Minnie and her mother, Mrs. Moulder, have an unspoken agreement that these two men should be treated differently. Though Minnie never leaves Guy and Laura's presence, she "was never sent for when Frank Heywood came; Laura herself could scarcely tell why; he was so like a brother, she said to herself; but Guy Bradford was different."[26]

Juxtaposed throughout with descriptions of Heywood's predicament are Lillie Blake's frequent, vituperative attacks upon the blatantly unfair place of women in this society. Blake demonstrates her greatest weaknesses as a storyteller in her heavy-handed method of depicting characters with a "message" for the world, and in her unfortunate predilection for halting the narrative in the midst of a dramatic moment in order to have a character harangue against the unfair system. She often seems overwrought in her efforts to spotlight a world in which women are abused in the areas of education, economics, politics, the law, and marriage. In addition, through the dialogue of a number of her more sympathetically depicted characters, Blake is forever reminding the reader that with votes for women will finally come sexual equality: a naïve view, albeit a view gleaned only through the lenses of hindsight.

But with Frank Heywood, Blake finds a most appropriate mouthpiece for these protestations against such horrible injustice, as in the following conversation between Frank and Laura. Laura has just returned from being denied an office job; the basis of this denial has been, of course, her sex. Naturally, Frank shows understanding. When Laura protests that Frank cannot possibly comprehend her helpless feelings accompanying this refusal, Frank insists, "'I do understand it better than you imagine, Miss Stanley.'"[27] There is, of course, a good deal of irony embedded in many of Frank's remarks, as in the preceding rejoinder, for he knows something that neither the other characters nor the reader as yet suspects. Moreover, like Mandy Oxendine, Frank has had to obliterate his past in order to maintain his disguise. So too, like Mandy, Frank exemplifies the total sacrifice required by a person who wants to forever erase just who s/he is and how s/he defines him/herself. For instance, as Frank prepares to accompany Rhoda and Maggie on their trip south, Laura inquires:

> "Shall you go to your home?" ...
> "No," said Heywood sadly; "I have no home to go to; that is, I have no parents or brothers or sisters. As for the rest of my people, I shall avoid them rather than seek them."[28]

Such melancholy, enigmatic commentary constitutes a sign of the invisible barrier that Frank has willingly erected between himself and even those for whom he cares. And it is a barrier of both sound as well as sight, for Frank lives in a silent enclosure of secrecy. He is like a frustrated, pre-verbal child, who wants to communicate with the adult world but who has no words for his longings. And Rhoda somehow understands what it is that his unspoken language conveys, though she does not live long enough to speak aloud what she does not dare say either to Frank himself or to anyone else.

But there is one other person who knows Frank's secret: Mrs. D'Arcy, a strong, independent woman who is also a physician — a rare creature indeed in the nineteenth century. She is also something of a cardboard character, notably concerned with making long speeches about women's need to gain the right to vote: a panacea that she thinks will remedy every wrong ever done to women by men. Although Mrs. D'Arcy's fervent beliefs seem naïve to a modern reader, this unusual professional woman was in the mainstream of liberal, feminist thinking of her own time. And she is an apt mentor for Laura.

One subject on which she gives Laura advice is one involving the character of Frank Heywood. Shortly after meeting Frank, Laura asks Mrs. D'Arcy many questions about him:

> "Have you known him long?" ...
> "Some twelve years," replied Mrs. D'Arcy. "His history is a very strange one; he has had trials and misfortunes that would have broken almost any spirit but his."
> "Are his parents living?"
> "No, they have been long dead..."
> "Poor fellow, how alone he must be!"
> "More alone than you can imagine. There are circumstances in his life that must always make him desolate. He has uncommon abilities, and his aim is very high, I only hope he will have the strength to make the sacrifice necessary to its accomplishment."
> "I admire him ever so much!" said Laura, heartily.
> "He is as true and faithful a friend as you could have," said Mrs. D'Arcy, with a slight emphasis on the word friend.[29]

That Mrs. D'Arcy realizes the impossibility of Frank's ever being more than a friend to any woman is a fact that becomes ever more clear as the novel progresses. In an echo of this previous scene, Mrs. D'Arcy talks to Laura sometime later about Frank, and asks a pointed question: "'I have heard of you sometimes from Frank Heywood; do you see him very often?'"[30] As Mrs. D'Arcy asks this seemingly innocuous question, she is described as looking at Laura "keenly."

> "Oh, yes!" answered Laura, unconsciously, "very often; I like him so much!"
> "An excellent friend for you," the doctor said; again with a slight accent on friend.[31]

Then again, when Mrs. D'Arcy speaks to Laura about both Guy Bradford and Frank Heywood, she consistently plays up the advantages of choosing Guy over Frank. In short, Mrs. D'Arcy clearly sees Guy as an eligible suitor, whereas she knows all too well that Frank must never be thought of in that way. On one occasion, as she and Laura are talking about Frank's talent as a writer and the fact that his editors at the *New York Trumpeter* are pleased with his reporting, Laura expresses her pleasure at Frank's accomplishments: "'I am so glad! ... He is such a noble fellow, he deserves to succeed.'"[32] But, as she has so often before, Mrs. D'Arcy replies hurriedly, her rejoinder once again carrying a subtextual caveat:

> "He does, indeed. But now that he is away, do you see much of Guy Brad-ford?" with a look, which she endeavored to make indifferent.
> Laura could not repress a vivid blush. "No," she said, "he has not called on me for a long while."
> "Hasn't he? why not?" then sharply: "You have not refused him, have you, Laura?"[33]

Mrs. D'Arcy's well-aimed queries reflect her keen desire to lead Laura away from an untenable partnership with Frank Heywood; further, at this point, only Mrs. D'Arcy knows the extent of this untenability, since sharp-eyed Rhoda is already dead. Yet only the most discerning reader can work his/her way through the subtext. Like all good mystery writers, though, Lillie Blake plays fair with her readers. For example, she places nothing in the story that might depict Frank as a typically dominant male; every detail she presents with respect to Frank's character and behavior points to the real reason for his being such a peculiar sort. Yet it is not until insight comes to Laura that the reader learns the truth as well:

> Laura regarded her companion for a moment with an astonished gaze; then a hundred little circumstances rushed to her memory —"You are a woman!" she cried, clapping her hands in delight; "that is glorious!" and she caught Frank around the neck with a hearty kiss.[34]

For his part, Heywood appears far less melancholy and wistful than he has previously seemed when he had been in Laura's presence. Perhaps now that he has disentangled himself from the ties that have bound him to his mask of pretense, he can afford to relax, at least when he is around this bright, sensible lady: "The young journalist looked really happy, and laughed light heartedly. 'It is rather a large practical joke isn't it! Some-times I keenly enjoy it.'"[35]

Yet Frank's reducing his transformation to the status of a joke is disin-genuous. There is nothing amusing about the way in which he has had to exist. Nor does his confession to Laura obviate in any way the need for him to continue the deception for the remainder of his life. Nor does Blake ever reveal Frank's real name. Both the little girl and young woman he had once been are long since dead: victims of a mercy killing. Unlike Mandy Oxendine, who reclaims her life as a black woman when she marries Tom Lowrey, Frank can never reclaim his past existence. To do so would be to deny all of the principles in which he believes and for which he has sacrificed so much. It is also tempting to see Frank as a symbol for Lillie

Blake's determination to give the lie to the myth of a woman's biology as her destiny. This myth is dissolved in her depiction of Frank, for he is the visual proof that, between men and women, there is no difference that cannot be conquered — provided, of course, that the woman becomes a crossdresser.

In her "Afterword" to the 1996 edition of *Fettered for Life*, Grace Farrell maintains that "Blake's use of the gender switch infers that gender itself is a surface detail."[36] Moreover, Farrell argues, Blake shows throughout her novel that the definition of femininity is bound by purely social constraints and prejudices:

> The fact that the woman who crossdresses and the man she pretends to be are the same person suggests that profound differences between the sexes, which are used to create a hierarchy and to justify social inequities, are themselves not preordained essences, but mere products of social circumstances.[37]

It is doubtless true that Blake shows Frank triumphant over those "mere products of social circumstances" and that she refuses to sanction the belief that women are preordained to be inferior. But Frank still walks a narrow, flimsy tightrope over a pit of male vipers. If he walks too near the edge, he will fall into the snake pit. He is always in danger of being discovered through some accident or illness that might force him to uncover his true sex. Such a misfortune is what had led him to Mrs. D'Arcy some three years before the action of the novel: thus, her discovery of his secret. So for Frank Heywood the world is a far more dangerous place than it is for Mandy Oxendine. It is far easier to hide one's race, as the fair-skinned Mandy does, than it is to hide one's gender. Small wonder that Frank often looks tired and sad.

And yet, Frank appears to have achieved at least a minimal degree of happiness; in addition, his state of mind, as depicted by Lillie Blake at the end of the novel, is understandable and even credible in light of Blake's feminist thinking. To illustrate her view of the bogus biological differences as promulgated by smug, hypocritical males, Blake presents two of her female characters deploring their own bodies: those physical traps set by nature. Flora Livingston is one such woman who ultimately chooses suicide because she cannot be her own person, especially after she enters into a loveless marriage with a rich but emotionally abusive and controlling husband. Early in the novel she complains to Laura about her limited life options as she bemoans the cause of such limitations: her biological destiny:

"I only wish I had something to do," she said, "some definite hope for the future, life sometimes seems to me very tasteless even now. I have often wished so intensely that I could change my sex, and go into business. Of course pa is rich, but then if I were a boy, I should be earning something for myself.[38]

Laura shares Flora's wish, although, for both women, the desire is a transitory one, expressed aloud only once by each of them. A short while after Flora's expression of regret that she can define herself only by her sex, Laura makes a similar comment to Mrs. D'Arcy: "'Sometimes I too feel like joining the cry that has gone up from so many women and uttering the useless wish that I were a man.'"[39]

This useless feeling takes a drastic form in Flora's case, for she ultimately is driven to suicide because she can find no outlet for her talents. When her wealthy husband learns that she has become a published author and thus has found a name for herself, an identity outside of his, he becomes so enraged that he literally tears up her work. So she chooses death over an anonymous and therefore purposeless existence.

No such outcome awaits her friend Laura, however, for Laura thinks that she knows what she wants from life; moreover, she is savvy enough to understand how to work the system. Yet the system itself ultimately remains more than she can handle. Though college educated, she can find only those few jobs that we characterize today as "women's work." She gives drawing lessons to young ladies and occasionally sells her paintings and artwork, but her income is never enough for her to be truly self-supporting. Thus, although Blake tries her best to present Laura as a forceful woman who wants nothing more than to subvert the system, Laura finally emerges as Cinderella at the end of the fairy tale. She finds her Prince Charming in the equivocal person of Guy Bradford, an ordinary enough "guy" who is trying his best to be liberal in his thinking about women but who still holds to old-fashioned notions about what separates the "good" women from the "bad" ones. What is more, the fact that Laura gets terribly flustered and squishy inside when she sees Guy is convincing evidence of her desire to belong to a man. In short, Laura Stanley is not as certain of her own worth as she would like the world to believe.

Ironically, Frank Heywood, boxed in by his deliberate choice of gender, is freer than Laura, for he has at least *made* a choice and changed his identity in order to become a part of the world of the dominant sex. While it is true that he has chosen a lonely path, he can still see down the road to a successful end, whereas Laura remains the rural girl from upstate New

York: the child of a tyrannical father and a doting, ineffectual mother. In many ways, she remains as unworldly at the novel's end as she was at the beginning.

To illustrate, when we first see her, she has come before the corrupt Judge Swinton. (And for author Blake, the pairing of the words *corrupt* and *judge* or *corrupt* and *politician* represents a tautology.) Because she has been seen alone on the streets at night, she is presumed to be worthy of arrest. When Judge Swinton "kindly" offers her a place to stay for the night, she naively believes that she will be safe in accompanying Swinton's courtroom friend, who is supposedly about to provide her with this cozy, safe place. In point of fact, though, this man will finally be exposed as a procurer for the typical, down-at-the-heels women who pass through Swinton's court. Yet we learn at the outset that Laura Stanley is not a typical denizen of these sordid premises.

In due course, however, Laura learns two significant lessons from her evening spent in this New York City lock-up. First, she is taught not to trust any man, especially one who is in an important political position. Second, she comes to realize that, in seeking asylum from the streets, she has made a very bad decision in her choice of a refuge. When she informs Judge Swinton of the circumstances surrounding her arrival in his legal domain, she is as yet unaware of the irony involved in her explanation:

> "I arrived here late last night, the train I was on was detained by an accident. When I reached the city, I went to a hotel, but could not get a room," her lip curling as if the remembrance aroused her indignation. "I soon found that it was not safe for me to be on the streets alone; I appealed to this policeman for protection and he brought me here."[40]

Laura will soon discover, however, that such "protection" as the legal system affords her is no protection at all. She might as well be on the streets as under the collapsible legal umbrella of Judge Swinton. And it is to escape such dangerous vulnerability that Frank Heywood changes his identity. As a man, he need not fear those terrors that haunted him when he went undisguised: a young woman prey to the most horrifying situations devised by men. For Frank Heywood had been humiliated by unwanted advances — even attempted rape.

In the present, however, he need not worry about discrimination in employment, in education, or in public places. He can visit restaurants and check into hotels by himself without arousing suspicion that he might be morally unfit. As in Wilkie Collins's London of the mid–1800s, New York City women of this time were looked upon with unmitigated disapproval on the occasions in which they were daring enough to venture into public places without a male escort. In fact, both Wilkie Collins and his friend and literary mentor Charles Dickens greatly enjoyed visiting Paris in the 1850s because they enjoyed freedoms unavailable in London, including the pleasure of watching unescorted women in restaurants and theaters.[41] To overcome the harsh restrictions placed on American women some twenty years after Dickens and Collins made the most of the Parisian entertainment available to curious, adventurous males, Frank Heywood places his own restriction upon himself. So by hiding and thus denying his true sexual identity, he can then make speeches in public, vote, and apply for professional positions without eliciting sly looks from prospective male employers. He can be out alone on the streets at night, and no one will offer to "protect" him by escorting him to the police court. In addition, as a journalist for a respected newspaper, he is allowed the freedom to travel freely about the country, gathering information so that he might write stories on important, substantive topics of the day. In short, as a man, he is permitted to be his own person. Indeed, as Blake presents her "hero," Frank is the only completely sympathetic and compassionate "man" in the novel — and this, significantly, because he is really female and, according to Blake's theory, only women can truly understand the impasse facing their own sex.

And yet for Frank, dark places remain, forever hidden in some deep corner of his brain, but always prone to reemerge, to remind him that he is not really the person that he appears to be — and yet, in some respects, he is. Both feminine and masculine instincts exist in him simultaneously. As a consequence, not for nothing does Frank Heywood seem melancholy, out of place, out of synch with himself and with the society of both sexes. Like Mandy Oxendine who, having been both black and white, belongs to neither race, Frank, having been both female and male, belongs to neither sex. While he necessarily sympathizes with the women who constitute his environment, he must also be one of the guys, for only by inhabiting their world can he succeed on their terms.

It is instructive to note that Lillie Blake never closely examines the price that Frank pays for his "success." What ultimately concerns Blake the most is the fate of Laura Stanley. And here, in the final presentation of Laura's character, Blake backs away from her protest against a woman's limited choices. So too, the author fails to carry to its logical conclusion one of her most deeply held convictions: a belief staunchly embodied in the character of Frank Heywood. For Frank comes to symbolize the possibility that a woman might actually deny the old lie that biology is destiny. Yet for Laura, biology *is* destiny, and her final destiny as depicted by Lillie Blake is in a union with that feminist sympathizer manqué, Guy Bradford.

The final scene of the novel emphasizes Laura's capitulation to the system as well as Lillie Blake's effort to provide a conventionally happy ending for her readers. After agreeing to marry Guy, Laura stumbles out of character and down a number of sexist steps as she offers the following hesitating, equivocating plea to her intended husband: "'I believe that you will not ask me to surrender my liberty entirely, and will permit me to follow out my own career in life.'"[42] Guy's answer is melodramatic and sentimental, and does not possess the quality of authentic, sincere reassurance:

> "My own darling," he replied, "your obligations to me shall be no greater than mine to you. We will make life's journey hand in hand, equals in all things, by God's blessing travelling together to the end, and finding an immortal happiness in an eternal heaven."[43]

On the other hand, Frank Heywood has renounced such "immortal happiness in an eternal heaven," for he can never ask a woman to be his wife. But is the fact that he must now for all time lead a chaste life necessarily a bad fate? This is a question that Blake does not pursue.

Moreover, as Blake constantly makes clear, Frank can never allow anyone to know his secret, with the exception of a select few whom he implicitly trusts. In short, Blake leaves the reader with the unanswered question: Has Frank Heywood paid too high a price for freedom? This is a significant issue that Lillie Blake never resolves satisfactorily. Frank is, after all, the only woman in the novel who is daring enough to change her sex, though at one point both Laura and her friend Flora express their desires to do that very thing. Their wish, however, is only a theoretical one. But it is tantalizing to contemplate how their stories might have had very different endings had they followed Frank's freethinking example. Flora would still have been alive at the novel's end, and Laura would not have been in the equivocal position of making such cautious, almost beseeching statements as the aforementioned: "'I believe that you will not ask me to surrender my liberty entirely, and will permit me to follow out my own career in life.'"[44] From this statement cum question, it is all too evident that Laura fears the very real possibility that Laura Stanley will be lost when she metamorphoses into Mrs. Guy

Bradford. And in the world as depicted by Lillie Blake, such a disappearance is quite likely.

So we are left, then, with the paradoxical dilemma of identity for women in the nineteenth century. Frank Heywood loses his identity by becoming a man, while Laura Stanley and Flora Livingston lose their identities by remaining women. Even the somewhat liberated physician, Mrs. D'Arcy, prefers to identify herself by her *late* husband's name, to use the married woman's designated prefix rather than her professional title. Thus, she is always identified as *Mrs.* rather than *Dr.*, even though the man whose name she continues to bear with some sort of misguided pride is long dead, a ghost who appears to have passed away many years before the events of the narrative begin.

Furthermore, we might conclude that Frank's victory in achieving a worthwhile male identity is a Pyrrhic one, for he has been forced into anonymity, just as surely as if he had stayed with the sex of his birth. In his own way, Frank has also been silenced, no less than Laura, who is marrying her Guy, who may or may not turn out to be a great guy; no less than Flora, who dies for want of an authentic life; and no less than a downtrodden, pathetic, woman aptly named Mrs. Bludgett, who is finally beaten to death by the husband who has systematically brutalized her for years. The fact that the words *blood* and *bludgeon* can be discerned in the name of this wretched woman only reinforces author Blake's insistence that a woman had no recourse to such vicious treatment save passivity, Bible-reading, and — all too often — death.

It is interesting to note at this juncture that a real-life counterpart of Frank Heywood may be found in the character of the French novelist George Sand. Born Amandine-Aurore-Lucile Dupin in 1804, she early demonstrated her androgynous nature by dressing as a boy in order to participate more freely in sports such as horseback riding; further, as she was growing up on the large family estate, she often cross-dressed, taking on male roles in local plays and going into the village dressed as a boy. Unlike Frank Heywood, however, Sand relished roles as both man and woman and appeared to enjoy her sexuality. At eighteen, she married a man who had many mistresses and who abused her. Undaunted, she herself took lovers of both sexes. Yet she seemed comfortable with herself. Unlike the "hero" of *Fettered for Life*, her crossdressing was not an attempt to disguise her identity; it was, rather, a celebration of her pride in nonconformity, of her uniqueness, of her celebration of herself as a sexual being. According to Carolyn Heilbrun, Sand enacted, through lovers and friends, all relationships from mother to master. She had the power both to give and to receive, to nurture and to be nurtured. Yet all who knew and admired her found themselves without language to describe or address her, without a story, other than her own unique one, in which to encompass her. Although she played every role, including conventionally female ones, although she wrote, in her letters, stereotypically romantic phrases, she did not herself become the victim of these roles or phrases.[45]

In short, for all of her attempts to be forceful and independent, Lillie Blake's Laura Stanley remains ambivalent toward herself as she tries to define herself and to set goals for herself. At bottom, unlike the daring nineteenth century novelist George Sand, she does indeed become a victim of the very roles and phrases that she has resisted most of her life, especially in her struggles following her arrival in New York City. While Sand appears to have had the best of both worlds, both Laura and Frank linger in a limbo: Laura because she chooses the feminine path; Frank because s/he chooses the masculine. Ironically, the lives of these two fictional characters mirror more closely the confining options available to most women of the nineteenth century than does the life of George Sand.

Yet, as Carolyn Heilbrun astutely observes in *Writing a Woman's Life*, even the most talented, independent women in the arts, sciences, or social services, have been ill served by biographers, who see these women as through a glass darkly — who believe that gifted, successful women manage to make it in a man's world only by forgoing their natural feminine instincts and by overcoming the angst that naturally comes with the crises accompanying their passage into early womanhood. And further, these same women put on disingenuous masks when they write about their own lives, when they try to create themselves through autobiography. They write of themselves as though their myriad accomplishments were the result of some lucky chance, some serendipitous outside agency. In addition, at some point, most of these talented women are forced to come to terms with and free themselves from their fathers, many of whom were imbued with patriarchal patterns of behavior that stifled their daughters' aspirations. Virginia Woolf, Adrienne Rich, Maxine Kumin, and Sylvia Plath are illustrations of such women who wrestled with identity questions in tandem with their efforts to deal with wrenching father-daughter relationships.[46]

In this connection, Lillie Blake does not allow Laura Stanley to resolve her conflicted feelings about her father, a hard-edged Yankee farmer who has eternally cowed her hardworking, beaten down mother, a woman of fifty who appears to have lived twice those years. While Laura is able to leave her family behind in rural New York State in order to try her luck in New York City, she is nonetheless unable to resolve her feelings of anger and bitterness at the way in which her father has continually abused her mother, both physically and emotionally. On a visit home, Laura thinks of the hard life of her two sisters and her mother — and of the father whom she regards with both bitterness and resignation. Watching her mother hasten into the kitchen in order to prepare for Mr. Stanley's arrival, "Laura looked after her sadly. She knew that with all these broad acres of productive land, her father was amply able to give the girls leisure for improvement, suitable clothing, and above all, to relieve her mother from the care and anxiety that had worn her out prematurely, and yet she knew also, that it was useless to hope for any such change."[47] Laura's parents, then, provide her with a negative example of married life, especially for the woman. Yet she still ultimately opts for marriage, though she knows that she gives up the right to her property, to her own earnings, to any children that she might have — indeed, to her very own body. Finally, then, Blake turns Laura into a feminist manqué, no more able to subvert the system in her way than Frank Heywood is in his/hers.

• *Seven* •

The Secret Life
of Lady Audley

Ah, the time will all too quickly come when, debased by her
fall, she will be no more to me than any other woman.
Choderlos de Laclos, *Les Liaisons Dangereuses* (1782)

The Death-Defining Spin of Fortune's Wheel

George Talboys, a melodramatic, sentimental, and elusive character
to whom we are soon introduced in Mary Elizabeth Braddon's 1862
novel *Lady Audley's Secret*, is a man obsessed with a mission: to be
reunited with his wife. He has spent three and one half years in Australia
making a fortune; now he is returning to England to reclaim the hauntingly beautiful wife and the young son that he had left behind. Though
he has not heard from his wife in all that time, he tells his shipmate,
a woman he has met on the long voyage back, that he is eager to return
to his "darling wife," a lady who, he is convinced, still awaits him with
a "'heart [that] is as true as the light of Heaven; and in whom I no
more expect to find any change than I do to see another sun rise in
to-morrow's sky?'"[1]

Talboys's innocent comment about his long-awaited reunion with his
wife — and his certainty that such a reunion will actually occur — ironically foreshadows the terrifying darkness to come. Furthermore, when Talboys notes with conviction that he does not expect to find any change in
this, the most devoted of wives; that he is as sure of her steadfastness as
he is that two suns will not rise in the sky the next morning, he has no
clue of the horror awaiting him. George Talboys will find that his wife

183

Helen has, in fact, undergone a most radical transformation. So too, George himself will soon change, for he is about to vanish, is on the brink of becoming an invisible man, thanks to the machinations of the woman he left behind. George Talboys is about to receive a bitter, horrifying homecoming.

George Talboys's slide into anonymity and near death begins almost immediately after his arrival back in England when he is informed that his adored wife, only twenty-two years old, has died just a few days earlier, leaving their young son. Or has she really? Throughout the novel, Braddon presents multiple clues that finally lead to the inevitable conclusion that the "late" Helen (Mrs. George) Talboys has been extremely busy during her husband's lengthy absence, and that *death*—at least her own death—has not been in her plans. Included, however, among her many activities during her husband's travels has been another marriage. She has reincarnated herself as Mrs. Michael Audley, a prosperous lady, wife of a very wealthy widower many years her senior. The title character of Braddon's novel is far more cruel, ruthless, and devious in her pursuit of a new identity than is any female character conceived by Wilkie Collins, Charles Chesnutt or Lillie Blake. In fact, Lady Audley would have made an ideal match for any of the many serpentine males that inhabit Blake's *Fettered for Life*. And she would have handily defeated all of the bombastic yet feeble-witted villains of that novel.

Just as with any number of Collins's female protagonists, Helen Talboys sloughs off her past in order to transform herself into an indulged lady of the British aristocracy. Unlike Collins's frequently misguided heroines, however, Helen (Lady Audley) needs no guide to show her the way to wealth. Though on at least two occasions she attempts murder as a way to avoid discovery, she never once questions either her means or her ends. Like author Lillie Blake in *Fettered for Life*, Mary Elizabeth Braddon builds a harrowing, suspenseful tale; in so doing, she grabs her reader's attention from the outset and, like her American contemporary does in *Fettered for Life*, skillfully presages the story's outcome, always pointing the way to the final revelation about switched identities. However, in this novel's depiction of the protagonist Lady Audley, we see a woman who is diabolically evil, a completely amoral woman with no ability to empathize: the quintessential narcissist. So too, unlike Frank Heywood, Lady Audley has more than one truly dreadful secret.

The Changing Face of Robert Audley

An essential ingredient for a good mystery story is a clear, consistent point of view. And such a viewpoint Braddon gives to Robert Audley, a nephew of the unfortunate Michael Audley, the man who becomes second husband of the chameleon who calls herself first, Lucy Graham — proper maiden lady and respectable governess — and then, triumphantly, Lady Audley. Through a tidy plot coincidence that nonetheless feels right, Robert Audley is an old school chum of George Talboys and is reunited with him almost immediately upon George's return to England. It is Robert who accompanies George to the grave of his recently deceased wife and who travels with his friend to visit George's pathetic, ne'er-do-well father-in-law and the young son whom he has not seen for over three years. By focusing on Robert Audley, the dispassionate but nonetheless loyal friend of the hapless George, Braddon has created a multi-dimensional, amateur detective who leads us through labyrinthine clues to shocking discoveries that are simultaneous with his own. And the surprises keep coming, even to the conclusion of the novel.

But more important than Robert Audley's primitive, plodding detective work following George's disappearance and presumed death is the fact that Robert Audley is transformed from a cold barrister to a sympathetic and careful man, one who is determined to find and avenge the person who, he is convinced, has killed his friend George. The cause of this disappearance finally surfaces at the novel's end: it is the very person whom Robert Audley has suspected all along — Lady Audley. But what a twisted path he must follow in order to prove that his theories are well grounded.

When the Time Is Ripe for Accounting

These twists begin with a description of the Audley estate in the novel's opening scene. In the second paragraph of Chapter I, Braddon describes the avenue leading up to the sumptuous Audley Court:

> At the end of this avenue there was an old arch and a clock tower, with a stupid, bewildering clock, which had only one hand — and which jumped straight from one hour to the next — and was therefore always in extremes. Through this arch you walked straight into the gardens of Audley Court.[2]

This clock with only one hand — the one that designates just the hours — presents a hint of the confusion to come. For in the world into which Robert Audley is thrust, the time is indeed out of joint. Built into this world is an inherent paradox: time moves forward at lightning speed, the hours — in tandem with this dysfunctional clock — jumping forward like minutes. However, time also appears to stop, suspended like an aborted embryo in formaldehyde, awaiting dissection by a dispassionate scientist — in this case, the barrister Robert Audley. The accelerated speed of time is evidenced by Lady Audley's haste in divesting herself of her past and recreating herself as a single, eligible woman. The suspension of time is revealed through Robert Audley's putting his life in abeyance immediately following George Talboys's disappearance — for Robert Audley wants very much to fit the puzzle pieces together. Moreover, time is suspended for George Talboys as well, a man for many months erroneously presumed dead.

Likewise, the manipulation of time is later symbolically represented by a gold watch. It is this timepiece that George Talboys, Jr. begs his grandfather to get back from wherever the old man periodically sends it. In an interview with Robert Audley, shortly after George, Sr.'s disappearance, the little boy confesses to the visitor that a "pretty lady" had given him the watch, but that it has temporarily disappeared.[3] Though the little boy is always told that the watch has been sent out to be "cleaned," and though we know that this cleaning is a euphemism for the watch's recurring stay at a pawnbroker's, we also understand that the gold watch symbolizes the suspension of time: in this case, time is frozen all the while that the watch is out of sight. It is also symbolic of the "pretty lady" who has given the child the watch: both a reminder of Lady Audley's wealth and, paradoxically, a sign of her father's economic efforts to just barely scrape by. So too, it is also undoubtedly the sign of a bribe. So long as Lady Audley slyly and secretively brings expensive tokens to the home of her father and her child, so long may she continue her daring charade without fear that her father will become discontented and give away her secret.

Another clue to the disjointed quality of this novel is revealed in an early description of the Audley house, the chambers of which are said to take on the appearance of a maze in which a person might be forever lost, even as that person doubles back upon himself/herself. Braddon's description of the architecture of the Audley mansion sounds much like the depiction of the arrangement of the castle rooms in Poe's eerie tale of the doomed revelers in "The Masque of the Red Death" (1842).

A noble place; inside as well as out, a noble place — a house in which you incontinently lost yourself if ever you were so rash as to attempt to penetrate its mysteries alone; a house in which no one room had any sympathy with another, every chamber running off at a tangent into an inner chamber, and through that down some narrow staircase leading to a door which, in its turn, led back into that very part of the house from which you thought yourself the furthest; a house that could never have been planned by any mortal architect, but must have been the handiwork of that good old builder, Time, who, adding a room one year, toppling down a chimney ... had contrived, in some eleven centuries to run up such a mansion as was not elsewhere to be met with throughout the county of Essex.[4]

In the manipulation of *time* in this novel, Mary Elizabeth Braddon demonstrates considerable skill. Even after we have negotiated the tangled narrative and figured out that Helen Talboys (née Helen Maldon) and Lucy Audley are one and the same, we find that, along the way, we will encounter some unsettling facts with respect to the chronology of Helen Talboys's timely metamorphosis. Yet, in another twist and turn of the paradoxical screw, it is Robert Audley's unpleasant duty to recreate the chronology of Lady Audley's fall and rise as completely and accurately as possible. For Robert Audley to trace Lucy Audley's movements backward in time and geographical space is of paramount importance. And with each twist and turn, he drives himself farther and farther down dark passages that he dreads, for he knows that at the end of each passage he may find that his suspicions are ever more justified and that a horrible fate has doubtless befallen his good friend, George Talboys.

Even so, the more he uncovers the facts about Helen Maldon Talboys, or Lucy Graham Audley, the more he realizes what a truly dangerous person she is. Here is a woman with no scruples whatsoever: a beautiful dissembler who can charm men, make them fall into a sublime fit of nearly uncontrollable passion, and then destroy them when it suits her own ends. Although she meets her match in the meticulous, cautious Robert Audley, the match begins as an unequal contest, with Lady Audley holding all of the most appropriate, most lethal weapons, unafraid to use them when Robert threatens to knock over the defiant but always precarious house of cards that she has built for herself in the days when her first husband was half a world away. The fact that Robert triumphs over his beautiful but cunning adversary is as much a tribute to his intelligent tenacity as it is a comment on Lady Audley's major weakness: her overweening hubris.

Indeed, it is this hubris that leads her to concoct the daring scheme of assumed and switched identities. And, as with her American contemporary Lillie Blake, Mary Braddon prepares the reader early on for this switch by providing clues that the world of her protagonists is just a little askew.

For instance, shortly after learning about his wife's "death," the tormented George Talboys, accompanied by Robert Audley, visits Ventnor, the town where, he has heard, his wife has just died. Here, the recent widower learns some peculiar facts surrounding Mrs. Talboys's final hours. For instance, when the grieving man questions the landlady of the house in which Helen Talboys died, he wants to know if his wife spoke of him at the end. To this, the forthright landlady gives an odd reply:

> "No, she went off quiet as a lamb. She said very little from the first; but the last day she knew nobody, not even her little boy, nor her poor old father, who took on awful. Once she went off wild-like, talking about her mother, and about the cruel shame it was to leave her to die in a strange place, till it was quite pitiful to hear her."[5]

To this speech, George muses naïvely: "'Her mother died when she was quite a child ... To think that she should remember her and speak of her, but never once of me.'"[6] That the dying woman knows neither father nor child will become a telling point, as will the fact that the dying woman has mentioned a living mother who, as George realizes, has long been dead. Nor does George, in his agony, note another anomalous curiosity that occurs when the landlady kindly offers George a long tress of Helen Talboys's hair, which she has taken from the "Helen" as she lay in her coffin. George is too distraught to solve the puzzle of incongruities, even as he "pressed the soft lock to his lips. 'Yes,' he murmured, 'this is the dear hair that I have kissed so often when her head lay upon my shoulder. But it always had a rippling wave in it then, and now it seems smooth and straight.'"[7] Something is peculiar about Helen Talboys's death.

More Secrets of Lady Audley

Even before the inconvenient return of George Talboys, Braddon hints of the strange events to come as she describes the appearance and manner of Lady Audley, the diabolical woman who harbors many secrets, which become apparent early in the novel. For instance, before her marriage to Sir Michael Audley — but while she is still the wife of George Talboys — she works as a governess in the home of a respected surgeon.

Though we as yet know nothing of the convoluted path taken by this madwoman to arrive at her current position, nonetheless we are led to suspect that there are some menacing clouds in this lady's past. As she thinks of the possibility that she might indeed have the chance to escape her present life of genteel poverty through a fortuitous marriage to a much older man, she reveals much through her appearance alone:

> She wore a narrow black ribbon around her neck, with a locket, or a cross, or a miniature, perhaps, attached to it; but whatever the trinket was, she always kept it hidden under her dress. Once or twice, while she sat silently thinking, she removed one of her hands from before her face, and fidgeted nervously with the ribbon, clutching at it with a half-angry gesture, and twisting it backward and forward between her fingers.[8]

Once Helen Talboys has accepted Michael Audley's marriage proposal, not without some trepidation, she silently rejoices in the thought that she has triumphed in leaving behind the hardness of her former life:

> "No more dependence, no more drudgery, no more humiliations," she said; "every trace of the old life melted away — every clew to identity buried and forgotten — except these, except these."
> She had never taken her left hand from the black ribbon at her throat. She drew it from her bosom as she spoke, and looked at the object attached to it.
> It was neither a locket, a miniature, nor a cross; it was a ring wrapped in an oblong piece of paper — the paper partly written, partly printed, yellow with age, and crumpled with much folding.[9]

Later, after Michael Audley has declared his love for her and proposed marriage, she has a brief moment of reflection, as she concentrates on something as yet unseen and unknown by the reader:

> Lucy Graham was not looking at Sir Michael, but straight out into the misty twilight and dim landscape far away beyond the little garden. The baronet tried to see her face, but her profile was turned to him, and he could not discover the expression of her eyes. If he could have done so, he would have seen a yearning gaze which seemed as it if would have pierced the far obscurity and looked away — away into another world.[10]

The other world into which the soon-to-be Lady Audley is gazing, of course, is the hardscrabble one that she has left behind, a world involving one young son, a down-at-the-heels father, and George Talboys, her absent husband. Moreover, it is a world that she has unhesitatingly chosen to relinquish in the name of self-aggrandizement. And, like many of the tortured, demented creations of Ambrose Bierce, Lady Audley is irrevocably mad: a woman existing in a twilight miasma of dark duplicity, outright lies, and attempted murder. Cunning, unscrupulous, intelligent, sexy, and manic — Lady Audley is also a victim of the same English society frequently depicted by Wilkie Collins. It is a society where to be poor is to be completely scorned, and to be rich is to be consummately pampered and adored. Furthermore, in the world of Victorian England, to be a woman was to be a victim of every law passed by man. So Lady Audley uses her only weapons at hand — her awesome beauty and her shrewd intellect — to dispose of one world and enter another. But Lady Audley will ultimately discover to her great chagrin that she cannot have it both ways. On her way to the perdition of a madhouse, however, she pulls some stunning maneuvers, beginning with the desertion of her son so that she can move forward to find a more prosperous way of life, one more suited to a lady of her beauty and refinement. In part, then, she resembles Magdalen Vanstone in Wilkie Collins's *No Name* (1862) but, unlike Magdalen, Helen Mallon Talboys Lucy Graham Audley has no heart.

How Lady Audley Pulls Off the Shift and Continues the Deception

As with Collins's *The Woman in White* (1861), there is an identity shift that takes place between the living and the dead. However, there is an important difference between the authors' approaches. In the Braddon novel, one of the ladies involved in the switch — whereby one woman is buried under the name of a still living woman — is instrumental in precipitating the name reversal. Indeed, Lady Audley devises this bit of chicanery when she learns to her horror that her husband is on his way home from Australia and that he will doubtless try to contact her. But by this time a complication has arisen: Mrs. George Talboys is a bigamist, having only recently made a fortuitous marriage, thereby assuming a different name as well as a supernumerary husband. Now she is the wealthy woman-to-be-envied: Mrs. Michael Audley. Meanwhile, her still smitten but benighted bridegroom remains blissfully oblivious to his young bride's former, eventful life. So, knowing that her extra husband will soon be hot on her trail, Lady Audley, who has already buried Mrs. George Talboys in spirit, vows to bury Mrs. George Talboys in body as well. Through a series of lucky breaks, she learns of a young woman, approximately her own age who is dying of an unnamed illness.

In due course, Lady Audley quickly arranges to have the nearly moribund woman transported to a town and into a house where neither this desperately sick woman nor the very much alive Mrs. Talboys is known. It is here that the terminally ill young lady is introduced to the landlady as Mrs. George Talboys; it is this Mrs. Talboys whom the landlady describes to the grieving husband and his friend Robert Audley when they ask about the late Mrs. Talboys just a few days after the young female inhabitant's death. So now Lady Audley is sure that she has disposed of George Talboys and his embarrassing inquiries.

But not quite. Robert decides to take George with him when he goes to visit Audley Court and Uncle Michael, for whom he has the greatest respect. Though George is still suffering from grief and remorse over the loss of his One True Love, he agrees to accompany Robert. Indeed, both George and Robert are curious to see Michael Audley's recently acquired bride. When Robert offers to fetch George so that the whole Audley family might welcome him, Lady Audley remains singularly cool-headed, even as she knows that she is about to be "discovered" unless she thinks fast. So, as Robert is about to bring George into the room where this recent widower would be stunned into silence at the physical manifestation of the lady whose grave he has just visited, Lady Audley demonstrates considerable savoir faire: "When Robert, therefore, was about to re-enter the inn, it needed but the faintest elevation of Lucy's eyebrows, with a charming expression of wariness and terror, to make her husband aware that she did not want to be bored by an introduction to Mr. George Talboys."[11] A short time after she has skillfully managed to avoid this meeting with her legal husband, Lady Audley plans a trip to London. But she is very careful about any signs of her presence that she might leave behind. Braddon again leaves subtle foreshadowing as Lady Audley circumspectly closes off a room containing some oil paintings. We later learn that these paintings include portraits of the lady herself; thus she must block any possible access by an intruder whose presence could handily destroy the tidy order of her present, shadowy world. Now, she thinks, she has efficiently hidden her mud-spattered tracks.

> Her suite of rooms ... opened one out of another and terminated in an octagon antechamber hung with oil-paintings. Even in her haste she paused deliberately at the door of this room, double-locked it, and dropped the key into her pocket. This door once locked cut off all access to my lady's apartments.[12]

But secrets are not so easy to shut out, as Lady Audley will learn to her dismay. As Braddon continually reminds us, when one means of access is cut off, another one opens to provide another means of discerning a different truth. Furthermore, it is not only through the perspective of Lady Audley that we receive tantalizing glimpses of her secret world. If we look carefully, we may even be able to work out the point at which George Talboys first learns that he has been the victim of a cruel deception.

George Talboys's Epiphany

This revelation occurs shortly after Lady Audley has taken the precaution of locking that door. What the lady of the house does not know is that her stepdaughter Alicia, for whom Mrs. Audley has little affection, has found another way into her stepmother's sacred chambers, a route unknown to Lady Audley herself. This route becomes a tortured path that nearly leads George Talboys to madness and ruin. What Talboys witnesses in this room is a portrait painting of Lady Audley: the primary reason for Lady Audley's precipitous caution in securing the room from intruders in her absence. Braddon draws some memorable images, as she guides her omniscient narrator to comment on the devastating, treacherous effect of Lady Audley's presence in art. Described memorably, paradoxically, as "a beautiful fiend," Lady Audley also takes on the aspect of an apparition from hell, carrying, in Poe-like fashion, her own red death in her wake:

> Her crimson dress, exaggerated like all the rest in this strange picture, hung about her in folds that looked like flames, her fair head peeping out of the lurid mass of color as if out of a raging furnace. Indeed the crimson dress, the sunshine on the face, the red gold gleaming in the yellow hair, the ripe scarlet of the pouting lips, the glowing colors of each accessory of the minutely painted background, all combined to render the first effect of the painting by no means an agreeable one.[13]

In addition, the passage carries with it a prescient phrase in its description of "her fair head peeping out of the lurid mass of color as if out of a raging furnace." By the conclusion of Lady Audley's journey, this "raging furnace" has become an apt metaphor for the madness of Lady Audley, whose fiery brain is evident in the many overwrought, desperate plots that she hatches in a futile effort to eliminate Robert Audley from the scene. First, she lies about his character, and then, failing in that, she makes a bold attempt to murder him in a "raging furnace" of her own making, as she starts a fire in the hotel where Audley is staying, hoping that he will die in the conflagration. Though her plot fails and Audley escapes, his timely exit is a matter of luck, not a failure of Lady Audley's carefully thought out plan.

But here, as we are reminded that "the first effect of the painting [is] by no means an agreeable one,"[14] we are drawn to George Talboys, staring at the painting. His trance-like state results from his recognition of the portrait's subject, for the woman whom he has just heard identified as the lady in the painting is the current mistress of Audley Court. Yet for George, such information is both superfluous and erroneous: the woman before him, looking so life-like, is his own late, lamented wife, now apparently very much alive and well, living in luxury, and living in sin as a bigamist. Braddon begins her description with a touch of irony:

> But strange as the picture was, it could not have made any great impression on George Talboys, for he sat before it for about a quarter of an hour without uttering a word — only staring blankly at the painted canvas, with the candlestick grasped in his strong right hand, and his left arm hanging loosely by his side.[15]

Yet impression it has indeed made. At this point, George Talboys descends into a state that is almost catatonic; in addition, Robert Audley, who is naturally unaware of the cause of his friend's apparent distress, fears that George has caught a cold or that he is suffering from some type of unnamed dread. Significantly, a lightning storm strikes that same night, Braddon making the obvious connection between the outer and inner turmoil suffered by the heretofore trusting and unsuspecting first husband of the lady in the portrait. Indeed, Audley attributes George's unsettled mental state to outright terror accompanying the storm. Yet when Audley confronts his friend with the suggestion that George is — in truth — afraid, George vehemently denies any such condition.

Despite these denials, torn by anguish and disbelief, George drives himself into the rainstorm. His behavior suggests that, by giving himself a thorough soaking, he can obliterate the memory of what he has just seen and, likewise, can melt himself away into oblivion as well: "He walked up and down, up and down, in the soaking shower for about twenty minutes, and then, re-entering the inn, strode up to his bedroom."[16]

That George is *striding* up to his bedroom suggests a purposefulness that he has previously lacked. Once again, however, Braddon gives only brief hints as to what George's next action might be. And when George disappears quite suddenly one afternoon, we are as puzzled and suspicious as his friend Robert Audley. We later learn that George's resolve had culminated when he had confronted his bigamous wife; in the course of their violent argument, George had fallen down a well and was presumed dead — at least as far as Lady Audley was concerned. In the meantime, Robert Audley begins a search for his missing friend; a search that goes down a tortured path, curving back upon itself, but always leading him to Lady Audley as the cause of his good friend's apparent vaporization.

All the while Robert Audley is engaged is his pursuit, Lady Audley is presented as a thoroughgoing villain, a madwoman with few redeeming qualities, save her haunting, Medusa-like beauty. Toward the end of the novel, we learn in Lady Audley's confession to Sir Michael that her mother was also mad; that Lady Audley, at the age of ten, had seen her mother in an asylum, and that she has carried the secret of her mother's madness ever since. If she offers this fact as an excuse for her subsequent yet incomprehensible and horrifying behavior, Sir Michael is not impressed. Rather, he wants nothing more to do with the woman who, he feels, has so betrayed his love and trust.

However, Sir Michael is not destined to ever fully comprehend the extent of Lady's Audley's betrayal nor of her crimes. In truth, one of the most provocative elements of this novel involves something in Lady Audley's past that is only hinted at. This mysterious secret is first suggested in the description of the black ribbon worn by Lady Audley around her neck, at the end of which a ring is attached. Author Braddon never tells the reader to whom this ring has belonged nor does she say what kind of a ring it is — whether a wedding ring, a signet ring, a child's ring to be worn on a chain around the neck, or some other type of ring. The blackness, however, is suggestive of sadness, loss, or mourning, and the ribbon itself carries with it the possibility of destruction, as it could very well be a loose end on which Lady Audley might ultimately hang herself.

Nowhere is this suggestion more obvious than in the scene where Sir Michael proposes to the woman whom he knows as Lucy Graham. Here is the future Mrs. Audley: clearly distraught, overcome by the turmoil of the moment:

> Beyond her agitation and her passionate vehemence, there is an undefined something in her manner which fills the baronet with a vague alarm. She is still on the ground at his feet, crouching rather than kneeling, her thin white dress clinging about her, her pale hair streaming over her shoulders, her great blue eyes glittering in the dusk, and her hands clutching at the black ribbon about her throat, as if it had been strangling her.[17]

The Most Heinous Crime of All

What, then, do this black ribbon and the ring at the end of it — a ring that Lady Audley wants no one to see — signify? We are initially tempted to conclude that the ring is Lady Audley's wedding band when she was Helen Talboys, the lawful wife of George Talboys. This conclusion is reinforced when we recall the earlier mentioned passage wherein Helen Talboys, now in the guise of Lucy Graham, bitterly contemplates the meaning of the black ribbon and the ring:

> "No more dependence, no more drudgery, no more humiliations," she said; "every trace of the old life melted away — every clew to identity buried and forgotten — except these, except these."
> She had never taken her left hand from the black ribbon at her throat. She drew it from her bosom as she spoke, and looked at the object attached to it.
> It was neither a locket, a miniature, nor a cross; it was a ring wrapped in an oblong piece of paper — the paper partly written, partly printed, yellow with age, and crumpled with much folding.[18]

That Helen Talboys despised her husband for not properly providing her with a respectable standard of living, despite his father's wealth, and that she equally disliked her child, are two incontrovertible facts. If these feelings are taken into consideration, then, it seems odd that Helen would want to carry with her such a tangible reminder of her marriage vows. Moreover, the paper wrapping the ring is "yellow with age," a description implying that the ring predates Helen Mallon's marriage to George Talboys. Additionally, what is written on this yellowed paper that wraps the ring, and why the words on it are "partly written, partly printed" are two questions contributing to the enigma. Is it perhaps a printed death notice that someone has made additional notes upon? If so, the black ribbon is an appropriate symbol for the deceased. But who has died? Might it be a dead infant? And why would the black ribbon be symbolically "strangling her"?

Beyond the matter of the ring, however, further complications arise regarding another memento that Lady Audley has kept, but kept in secret: a baby shoe, along with a lock of yellow hair, presumably taken from this same baby. Her maid Phoebe discovers these treasures in a locked drawer in her mistress's room, after Helen has become Lady Audley. Looking in the drawer, Phoebe sees that there "was not much in it; neither gold nor gems; only a baby's little worsted shoe rolled up in a piece of paper, and a tiny lock of pale and silky yellow hair, evidently taken from a baby's head."[19]

Again, we might make the obvious assumption that the shoe and the lock of hair belong to the child that Lady Audley left behind: young George Talboys, Jr. Yet we know that she has no sentimental feelings for the little boy. In her later "confession" to Sir Michael, a confession that she has no choice but to make when she finally realizes that the game is over and that she has lost, she admits her dislike for the boy. After George has left her and she is reduced to poverty, she admits: "I did not love the child, for he had been left a burden upon my hands."[20] A further complication embedded within this "tiny lock of pale and silky yellow hair" is directly related to the physical appearance of George Talboys, Jr. We know from a previous description that George, Jr. is "a handsome boy, with his father's brown eyes and dark waving hair."[21] So the boy has dark hair, not "silky yellow." In short, then, if the lock does not belong to her child by George Talboys, whose lock is it? And if the ring is not that which tied her to George Talboys in marriage, whose ring is it?

In order to answer these questions and to further penetrate the mystery of Lady Audley, it is necessary to probe further into the lady's ancestry. We learn that her mother went insane shortly after the daughter's birth, and that Lady Audley's grandmother was also tainted with this hereditary insanity. Lady Audley herself gives these facts in her confession to her deluded and disillusioned husband. She also confides to him a detailed portrait of her mother, the first time that Helen can ever recall having seen her unfortunate mother. Taken by her father to the asylum when she is ten, she is surprised not to see a maniacal creature in chains but instead "a golden-haired, blue-eyed, girlish creature, who seemed as frivolous as a butterfly, and who skipped toward us with her yellow curls decorated with natural flowers, and saluted us with radiant smiles, and gay, ceaseless chatter."[22] So it is both the mother and Lady Audley herself who have the golden hair and yellow curls — not the child, not George Talboys, Jr. So, in her abandonment of her past and her recreation of herself in the present, just what sorts of personal accessories and artifacts do we need to be cognizant of? What *is* it that the narcissistic Lady Audley is hiding?

The answers to these questions are not really clear. A writer such as Wilkie Collins would have carefully tied up all the loose ends of the narrative, but Mary Elizabeth Braddon leaves some puzzling and frustrating ambiguities. All the same, the reader can pursue some provocative speculation and try to answer a number of the more perplexing riddles, all of which simply reinforce the picture the author is drawing of

Lady Audley's madness. One of these puzzles involves that ring, the baby shoe, and the lock of silky yellow hair; in her confession to the stunned Sir Michael, Lady Audley herself alludes to the conundrum. She admits to having left school before she was seventeen and moving with her father, who had retired and was living on half pay, to a remote village called Wildernsea.

At this point, even Lady Audley finds it necessary to hasten her story, lest she reveal something too awful to give away, though she knows that she might very well tell all — her accumulation of crimes has already reached the summit of the most diabolical of peaks: "I had not been there a month before I discovered that even the prettiest girl might wait a long time for a rich husband. I wish to hurry over this part of my life. I dare say I was very despicable."[23]

What is so despicable about her existence at this point is a matter of conjecture. That her earliest "secret" might be connected to the origins of the ring, the lock, and the baby shoe presents a seductive possibility. One such scenario includes the possibility that Lady Audley had engaged in some non-exemplary behavior less than a month after her arrival at Wildernsea. We have been told that she left school "before she was seventeen," so we cannot be sure of her exact age upon her arrival at Wildernsea. If we assume that she is in her mid-teens, around fifteen or so, then it is entirely possible that her despicable behavior had consisted of a hasty sexual encounter, engaged in while she was passing those long hours in looking for a wealthy husband. Such an activity would presumably not have caused much distress to a woman of Lady Audley's not too discriminating sensibilities.

Yet Braddon hints that these three mementos may very well have belonged to a possible complication of such an encounter: an infant who antedates George Talboys, Jr. If young Master Talboys, the dark-haired, legitimate son of Lady Audley's former life as Helen Talboys, is not the infant associated with Lady Audley's secret mementos, then this earlier child hints at an even darker secret, a former identity preceding Helen Maldon's life with her first husband.

Suppose, then, that shortly following Helen's arrival at Wildernsea, she had snatched the most available man, though one without the requisite fortune, had subsequently borne a child, and had, through fair means or foul, disposed of the infant. Such a scenario would more than account for a motif that pervades the novel: the emptiness at the center of Lady's Audley's soul.

The Woman Writer and Victorian Sensibilities

Moreover, if we remember that Mary Elizabeth Braddon was writing within the constraints imposed by Victorian morality and censorship, we can even more readily give credence to this possibility of infanticide. That is, Braddon need only hint at something nameless and reprehensible in Lady Audley's adolescent, post-schoolgirl past; she then leaves it to her readers to fill in those blank, immoral spaces. As Ellen Miller Casey has argued, Braddon's various "struggles with the restraints of conventional morality reveal much about both the Victorians and their novels."[24] If we are not privy to the intimate details of Helen Maldon's behavior pre–George Talboys, it is because of Braddon's reticence to counter Victorian standards: "There is no simple, enjoyable fornication in Braddon's novels. Always the appearances are preserved."[25]

So we can see, then, that Braddon was canny enough to understand the popular tastes of the day; consequently, her early novels of sensation, including *Lady Audley's Secret*, are filled with tantalizing tidbits about plot and character that are nonetheless never explicitly drawn, no more than tempting outlines and shadows. As frustrating as these shadows are to a modern reader, they linger as a reminder of another time, another perspective on society's dictates, now all but vanished from the western world:

> Her subjects were shocking, but she maintained the proprieties by limiting the amount of detail which she provided, by legitimatizing passion with marriage, even if a bigamous one, and by taking care that at the end of the novel the good were rewarded and the evil punished. In other words, she provided a stimulus to Victorian imaginations with a wink for the knowing and a carefully proper surface for the censors.[26]

If Braddon was forced by the times to maintain the proprieties, she was limited even more drastically by her social position as a nineteenth century woman writer. Though Wilkie Collins, her male British contemporary, shared some of her ideas about the unfairness of the laws which legally shackled women, and though he too created credible female characters who found that the only way to assert themselves was through disguise, Collins nonetheless had some male prerogatives that Braddon lacked. Whereas Braddon was socially ostracized due to her unconventional living arrangements with her married lover, Collins was not equally stigmatized when he lived openly with two mistresses and fathered three children by his second. In fact, Collins appears to have been less than empathetic toward these women whom he invited to share his bed and his unconventional ideas, even as they accepted their place on the margins of respectable society.

At one time, Collins even kept two mistresses at once; his earlier lover, Caroline Graves, inexplicably left her second husband and returned to the home that she and Collins had made together in Gloucester Place. At the same time, however, Collins was keeping intimate company with Martha Rudd, who had already borne him two children.[27] Collins used the pseudonym of Dawson when he signed bills and legal papers pertaining to his relationship with Martha, though he never tried to keep their liaison a secret; however, he was never excluded from polite society. So too, with the more polished, popular Caroline, he still held the upper hand socially. The two of them were often entertained in the homes of friends, but these same friends did not welcome Wilkie and Caroline's company at public functions. "Wilkie and Caroline knew the problem though in Wilkie's case only Caroline seems to have suffered, for he was wined and dined without hesitation, provided that he went alone."[28]

So it is through such a cultural double standard that the British Mary Elizabeth Braddon and the American Lillie Devereux Blake shared some of these gender-biased preconceptions and were thus forced by nineteenth century society's expectations of proper female behavior to be quite circumspect in their depiction of women living on the edge. Like Lillie Devereux Blake in *Fettered for Life*, Braddon found that there were certain gender lines that she dared not cross. For Lillie Blake, her important creation of Frank Heywood becomes the metaphorical representation of the nineteenth century male-dominated profession of writing. Because female authors were condescended to and patronized as mere "bluestockings" and "scribblers," the character who comes to be known as Frank Heywood must perforce nominally change her sex in order to be a success as a newspaper reporter.

But, no matter how daring Frank Heywood's irrevocable decision to leap through gender hoops and emerge as the "correct" sex, Blake will not even hint at the sexually repressive implications of a woman such as Frank, one who dares not reveal her true sex, nor even divulge her birth name, lest the knowledge of her identity transformation endanger not only her writing career but her very life. Commenting on the traditional male domain that gives male *authors* the "*author*ity" and power to create while simultaneously barring the inferior females from allowing free rein to their desire to be equally creative writers, the literary historians Sandra M Gilbert and Susan Gubar have observed: "The pen, therefore, is not only mightier than the sword, it is also *like* the sword in its power — its need, even — to kill. And this last attribute of the pen once again seems to be associatively linked with its metaphorical maleness."[29]

By the same token, Mary Elizabeth Braddon cannot use her pen (the metaphorical penis) to assert her power and therefore is not allowed to blatantly proclaim any early sexual misdeeds of Helen Maldon Talboys. For Helen is indeed a woman who, we are led to understand, has not always made passion legitimate. Thus, the author only suggests the veiled significance of the ring, the lock, and the shoes: only intimates what these might represent to Lady Audley. But it would not have been particularly difficult for newcomers to this remote spot called Wildernsea to remain unnoticed. According to Lady Audley, this location was "at the other extremity of England."[30] Here was where she moved with her father, "who had retired upon his half-pay, and had established himself at Wildernsea, with the idea that the place was cheap and select."[31]

So in such an out-of-the-mainstream locale, it would have been fairly easy for the young Helen to escape notice, even as she engaged in a brief romance, got pregnant, had a baby, nurtured the child for a short while, and then watched it die. Whether death by accident, by disease, or by deliberate means, Helen might well have been sentimental enough to hold onto the tokens of this lost child, though such tokens were indeed strangling her. And her comparative isolation with her father in a place where they were both newcomers, where neither was intimately known, would have ensured that gossip did not follow her when she moved away. Nor would George Talboys have had the opportunity to hear many stories about Helen. By Lady Audley's later confessional account to Sir Michael, George was only passing through this secluded part of England when he was smitten by her: "The wandering prince came.... Mr. George Talboys was a cornet in a dragoon regiment. He was the only son of a rich country gentleman. He fell in love with me, and married me three months after my seventeenth birthday."[32]

If these three reminders are tokens of a lost infant; are, in fact, remnants of Lady Audley's very sordid early years, indeed of an act of infanticide, then small wonder that she eventually goes mad in her pursuit of wealth and in her concomitant escape from self.

The fact remains, however, that a number of questions are left behind for the reader to mull over. And, while it must be conceded that Mary Elizabeth Braddon lacks the skillful plotting ability of both Wilkie Collins and Robert Louis Stevenson, she nonetheless has created in *Lady Audley's*

Secret a story of incredible vitality, with psychologically dazzling characters. Furthermore, she shares with Stevenson the dubious distinction of having her work dramatized on film, with similarly dreadful results.[33]

For instance, one is not likely to find the answers to the questions raised by Braddon's convoluted narrative structure through a viewing of the movie version of *Lady Audley's Secret*, made for television and released in 2000. This effort to recreate onscreen the struggles of the mad Lady Audley is seriously flawed. To begin, the story is badly truncated, running about 100 minutes, and is thus nearly unrecognizable. Someone who has not read the book will have difficulty in following the bits and pieces of narrative tossed out by the screenwriters. We catch brief glimpses of George Talboys, Jr., of Lady Audley's insane mother — seen ranting and raving in a madhouse. On the other hand, the Lady Audley of the novel tells us that, when she visited her mother in the asylum, she was struck by the fact that her mother presented a carefree, girlish appearance as she "skipped toward us with her yellow curls decorated with natural flowers, and saluted us with radiant smiles, and gay, ceaseless chatter."[34] Since Lady Audley has no reason to lie about her mother's demeanor, we can only conclude that the modern filmmakers must have wanted to heighten the film noir appearance of their movie by depicting Mrs. Maldon as a wild harridan.

There is one especially suspenseful moment in the novel when Lady Audley uses all her craft and guile to set fire to the inn where she knows that Robert Audley is staying. Furthermore, convinced that Audley is secure in his room, she fastens it from the outside, thus ensuring that he cannot escape the coming inferno. Except that he isn't in his room and he does escape, more determined than ever to see his would-be executioner held accountable for her crimes. The film, however, has only a brief scene depicting her attempt at murder. The scene comes and goes apropos of nothing, and so lacks the dramatic intensity of the original. Nor does the Robert Audley of the novel ever lust after Lady Audley, whereas the film shows several instances of the two kissing in a passionate embrace. Finally, where the novel tells of Lady Audley's fitting death in a madhouse, the movie ends with Robert Audley catching a quick look at the lady entering her carriage with another gentleman, doubtless the next catch on her list of many eligible men.

Given the many liberties taken by the filmmakers in their version of *Lady Audley's Secret*, it is not at all surprising that the only secret that we are privy to in this account of the elegant courtesan is the fact that she has changed her identity from Helen Talboys to Lady Michael Audley. Other aspects of her colorful past are only suggested, and these in a confusing, inchoate manner. Moreover, although George Talboys returns at the film's end, just as he does in the novel, the movie George is left in an uncertain state at the final credits, whereas author Braddon guides her fictional George to a happy finish. We learn at the novel's end that George had left England following his miraculous, improbable escape from the well down which he had tumbled in his argument with his reincarnated wife. Nevertheless, he returns in time to be reunited with his son. And so George Talboys is a contented man at last, now that his wife is really, truly dead.

Despite its occasionally flawed plot, *Lady Audley's Secret* received widespread notice on its initial publication in 1862. In fact, by 1863, it had already gone through nine editions.[35] It is a memorable, engrossing novel with a strong — albeit demented — heroine. Lady Audley is one of those incredible women who remind modern readers that, no matter how hard we try, we can never completely erase our heritage, no more than we can peel away our skin in search of a different person underneath. Both actions are fraught with incalculable moments of terrible pain.

Chapter Notes

Preface

1. Ernest Becker, *The Denial of Death* (New York: Free Press Paperbacks, 1973), 87.

Introduction

1. Louis Menand, *The Metaphysical Club: A Story of Ideas in America* (New York: Farrar, Straus and Giroux, 2001), 49.
2. Menand, 49.
3. Menand, 64.
4. Menand, 62, 65.
5. Quoted in Menand, 60.
6. Quoted in Menand, 69.
7. Lacey Baldwin Smith, *Fools, Martyrs, Traitors: The Story of Martyrdom in the Western World* (New York: Alfred A. Knopf, 1997), 251.
8. Smith, 248–49.
9. Roy Morris, *Ambrose Bierce: Alone in Bad Company* (New York: Crown, 1996), 19.
10. Leon Edel, *Henry James: The Untried Years 1843–1870,* Vol. I, *The Life of Henry James,* 5 vols. (New York: Avon, 1953), 175.
11. Morris, 169.
12. Edel, *The Untried Years: 1843–1870,* 74.
13. Menand, 120.
14. James, *The Will to Believe,* New York: Longmans, 1912, ix. Quoted in Cathy Notari Davidson, *The Poetics of Perception: A Semantic Analysis of the Short Fiction of Ambrose Bierce,* dissertation (State University of New York at Binghamton, 1974), 2.
15. Edel, Vol. I, 209.
16. *Henry James: Complete Stories 1892–1898* (New York: Library of America, 1996), 354.
17. Norman Donaldson, "Introduction to the Dover Edition," *Lady Audley's Secret* (New York: Dover, 1974), xi–xii.
18. Morris, 116.

19. Grace Farrell, "Afterword," *Fettered for Life* by Lillie Devereux Blake (New York: The Feminist Press, 1996), 414.
20. *Dr. Jekyll and Sister Hyde.* Dir. Roy Ward Baker, Hammer Film Productions. With Ralph Bates (Jekyll) and Martine Beswick (Sister Hyde).
21. Menand, 365.
22. Menand, 365.
23. Menand, 366.
24. Alvin Toffler, *Future Shock* (New York: Bantam, 1970), 98–99.

Chapter One

1. *The Complete Short Stories of Ambrose Bierce,* compiled by Ernest Jerome Hopkins (Lincoln: University of Nebraska, 1970), 72.
2. Bierce, 77.
3. Bierce, 80.
4. Bierce, 80.
5. Bierce, 80.
6. Bierce, 81.
7. Bierce, 77.
8. Bierce, 72.
9. Bierce, 76.
10. Bierce, 81.
11. Bierce, 81.
12. Bierce, 73.
13. Bierce, 80.
14. Bierce, 79.
15. Bierce, 81.
16. Cathy N. Davidson, *The Experimental Fictions of Ambrose Bierce* (Lincoln: University of Nebraska, 1982), 45.
17. Hopkins, *The Complete Stories,* 21.
18. Roy Morris, Jr., *Ambrose Bierce: Alone in Bad Company* (New York: Oxford University, 1998), 88.
19. Morris, 91.
20. Bierce, 127.
21. Bierce, 127.

22. Bierce, 127.
23. Bierce, 128.
24. Bierce, 128.
25. Bierce, 128.
26. Bierce, 128.
27. Bierce, 129.
28. Bierce, 129.
29. Bierce, 130.
30. Bierce, 131.
31. Bierce, 131.
32. Bierce was morbidly fascinated with suicide, especially by the various peculiar methods people chose to end their lives. As a writer for the San Francisco *News Letter* in the late 1860s, he chronicled with a sort of gruesome glee the efforts at self-murder perpetrated by the local citizens. (Morris, 121–22) Additionally, he was never deluded into thinking that marriage could provide him with eternally blissful rewards. His own marriage to a socially prominent woman, Mollie Day, was singularly miserable for both of them. (Morris, 132–46) Perhaps he wanted to save John in "One of Twins" from just such an unhappy fate. One wonders if Bierce truly believed that suicide was preferable to marriage.
33. Bierce, 131–32.
34. Bierce, 132.
35. Bierce, 132.
36. Morris, 51–52.
37. Bierce, 188.
38. Bierce, 188.
39. Bierce, 188.
40. Bierce, 189.
41. Morris, 30.
42. Bierce, 189.
43. Bierce, 190.
44. Bierce, 190.
45. Bierce, 190.
46. Bierce, 191.
47. Bierce, 192.
48. Stephen Nacco, "The Double Motif in the Short Stories of Ambrose Bierce," unpublished dissertation (Fordham University, 1991), 30.
49. Nacco, 31–32.
50. Bierce, 388.
51. Bierce, 389.
52. Bierce, 389.
53. Bierce, 390.
54. Bierce, 391.
55. Bierce, 391.
56. Morris, 54.
57. Bierce, 391.
58. Bierce, 392.
59. Bierce, 392.
60. Bierce, 392.
61. Bierce, 392.
62. Bierce, 392–93.

63. Bierce, 393.
64. Bierce, 393.
65. Bierce, 393.
66. Morris, 52.
67. Bierce, 394.
68. Bierce, 394–95.
69. Bierce, 395.
70. Bierce, 395.
71. Bierce, 393.
72. Bierce, 367.
73. Bierce, 367.
74. Bierce, 368.
75. Bierce, 366.
76. Bierce, 368.
77. Nacco, 86.
78. Nacco, 92.
79. Stuart C. Woodruff, *The Short Stories of Ambrose Bierce: A Study in Polarity* (Pittsburgh: University of Pittsburgh, 1964), 76.
80. Lawrence Ivan Berkove, *Ambrose Bierce's Concern with Mind and Man.* University of Pennsylvania, 1962, dissertation (Ann Arbor, Michigan, University Microfilms), 75.
81. Berkove, 88.
82. Nacco, 18.
83. Cathy Notari Davidson, *The Poetics of Perception: A Semantic Analysis of the Short Fiction of Ambrose Bierce*, dissertation (State University of New York at Binghamton, 1974), 11.
84. Davidson, 12.
85. Davidson, 13.
86. Woodruff, 20.
87. Woodruff, 21.
88. Edmund Wilson, *Patriotic Gore* (New York: W.W. Norton, 1994), 622.
89. Wilson, 623.
90. Quoted in Barry Werth, *The Scarlet Professor, Newton Arvin: A Literary Life Shattered by Scandal* (New York: Doubleday, 2001), 293.

Chapter Two

1. James gives to Alice Staverton the first name of his sister and his sister-in-law. Leon Edel, *Henry James: The Master 1901–1916* (New York: Avon, 1972), 315.
2. Henry James, "The Jolly Corner," in *The Jolly Corner and Other Tales*, ed. with an introduction and notes by Roger Gard (New York: Penguin, 1990), 162.
3. James, 162.
4. James, 169.
5. James, 170.
6. James, 171.
7. James, 171.
8. James, 174.
9. Daniel Mark Fogel, "A New Reading of Henry James's 'The Jolly Corner,'" in *Crit-*

ical Essays on Henry James: The Late Novels, ed. James W. Gargano (Boston: G.K. Hall, 1987), 197.

10. James, 174.
11. James, 176.
12. James, 177.
13. James, 178.
14. James, 178.
15. James, 178.
16. James, 166.
17. James, 166.
18. James, 179.
19. James, 179.
20. James, 181.
21. James, 186.
22. James, 187.
23. James, 187.
24. James, 188.
25. James, 188.
26. James, 188.
27. James, 192.
28. James, 193.
29. Fogel, 196.
30. Leon Edel, *Henry James: The Master 1901–1916* (New York: Avon, 1972), 315.
31. James, 193.
32. Eric Savoy, "Spectres of abjection: 'The Jolly Corner,'" in *Spectral Readings: Towards a Gothic Geography*. Ed. Glennis Byron and David Punter (New York: St. Martin's, 1999), 172.
33. Savoy, 173.
34. James, 170.
35. James, 170–71.
36. James, 171.
37. James, 171.
38. James, 171.
39. James, 187.
40. Savoy, 173.
41. Fogel, 198.
42. James, 193.
43. James, 193.
44. James, 193.
45. Elaine Showalter, *Sexual Anarchy: Gender and Culture at the Fin de Siècle* (New York: Viking, 1990), 8.

Chapter Three

1. Kenneth Robinson, *Wilkie Collins, A Biography* (London: Bodley Head, 1951), 169.
2. Robinson, 170.
3. William M. Clarke, *The Secret Life of Wilkie Collins* (Chicago: Ivan R. Dee, 1988), 92.
4. Robinson, 132.
5. Clarke, 92.
6. Robinson, 134.
7. Robinson, 135.
8. Wilkie Collins, *No Name*, ed. with an introduction and notes by Mark Ford (New York: Penguin, 1994), 144.
9. Collins, *No Name*, 109.
10. Robinson, 171.
11. Collins, *No Name,* 194.
12. Collins, *No Name*, 196.
13. Deidre David, "Rewriting Male Plot in *No Name*," in *Wilkie Collins*, ed. Lyn Pykett (New York: St. Martin's, 1998), 145.
14. Collins, *No Name*, 166.
15. Collins, *No Name*, 167.
16. Collins, *No Name*, 162.
17. Collins, *No Name*, 320.
18. Collins, *No Name*, 255.
19. Collins, *No Name*, 257.
20. Collins, *No Name*, 358.
21. Collins, *No Name*, 387.
22. Robinson, 164.
23. Robinson, 281.
24. Collins, *No Name*, 440.
25. Collins, *No Name*, 440.
26. Collins, *No Name*, 484.
27. Collins, *No Name*, 451.
28. Collins, *No Name*, 575.
29. Collins, *No Name*, 576.
30. Collins, *No Name*, 610.
31. Dickens had even given Collins some advice about plotting, suggesting that he have Mrs. Lecount destroy the laudanum bottle upon her discovery of it among Magdalen's belongings. Writing to Collins on 14 October 1862, Dickens recommends: "I think Mrs. Lecount should break it before Noel Vanstone's eyes. Otherwise, while he is impressed with the danger he supposes himself to have escaped, he repeats it, on a smaller scale, by giving Mrs. Lecount an inducement to kill him, and leaving the means at hand." (Notes to *No Name*, 614, note 1)
32. Collins, *No Name*, 605.
33. Collins, *No Name*, 586.
34. Collins, *No Name*, 586.
35. Collins, *No Name*, 162.
36. David, "Rewriting the Male Plot in *No Name*, 146.
37. Quoted in Leon Edel, *Henry James, The Conquest of London: 1870–1881* (New York: Avon, 1962), 275.
38. Edel, *Henry James, The Conquest of London: 1870–1881*, 275.
39. Collins, *No Name*, 148.
40. Robinson, 166.
41. Virginia Blain, "The Naming of *No Name*," *Wilkie Collins Society Journal*, Vol. 4, 1984, 25.
42. Robinson, 162.
43. Blain, 26.
44. Blain, 28.

45. Edel, *Henry James, The Conquest of London: 1870–1881*, 276.
46. Collins, *Hide and Seek*, intro. Norman Donaldson (New York: Dover, 1981), 1.
47. Collins, *Hide and Seek*, 224–25.
48. Collins, *Hide and Seek*, 107.
49. Collins, *Hide and Seek*, 337.
50. Collins, *Hide and Seek*, 337.
51. Collins, *Hide and Seek*, 339.
52. Clarke, 147.
53. Robinson, 261.
54. Wilkie Collins, *The New Magdalen* (Chicago: M.A. Donohue, n.d.), 232.
55. Collins, *The New Magdalen*, 236.
56. Collins, *The New Magdalen*, 237.
57. Collins, *The New Magdalen*, 237.
58. Collins, *The New Magdalen*, 237.
59. Collins, *The New Magdalen*, 7.
60. Collins, *The New Magdalen*, 7.
61. Collins, *The New Magdalen*, 5.
62. Collins, *The New Magdalen*, 5.
63. Collins, *The New Magdalen*, 152.
64. Collins, *The New Magdalen*, 152.
65. Robinson, 260–61.
66. Quoted in Clarke, 166.
67. Appearing a few years before *The Woman in White*, Fanny Fern's novel *Ruth Hall* (1855) chronicles the appalling conditions for women in America who are cast aside into these asylums. One of these, Mary Leon, had been a wealthy, pampered, envied lady. She eventually goes mad and dies after her husband has her committed in order that he might travel to Europe, unencumbered. See *Ruth Hall* (New York: Penguin, 1997), 138–41.
68. Wilkie Collins, *The Moonstone* and *The Woman in White* (New York: Random House, 1937), 832.
69. Collins, *The Woman in White*, 832.

Chapter Four

1. R. L. Stevenson, "The Body Snatcher," in *The Strange Case of Dr Jekyll and Mr Hyde and Other Stories* (London: J.M. Dent, 1992), 15.
2. "The Body Snatcher," 22.
3. "The Body Snatcher," 20–21.
4. "The Body Snatcher," 23.
5. "The Body Snatcher," 23.
6. "The Body Snatcher," 23.
7. "The Body Snatcher," 23.
8. "The Body Snatcher," 23.
9. "The Body Snatcher," 23.
10. "The Body Snatcher," 23.
11. "The Body Snatcher," 24.
12. "The Body Snatcher," 26.
13. "The Body Snatcher," 27.
14. "The Body Snatcher," 28.
15. "The Body Snatcher," 28.
16. "The Body Snatcher," 30.
17. "The Body Snatcher," 30.
18. "The Body Snatcher," 18.
19. See Erik Larson, *The Devil in the White City* (New York: Crown, 2003), for a compelling account of Holmes's nefarious deeds and the times in which he operated.
20. Philip Callow, *Louis: A Life of Robert Louis Stevenson* (Chicago: Ivan R. Dee, 2001), 161.
21. Lettice Cooper, *Robert Louis Stevenson* (Denver: A. Swallow, 1948), 56.
22. *R. L. Stevenson: A Critical Study* (New York: Kennikat, 1915), 120.
23. Swinnerton, 49.
24. John Mason Brown, "Introduction," *Strange Case of Dr. Jekyll and Mr. Hyde* (New York: Heritage, 1952), xii.
25. Patricia Cornwell, *Portrait of a Killer* (New York: G. P. Putnam's Sons, 2002), 155.
26. G. B. Stern, *Robert Louis Stevenson*, Writers and their Work, No. 27 (London: Longmans, Green, & Co., 1952), 7.
27. James L. Limbacher, *Haven't I Seen You Somewhere Before? Remakes, Sequels and Series in Motion Pictures and Television, 1896–1978* (Ann Arbor: Pierian, 1979), 52.
28. *Voyage to Windward: The Life of Robert Louis Stevenson* (New York: William Sloane Associates, 1951), 21–22.
29. Stevenson, *The Strange Case of Dr. Jekyll and Mr. Hyde*, in *The Strange Case of Dr. Jekyll and Mr. Hyde and Other Stories* (London: J. M. Dent, 1992), 109.
30. Callow, 79.
31. Callow, 114.
32. *The Strange Case of Dr. Jekyll and Mr. Hyde*, 99.
33. *The Strange Case of Dr. Jekyll and Mr. Hyde*, 100.
34. *The Strange Case of Dr. Jekyll and Mr. Hyde*, 100.
35. *The Strange Case of Dr. Jekyll and Mr. Hyde*, 101.
36. *The Strange Case of Dr. Jekyll and Mr. Hyde*, 104–105.
37. David Daichos, *Stevenson and the Art of Fiction*, New York: Privately Printed, 1951, 9.
38. *The Strange Case of Dr. Jekyll and Mr. Hyde*, 105.
39. *The Strange Case of Dr. Jekyll and Mr. Hyde*, 110.
40. *The Strange Case of Dr. Jekyll and Mr. Hyde*, 119.
41. *The Strange Case of Dr. Jekyll and Mr. Hyde*, 120.
42. *The Strange Case of Dr. Jekyll and Mr. Hyde*, 121.

43. *The Strange Case of Dr. Jekyll and Mr. Hyde*, 121–22.

44. Elaine Showalter, *Sexual Anarchy* (New York: Viking, 1990), 110.

45. *The Strange Case of Dr. Jekyll and Mr. Hyde*, 141.

46. In order to maintain a respectable appearance, Symonds did have a wife and four children.

47. Callow, 157–58.

48. *Voyage to Windward: The Life of Robert Louis Stevenson* (New York: William Sloane Associates, 1951), 39.

49. Claire Harman, *Myself and the Other Fellow: A Life of Robert Louis Stevenson* (New York: HarperCollins, 2005), 54.

50. *The Strange Case of Dr. Jekyll and Mr. Hyde*, 105.

51. *The Strange Case of Dr. Jekyll and Mr. Hyde*, 111.

52. *The Strange Case of Dr. Jekyll and Mr. Hyde*, 122.

53. *The Strange Case of Dr. Jekyll and Mr. Hyde*, 122.

54. Callow, 17.

55. Callow, 11–12.

56. Callow, 202.

57. Callow, 203.

58. Callow, 205.

59. *Sexual Anarchy*, 115.

60. *Sexual Anarchy*, 116.

61. *The Strange Case of Dr. Jekyll and Mr. Hyde*, 143.

62. *The Picture of Dorian Gray* (Cleveland: World, 1946), 180.

63. A. C. Bradley, *Shakespearean Tragedy* (New York: Macmillan, 1949,) 209.

64. *The Strange Case of Dr. Jekyll and Mr. Hyde*, 144.

65. *The Strange Case of Dr. Jekyll and Mr. Hyde*, 144.

66. *The Strange Case of Dr. Jekyll and Mr. Hyde*, 99.

67. *The Strange Case of Dr. Jekyll and Mr. Hyde*, 105.

68. *The Strange Case of Dr. Jekyll and Mr. Hyde*, 141.

69. *The Strange Case of Dr. Jekyll and Mr. Hyde*, 141.

Chapter Five

1. Richard O. Lewis, "Romanticism in the Fiction of Charles W. Chesnutt: the Influence of Dickens, Scott, Tourgée, and Douglass," *CLA Journal*, XXVI: (December 1982), 153.

2. Sylvia Lyons Render, *Charles W. Chesnutt* (Boston: G. K. Hall, 1980), 17–18.

3. J. Noel Heermance, *Charles W. Chesnutt: America's First Great Black Novelist* (Hamden, Connecticut: Archon, 1974), 11.

4. Heermance, 16.

5. Sylvia Lyons Render, *Charles W. Chesnutt* (Boston: G. K. Hall, 1980), 55.

6. Quoted in Render, 32.

7. "Introduction," *Mandy Oxendine* (Urbana: University of Illinois, 1997), xviii.

8. Charles Duncan, "The White and the Black: Charles W. Chesnutt's Narrator-Protagonists and the Limits of Authorship," *The Journal of Narrative Technique*, 28 (Spring 1998), 119.

9. Duncan, 119.

10. Render, 16.

11. Render, 16.

12. Charles W. Chesnutt, *Mandy Oxendine*, ed. Charles Hackenberry (Urbana: University of Illinois, 1997), 29.

13. Chesnutt, 27.

14. Chesnutt, 7.

15. Chesnutt, 7.

16. Chesnutt, 39.

17. Chesnutt, 31.

18. Chesnutt, 40.

19. Chesnutt, 36.

20. Chesnutt, 39.

21. Chesnutt, 73.

22. Chesnutt, 73.

23. Chesnutt, 94.

24. Chesnutt, 94.

25. Chesnutt, 86–87.

26. Chesnutt, 46.

27. See Render, 53–55, for a discussion of Chesnutt's ability to recreate the speech patterns of different races and classes.

28. Chesnutt, 109.

29. Chesnutt, 109.

30. Chesnutt, 110.

31. Chesnutt, 110.

32. Chesnutt, 36.

33. Render, 93.

34. Chesnutt, 111.

35. Chesnutt, 112.

Chapter Six

1. See Michelle Stacey, *The Fasting Girl* (New York: Jeremy P. Tarcher/Putnam, 2002) for a fascinating account of Fancher's bizarre life.

2. Lillie Devereux Blake, *Fettered for Life* (New York: Feminist Press, 1996), 366.

3. Blake, 10.

4. Blake, 25.

5. Blake, 26.

6. Blake, 28.

7. Blake, 198.

8. Blake, 168.
9. Blake, 218.
10. Blake, 169.
11. Blake, 221.
12. Blake, 222.
13. Blake, 223.
14. Blake, 277.
15. Blake, 302.
16. Blake, 134.
17. Blake, 134.
18. Blake, 291.
19. Blake, 149.
20. Blake, 216.
21. Blake, 216.
22. Blake, 216.
23. Blake, 216–17.
24. Blake, 282.
25. Blake, 253.
26. Blake, 134.
27. Blake, 53.
28. Blake, 215.
29. Blake, 65.
30. Blake, 139.
31. Blake, 139.
32. Blake, 259.
33. Blake, 259.
34. Blake, 364.
35. Blake, 364.
36. Blake, 394.
37. Farrell, 394.
38. Blake, 43.
39. Blake, 64.
40. Blake, 9.
41. William M. Clarke, *The Secret Life of Wilkie Collins* (Chicago: Ivan R. Dee), 80.
42. Blake, 379.
43. Blake, 379.
44. Blake, 379.
45. Carolyn Heilbrun, *Writing a Woman's Life* (New York: Ballantine), 1988, 36.
46. Heilbrun, 65–69.
47. Blake, 313–14.

Chapter Seven

1. Mary Elizabeth Braddon, *Lady Audley's Secret*, introduction by Norman Donaldson (New York: Dover, 1974), 12.
2. Braddon, 1.
3. Braddon, 62.
4. Braddon, 2.
5. Braddon, 28.
6. Braddon, 28.
7. Braddon, 28.
8. Braddon, 6.
9. Braddon, 8–9.
10. Braddon, 7.
11. Braddon, 10.
12. Braddon, 40.
13. Braddon, 47.
14. Braddon, 47.
15. Braddon, 48.
16. Braddon, 49.
17. Braddon, 8.
18. Braddon, 8–9.
19. Braddon, 21.
20. Braddon, 232.
21. Braddon, 61.
22. Braddon, 230.
23. Braddon, 231.
24. Ellen Miller Casey, "'Other People's Prudery': Mary Elizabeth Braddon," *Tennessee Studies in Literature* (1984), 73.
25. Casey, 74.
26. Casey, 73.
27. William M. Clarke, *The Secret Life of Wilkie Collins* (Chicago: Ivan R. Dee, 1988), 130–31.
28. Clarke, 133.
29. Sandra M. Gilbert and Susan Gubar, *The Madwoman in the Attic* (New Haven, Yale University), 1979, 14.
30. Braddon, 231.
31. Braddon, 231.
32. Braddon, 231.
33. Many of Wilkie Collins's novels have also been dramatized on stage and in film. In addition to *The New Magdalen,* which was well received when it was produced on stage in the nineteenth century, both *The Moonstone* and *The Woman in White* have been adapted for the movies.
34. Braddon, 230.
35. Sara Keith, "The 'Athenaeum' as a Bibliographical Aid: Illustrated by 'Lady Audley's Secret' and Other Novels," *Victorian Periodicals Newsletter,* Vol. 8, 26.

Bibliography

Becker, Ernest. *The Denial of Death.* New York: Free Press Paperbacks, 1973.

Berkove, Lawrence Ivan. *Ambrose Bierce's Concern with Mind and Man.* University of Pennsylvania 1962 dissertation. Ann Arbor, MI: University Microfilms.

Bierce, Ambrose. *The Complete Stories of Ambrose Bierce.* Compiled by Ernest Jerome Hopkins. Lincoln: University of Nebraska Press, 1970.

Blain, Virginia. "The Naming of *No Name,*" *Wilkie Collins Society Journal,* Vol. 4 (1984), 25.

Blake, Lillie Devereux. *Fettered for Life.* New York: Feminist Press, 1996.

Braddon, Mary Elizabeth. *Lady Audley's Secret.* Intro. Norman Donaldson. New York: Dover, 1974.

Bradley, A.C. *Shakespearean Tragedy.* New York: Macmillan, 1949.

Brown, John Mason. "Introduction." *Strange Case of Dr. Jekyll and Mr. Hyde.* New York: Heritage, 1952.

Callow, Philip. *Louis: A Life of Robert Louis Stevenson.* Chicago: Ivan R. Dee, 2001.

Casey, Ellen Miller. "'Other People's Prudery'": Mary Elizabeth Braddon," *Tennessee Studies in Literature* (1984), 72–82.

Chesnutt, Charles W. *Mandy Oxendine.* Ed. Charles Hackenberry. Urbana: University of Illinois Press, 1997.

Clarke, William M. *The Secret Life of Wilkie Collins.* Chicago: Ivan R. Dee, 1988.

Collins, Wilkie. *Hide and Seek.* Intro. Norman Donaldson. New York: Dover, 1981.

_____. *The Moonstone* and *The Woman in White.* New York: Random House, 1937.

_____. *The New Magdalen.* Chicago: M.A. Donohue, n.d.

_____. *No Name.* Ed. Mark Ford. New York: Penguin Books, 1994.

Cooper, Lettice. *Robert Louis Stevenson.* Denver: A. Swallow, 1948.

Cornwell, Patricia. *Portrait of a Killer.* New York: G.P. Putnam's Sons, 2002.

Daiches, David. *Stevenson and the Art of Fiction.* New York: Privately printed, 1951.

David, Deirdre. "Rewriting Male Plot in *No Name,*" in *Wilkie Collins.* Ed. Lyn Pykett. New York: St. Martin's, 1998.

Davidson, Cathy N. *The Experimental Fictions of Ambrose Bierce.* Lincoln: University of Nebraska Press, 1982.

_____. *The Poetics of Perception: A Semantic Analysis of the Short Fiction of Ambrose Bierce.* Dissertation. State University of New York at Binghamton, 1974.

Donaldson, Norman. "Introduction." *Lady Audley's Secret*. New York: Dover, 1974.

Duncan, Charles. "The White and the Black: Charles W. Chesnutt's Narrator-Protagonists and the Limits of Authorship." *The Journal of Narrative Technique*, Vol. 28 (Spring 1998), 119.

Edel, Leon. *The Life of Henry James*. 5 vols. New York: Avon, 1953.

Farrell, Grace. "Afterward." *Fettered for Life*. New York: Feminist Press, 1996.

Fern, Fanny. *Ruth Hall*. New York: Penguin Books, 1997.

Fogel, Daniel Mark. "A New Reading of Henry James's 'The Jolly Corner,'" in *Critical Essays on Henry James: The Late Novels*. Ed. James W. Gargano. Boston: G. K. Hall, 1987.

Furnas, J.C. *Voyage to Windward: The Life of Robert Louis Stevenson*. New York: William Sloane Associates, 1951.

Gilbert, Sandra M., and Susan Gubar. *The Madwoman in the Attic*. New Haven: Yale University Press, 1979.

Hackenberry, Charles. "Introduction." *Mandy Oxendine*. Urbana: University of Illinois Press, 1997.

Harman, Claire. *Myself and the Other Fellow: A Life of Robert Louis Stevenson*. New York: HarperCollins, 2005.

Heermance, J. Noel. *Charles W. Chesnutt: America's First Great Black Novelist*. Hamden, CT: Archon Books, 1974.

Heilbrun, Carolyn. *Writing a Woman's Life*. New York: Ballantine Books, 1988.

Hopkins, Ernest Jerome, ed. *The Complete Short Stories of Ambrose Bierce*. Lincoln: University of Nebraska Press, 1970.

James, Henry. *The Jolly Corner and Other Tales*. Ed. Roger Gard. New York: Penguin, 1990.

James, William. *The Will to Believe*. New York: Longmans, 1912.

Keith, Sara. "The 'Athenaeum' as a Bibliographical Aid: Illustrated by 'Lady Audley's Secret' and Other Novels," *Victorian Periodicals Newsletter*, Vol. 8, 25–28.

Larson, Erik. *The Devil in the White City*. New York: Crown, 2003.

LeFanu, Joseph Sheridan. *Uncle Silas*. New York: Dover, 1966.

Lewis, Richard O. "Romanticism in the Fiction of Charles W. Chesnutt: the Influence of Dickens, Scott, Tourgée, and Douglass, *CLA Journal*, XXVI (December 1982), 153.

Limbacher, James L. *Haven't I Seen You Somewhere Before? Remakes, Sequels and Series in Motion Pictures and Television, 1896–1978*. Ann Arbor, MI: Pierian Press, 1979.

Menand, Louis. *The Metaphysical Club: A Story of Ideas in America*. New York: Farrar, Straus and Giroux, 2001.

Morris, Roy, Jr. *Ambrose Bierce: Alone in Bad Company*. New York: Crown, 1996.

Nacco, Stephen. *The Double Motif in the Short Stories of Ambrose Bierce*. Dissertation. Fordham University, 1991.

Render, Sylvia Lyons. *Charles W. Chesnutt*. Boston: G. K. Hall, 1980.

Robinson, Kenneth. *Wilkie Collins: A Biography*. London: Bodley Head, 1951.

Savoy, Eric. "Spectres of abjection: 'The Jolly Corner,'" in *Spectral Readings: Towards a Gothic Geography*. Ed. Glennis Byron and David Punter. New York: St. Martin's, 1999.

Showalter, Elaine. *Sexual Anarchy: Gender and Culture at the Fin de Siècle*. New York: Viking, 1990.

Smith, Lacey Baldwin. *Fools, Martyrs, Traitors: The Story of Martyrdom in the Western World.* New York: Alfred A. Knopf, 1997.

Stacey, Michelle. *The Fasting Girl.* New York: Jeremy P. Tarcher/Putnam, 2002.

Stern, G.B. *Robert Louis Stevenson.* Writers and their Work. No. 27. London: Longmans, Green, & Co., 1952.

Stevenson, Robert Louis. *The Strange Case of Dr. Jekyll and Mr. Hyde and Other Stories.* London: J. M. Dent, 1992.

Swinnerton, Frank. *R.L. Stevenson: A Critical Study.* New York: Kennikat, 1915.

Toffler, Alvin. *Future Shock.* New York: Bantam, 1970.

Werth, Barry. *The Scarlet Professor, Newton Arvin: A Literary Life Shattered by Scandal.* New York: Doubleday, 2001.

Wilde, Oscar. *The Picture of Dorian Gray.* Cleveland: World, 1946.

Wilson, Edmund. *Patriotic Gore.* New York: W.W. Norton, 1994.

Woodruff, Stuart C. *The Short Stories of Ambrose Bierce: A Study in Polarity.* Pittsburgh: University of Pittsburgh Press, 1964.

Index